ESSAY ON THE INEQUALITY
OF HUMAN RACES

ESSAY ON
THE INEQUALITY
OF HUMAN RACES

BY
JOSEPH-ARTHUR DE GOBINEAU

TRANSLATED FROM THE FRENCH
BY ADRIAN COLLINS, M.A.

INTRODUCTION BY DR. OSCAR LEVY,
EDITOR OF THE AUTHORIZED ENGLISH
VERSION OF NIETZSCHE'S WORKS

First published 1855
Translation first published 1915
This edition © 2020
All Rights Reserved.

ISBN: 979-8-6817-7451-8

CONTENTS

THE LIFE WORK AND INFLUENCE OF COUNT JOSEPH-ARTHUR DE GOBINEAU

AN INTRODUCTORY ESSAY
BY DR. OSCAR LEVY

I

It has been generally thought and stated that the past century was a profoundly irreverent and irreligious age, the age of the twilight of old gods, the shattering of old idols, the ruin of an old and holy creed Nothing, however, could be further from the truth. In every department of human knowledge, in philosophy, in science, and in politics as well as in art, the nineteenth century was deeply imbued with religious ideas; nay, spoilt by what may almost be called a spiritual intoxication. It was the only century known to history in which theology and its favorite offspring, morality, had swamped everybody and everything. Whether it paraded itself as cold and scientific, as warm and humanitarian, as lukewarm and agnostic, as progressive and liberal, as ethical and socialistic, as anarchical and revolutionary, as conservative and reactionary, as rationalistic and freethinking or as romantic and artistic, there was always one and the same personality behind that cloak of many colors, behind that medley of divers fashions; and that personality was a good man, a religious man—a Christian.

Thank heaven, this good man is growing wiser and a little wickeder. Thank heaven, that gloomy and oppressive century is past! Thank God, the spiritual deluge of the nineteenth century is fast dispersing! How that religious flood roared and rushed, how it deafened our ears, how it drowned the voice of our innermost heart, how it frightened every one of us into submission! And now—unknown, of course, as yet to the great majority—the ebb of that movement has set in, and we are able to discern, with a calmer mind, the object of our terror. There it is: receding before our feet, crawling back into eternity, carrying its constituents away with it to the deep sea of oblivion—water, plenty of water, froth, plenty of froth, and sand, plenty of sand. And there are also a number of pebbles among the outgoing tide, and these pebbles are the great celebrities of the past century, the heroes who were acclaimed as superior and representative men, as leaders of mankind by their religious contemporaries, who proved once more their superabundance of faith by the selection of their celebrities. Good-bye, good pebbles; good-bye and away with you forever into the watery limbo!

But what is that strange sight yonder? The sand and the water and the froth and the pebbles are disappearing fast before our eyes, but some firm rocks, which no one has ever yet seen, or even suspected, are left standing in lonely majesty between the receding waves. They seem to be firmly established, and like everything firm and self-centered, they are respected by the waves and the sands, which are flowing round them as if in awe and veneration, nay, which seem to flee from them as fast as they can as if frightened by a bad conscience. And well might they have a bad conscience, for while the flood was reigning, they had hidden from everybody's view these mighty rocks, pretending they were not there, they had danced merrily over them, roaring out of their myriad throats: they, the little pebbles, and the microscopic sands, and the babbling waves. But they could only hide for a time those mighty rocks, they could not move them—and now, when the ebb has set in, these rocks spring into everybody's sight, and grave and erect they stand above their surroundings, smiling grimly at the tiny pebbles and the loquacious waters at their feet. Away with you, ye ephemeral waters, away with you—and make room for the eternal rocks!

Take close heed of these rocks, you younger generation of the twentieth century! These rocks can no longer be ignored, as they were by your fathers and grandfathers: rocks that are ignored are dangerous! But if you pay due attention to them, they will be of welcome service to you; for these rocks, which your blind and superstitious ancestors did not notice, or did not wish to notice, are the only firm structure left to your youth, to the New Age, to the century which you one day will have to direct Upon these rocks, upon this mighty foundation of granite, you shall henceforth build, you *must* build, for they alone, and not the pebbles and the sands that your forefathers thought eternal, will offer you a fitting and lasting foundation for the palace of the future.

One of those men, who, like those mighty rocks, is only now beginning to appear above the waters of the receding nineteenth century, is Count Arthur de Gobineau.

Joseph Arthur, Comte de Gobineau, was born at Ville d'Avray, on the 14th of July, 1816. He was the descendant of a family that had remained loyal to the ancient dynasty of the Bourbons, and his father, Louis de Gobineau, an officer of the Royal Guard, had followed Louis XVIII. into exile during the hundred days of Napoleon's return. It was told of him that he considered Voltaire as the devil and Charles X. as a saint, but that he was enough of an independent thinker to love the Devil Monsieur de Voltaire, as well as the Saint Charles X.

The grandfather of our Count, who was a Councillor to the Parliament of Bordeaux, had a remarkable wife, who may have transmitted some of her qualities to her famous grandson. Her name was Victoire de la Haye, and she was a descendant of a Norman family of great wealth. A story is circulated about her that one day when she saw her son Thibault-Joseph fall from a horse upon the stone-pavement, she went up to him and coolly asked him, "Monsieur, did you do yourself any injury?" "No, mother." "Well then, get on again" Thibault-Joseph never forgot the scene and always spoke with the greatest reverence of his mother and her unusual strength of character.

This uncle, Thibault-Joseph, who was destined to play a certain part in Arthur's life, was another noteworthy member of the family. When he was a pupil at the college of Guyenne, he was ignominiously sent away from that school, because one day he had tried to set fire to the school-house—which may certainly be considered as a proof that neither intelligence nor energy was wanting in this remarkable stock. Later on he fought under Dugommier in Spain and excelled in deeds worthy of those feudal knights from whom his famous nephew always imagined himself to descend Almost single-handed he is said to have captured an English brig. He was a violent anti-Jacobin and legitimist, and after the ninth of Thermidor he did everything to re-establish the old order.

After a long journey in Germany with his mother, and having attended school at the College of Bienne, in Switzerland, Arthur Gobineau was sent to Paris to live with this marvellous uncle of his. The latter, however, in the course of time, had become more and more a quaint fellow: his whole occupation now apparently consisted in cursing the upstart Louis Philippe and in loose talking about the re-establishment of the legitimate kings of France. He spent his days on a sofa, his head hidden behind big newspapers, and without troubling in the least about his nephew, whom his valet was supposed to look after. Arthur Gobineau endured this life for three weeks and then went up to his uncle and frankly declared that he would commit suicide on the spot, and before his eyes, if the uncle did not change his behaviour towards him. Then, and only then, is the strange man reported to have given in and paid more attention to his nephew, whom he certainly must have recognized as belonging to his own breed.

On account of his Conservative political views, Gobineau, of course, never thought of playing a part under the new democratic regime of France. All the time he was staying with his uncle, in the years 1835-1848, he occupied himself with literary work and thus acquired, during the most important years of his life, a knowledge which was all the more vast in that no spur to honor and bread forced him to specialize, and all the more useful and deep in that the love of study alone had caused him to acquire it It is to this training, which Gobineau gave himself—the only training for a man worth having nowadays—that he owes his freedom from many of the popular or academic prejudices of his time and country.

While thus occupied with his studies in Paris, the young Count made the acquaintance of Alexis de Tocqueville, the famous author of *La Démocratie en Amérique,* who in 1848 became Minister of Foreign Affairs. Tocqueville appointed Gobineau his private secretary, and soon afterwards chief of his Cabinet. Thus Gobineau, who had never dreamt of taking active part in political affairs, saw himself launched upon a career which was—in its diplomatic variety—to become the career of his life.

De Tocqueville did not retain his post for long. On retiring, however, he recommended his young friend to his successors, with each of whom Gobineau remained popular. One of them, General Marquis d' Hautpoul, nominated him to be first secretary to the French Embassy at Berne.

This, no doubt, was an easy post and thus quite suitable to the literary propensities of Arthur Gobineau. It was here and later on at Hanover and Frankfort that he wrote from the notes collected during his Parisian studies his famous *Essai sur l'inégalité des races humaines.* This book, which he published in two volumes, one in 1853 and the other in 1855, gives us the key to Gobineau's personality and the quintessence of all his thought

In Frankfort Gobineau made the acquaintance of Bismarck, but the Prussian politician, as was to be expected, took notice neither of the young diplomatist nor of his extraordinary ideas. Bismarck apparently was so busy fighting the Austrian preponderance and pretensions to supremacy that he quite overlooked the man who was destined, more than himself, to give new blood and new beliefs to the future, just as he overlooked Schopenhauer, who, already famous, was then living at Frankfort. Thus in the long run the politician, even the politician of genius, is always beaten by the man of thought, the creator of ideas: empires vanish, but thought is immortal. Much more interest in Gobineau was taken by Bismarck's enemy and antagonist, Baron von Prokesch-Osten, who was not only a diplomatist but likewise an eminent writer on Oriental subjects. He was a very able disciple of Metternich and became well known later on as Austrian Ambassador in Constantinople. "Is the Gobineau who has written the book on the Inequality of the Human Races one of your relatives?" the old gentleman once asked the Count "I have written it myself." "What—and so young?" was the astonished answer. Throughout his life Gobineau maintained cordial relations with the Baron, and kept up a most interesting correspondence with his admirer, who lived to a very great age.

In 1854 Gobineau was nominated first secretary to the Embassy in Teheran, and took with him his wife, whom he had married eight years previously, and his little daughter. He was delighted to go there, for, in spite of his Germanic propensities, the Orient, from his youth upwards, had always greatly attracted him. He went there with the firm resolution—so rarely found in a European diplomatist—to try to understand the Asiatics. He learned the language of the country, he sought the acquaintance of erudite Persians, he cultivated friendship with anyone who could be of use to his eager, searching mind. "I have tried to banish from my .mind any idea of true or false superiority over the people that I have studied. Before delivering judgment on them and on their peculiarities, I have attempted to get into their habits of thought, I have tried to see things from their point of view." Thus Gobineau wrote in his book "Three Years in Asia," which he published in 1856 on his return to France. But another and more important book was the fruit of his Persian sojourn, a book which had some success even during the author's lifetime. It is entitled "The Religions and Philosophies of Central Asia," and certainly ranks amongst the best that Gobineau has ever written. We shall hear more of it later on.

On his return to France, Gobineau was sent on a French man-of-war to Newfoundland in order to settle the eternal question of the fishing rights with the representatives of the British Government. He again profited from this journey, and brought back a book, "Voyage to Newfoundland." In a little book published later, under the title "Reminiscences of Travel," which contained three little stories, there is one that has its scene in Newfoundland. It is the story of a vain Parisian, a man about town, with whom a British Colonial girl falls in love, and who thus—quite contrary to his expectation—sees himself taken seriously by the simple Anglo-Saxon temperament, and threatened with that Waterloo of all philanderers and poets, to wit, matrimony. This story could only be written by a good European, that is to say by a man who, like Gobineau, understood the weaknesses of his own as well as the virtues and shortcomings of other peoples. He was entirely above the two nations and was thus enabled to describe them with all that bonhomie and true satire which is and always must be the outcome of a certain good-natured contempt for its object

In the year 1861 Gobineau was sent again to Teheran, this time as chief of the French Embassy, and here he passed two years in succession. During this time he tried to make use of his great personal influence in Persian circles to gain a footing for France in that country, where Russia and England were not yet so firmly established as they are today. But in Paris his ideas were considered those of a dreamer: in this world the rare man of healthy imagination is usually ranked among the idealists, while the real idealists always appeal strongly to the men in power, who usually are Philistines and stand in sore need of a little romanticism as a welcome antidote to their prosaic souls. The French *bureaux,* the seat of power in modern France, had always distrusted the Count, whom they could not forgive, because, besides an anti-democrat, he was also a "scribbler," a fact which, combined with the want of success even in this inferior direction, was a sure sign of a wild personality. Long ago a friendly Minister of Foreign Affairs had said to Gobineau, alluding to his essay: "A scientific book of such importance will do your diplomatic career no good; on the contrary it may do you a great deal of harm!"

Gobineau soon discovered that this Minister was right, and that neither his books nor his political ideas had influenced the central authorities in his favor. When, in 1864, he applied for an appointment in Constantinople, his request was not granted. He was sent to Athens instead, where he published the two books mentioned above, his "Reminiscences of Travel" and "The Religions and Philosophies of Central Asia." He wrote and published some other books besides during his stay at Athens: "The History of the Persians," the "Asiatic Novels," and a number of poems, which received the title of "Aphroessa."

In the year 1868 the count was transferred from Athens to Rio de Janeiro, where he suffered a great deal from uncongenial surroundings. It may be easily imagined that an aristocratic nature, a firm believer in good blood, could not but he shocked and horrified by the aspect of that mixed population (all the more repugnant because it is a prosperous mixed population) which the two Americas, those of the north and south, offer to a cultured European. His only consolation was the friendship with the Emperor Dom Pedro, who seems to have suffered from his exile as much as Gobineau, and who probably complained to the French Count often enough in the orthodox Ovidian strain about his Brazilian isolation:

"Barbaras hic ego sum, quia non intelligor ulli."
(Here I am a barbarian, because there is nobody who understands me.)

The Emperor seems to have had an intimate knowledge of Count Gobineau's books, and every Sunday the two, the Monarch and the French Ambassador, met for long conversations. Even after Gobineau—for reasons of health—had left Brazil, this friendship was maintained by means of a long correspondence, a correspondence which was only interrupted by the prolonged stay of the Emperor in Europe during the years 1871, 1876 and 1877.

The war of 1870 found Count Gobineau in France. He had inherited a fortune from his uncle Thibault-Joseph, and had with part of the money bought the castle of Trye-en-Vexin, which he considered as the cradle of the Norman House of Goumay, the house from which his mother was descended. As the Mayor of Trye he was able to do a great deal for his fellow-citizens during the war. He spoke German fluently, he had a good knowledge of the German character, and was able by means of successful parleys with the victorious generals to shield his district from a great deal of severe treatment. Unlike Taine and Renan and so many other Frenchmen, he had foreseen the defeat of his country: he likewise thought that France, on account of her rampant democracy, had thoroughly deserved that defeat But his aversion to democratic France did not prohibit him from doing what he could for her in the hour of danger, and thus this despiser of patriots and democrats was of more use to his fatherland than many of its enthusiastic and well-meaning, but less intelligent worshippers. When the war was over the town of Beauvais publicly acknowledged its gratitude to the Count His grateful fellow-citizens even wished to send him to Parliament or to the Senate, an honor which Gobineau, as *gentilhomme* and *honnête homme* and disbeliever in the divine right of the people and its votes, had to decline with polite though determined thanks.

In 1872 Gobineau was sent to Stockholm. There, as elsewhere, he does not seem to have found many congenial friends amongst his colleagues and apparently led a very solitary life. And these colleagues themselves do not seem to have had at any time much knowledge of the Count's ideas and doings. One day, for instance, Gobineau in a certain drawing-room met another diplomatist, a former acquaintance of his German days. This colleague was asked by the lady of the house whether he knew the Count. "Oh, yes," was the reply, "the worthy Gobineau, of course, I know him." "You see," whispered Gobineau (who was, of course, highly amused at being called "worthy" while propagating so many daring ideas), "you see, madam, how well-known I am," and in his simple and good-natured manner he

11

heartily shook hands with the great connoisseur of human character. It must be added, however, that Gobineau himself was apparently not desirous of leading people on to the right track about himself and his literary achievements. He was not a man of letters, but a gentleman of letters, and as such was not given to talking overmuch of his printed offspring. He also, no doubt, knew what kind of literary people a democratic age brings to pre-eminence, and in order not to be mistaken for one of the geniuses of the day he may not have cared to acknowledge his authorship in public. He never looked a genius either: like young Professor Nietzsche, he had something military in his bearing as well as in his manner, so that a flunkey in the Tuileries, whom he had asked a question one day, replied to him, "Oui, mon général!"

In 1876 Gobineau received leave of absence from his government, which enabled him to accompany the Emperor of Brazil on a journey to Russia, Turkey, and Greece. They returned by way of Rome, where Gobineau for the first time met Richard Wagner, who, as the Count's discoverer, was destined to play a certain part in his life. It was, however, not a case of appreciation "at first sight"; it was not until a year later, when Wagner had read Gobineau's book on the Renaissance, that he knew, or thought he knew, who the French Count really was. But from this time a rather close friendship sprang up between the composer and the ambassador, a friendship which led to a great deal of personal intercourse and was destined to last till the end of Gobineau's life.

This end, however, was hastened by the ill-use to which Gobineau was subjected on the part of his old enemies the governmental *bureaux* in Paris. They apparently knew what an enemy of their order and class they had to deal with, and pensioned the independent

Count off before his time. As if wishing to poison the wound they thus inflicted, they nominated as his successor the Marquis de Tamissier, whose real name was Carrier. This Carrier was a grandson of the notorious Carrier who, when sent as commissioner by the Convention to Nantes, had thousands, of people executed, some by the rapid method of drowning in the Loire. "The grandson of the Carrier of the *Noyades de Nantes,*" wrote Gobineau to a friend, "the Carrier of the 'Republican Marriages' (the drowning of a man and woman bound together was called by the popular wit a 'Republican Marriage') it is he who is going to be my successor." Thus ran the complaint of our anti-Jacobin ambassador, whose manly heart must have been sore at the double affront offered him. Soon afterwards his health broke down, his eyes began to trouble him, and he likewise suffered some heavy monetary losses. He went to Rome, where he led a very simple life, occupying himself with sculpture, which since his residence in Athens had been a constant source of pleasure to him. From time to time he went to Bayreuth, where he enchanted the Germans by his tales of many lands—but it must not be forgotten that he was an old and broken man, and that only thus can the friendship between such a fantastic thinker as Wagner and such a profound mind as Gobineau be satisfactorily explained.

During the winter of 1881-1882 his health deteriorated more and more. In the spring he went to Bayreuth, but could not stop more than two days. He then went to Gastein, where he slightly improved. During the summer he visited his friends the Count and Countess de la Tour in their *château* in the Auvergne. When the autumn came he wished to return to Italy and left his hosts on October nth to go to Pisa. In Turin, on the 13th, while trying to get into the railway carriage, he had a sudden seizure and had to be carried back to the hotel. A priest was called who administered the last consolation of the Church, but stated later on that the Count was already unconscious and unable to appreciate the benefit conferred upon him The power of the great freethinker's mind was such that it could even give way at the right moment!

II

When Gobineau was an old man, his *Essay on the Inequality of Human Races* went into a second edition, to which he prefixed a new introduction. In this he declares: "I leave these pages just as I wrote them many years ago, when the doctrine they contain sprang out of my mind just like a bird that puts its head out of its nest and then seeks its way in illimitable space." This poetical sentence alone gives the reader a hint of the great value of the book, a value which at first sight might not seem so obvious. For there is no doubt that the Essay is not free from faults. It is very long, it is rather chaotic, and it is dry reading in places. It suffers from great prejudices and from some omissions. Neither its facts, nor its theories, nor its judgments are wholly admirable or even true. But what is wholly admirable is the spirit in which the book is written. It is one of the few books that had to be written—the author's heart, one feels, would have burst in the fulness of its ecstasy, if it had not found an outlet on paper. The book is full of inward fire, of fire only half hidden and breaking out again and again from underneath the grey ashes of scientific, archaeological, historic, linguistic and other facts. It is a rebellious book, but the rebel in this case is a creative rebel, a rebel from above, a rebel against the rebels of his time, and, let me add, of our own time. He is an aristocratic rebel, who has deduced and proves from history a terrible truth which he throws like a bomb into the faces of the victorious heretics, reformers, radicals, socialists, and other Philistines and Pharisees of revolution. This truth discovered by Gobineau is the all-importance of race. This truth is the neglect of the principle of race under democratic conditions. This truth is the refutation of the democratic idea that by means of an improvement in environment a healthy and noble people could be produced out of a rotten stock.

Gobineau's "system," as explained in the Essay, is the following: "The history of mankind proves that the destinies of people are governed by a racial law. Neither irreligion, nor immorality, nor luxurious living, nor weakness of government is causing the decadence of civilizations. If a nation goes down, the reason is that its blood, the race itself, is deteriorating. Now, there has been only one race that was able to create a civilization, because it alone possessed the element of order and a certain healthy imagination, and that was the white race —the Aryans. If there had only been Aryans on earth, humanity would have been easily and forever perfectible. But there were inferior races as well, the yellow and the black races, which always and everywhere adulterated the pure white blood. These mixtures, no doubt, have benefited the yellows and the blacks, and thus even these mixtures have created something in this world. But the Aryan blood, again and again rejuvenating inferior peoples, has finally exhausted itself. There is consequently nothing left in this world of ours but half-castes, that is to say, cowardly and impotent people, ready to adapt themselves to any law and any master, and not minding the loss of their personality, because they do not happen to possess one."

History, philology, archaeology, anthropology, are called in by the author to support his thesis, or rather his cry of alarm. For the poet again and again peeps out from behind his pedantic, dry, and scientific mask, and this long epic, which might fitly be called "The Twilight of the Aryan," rings out in a noble and passionate complaint, worthy of a great author and laying bare the bleeding heart of a Jewish prophet:

"Not death, but the certainty of dying in degradation, is the gloomy prospect in store for us; and perhaps this disgrace that is doomed to fall upon our posterity might leave us cold, did we not feel, with a hidden thrill of terror, that the clawing hands of destiny are already upon our shoulders."

If we wish to gauge the importance and novelty of this idea, we must go back to the nineteenth century and remember the two main currents of thought regarding men, currents which we shall understand all the better as they are still flowing, though with diminished strength, through the thought of our own day. One of these is the spiritualistic current of Christianity, the Christianity that wishes to save every soul because it thinks everyone perfectible and possibly, if converted to the eternal truth, equal to everybody else. In opposition to this trend of thought stands the materialistic school of the natural scientist, a school based upon the ideas of Montesquieu, Herder, and Hegel, or in this country, of Buckle and John Stuart Mill, according to which a human being is an unstable entity dependent upon outside circumstances and changing with them—a creature, in short, of chance and environment. In opposition to both these schools, the spiritualistic and the materialistic, Count Gobineau had the courage to declare, in the midst of his dark age, that the environment scarcely mattered, that the "eternal truth" was an impotent assumption, and that everything, perfectibility as well as history, depended upon the blood, upon the race. His conclusions were the same as

Disraeli's, who probably had never heard of him: "All is race, there is no other truth."

From this little glimpse at the Essay alone we may perceive that we have to do with an author of the aristocratic school, that is to say, of a school that heartily despises the values of modern morality. Gobineau, it will be seen, belongs to the same school as Nietzsche, and thus he not only despises our current opinions on "good and evil" but he fears and loathes them on account of their deleterious effect upon humanity. For Gobineau as well as Nietzsche had noticed fifty years ago what the most cultured people of today are only beginning to suspect, that our moral values, the values of Democracy, Socialism, Liberalism, Christianity, lead to the survival of a type of man who has no right to survive, or who ought only to survive on an inferior plane. Gobineau as well as Nietzsche knew that "good" under the present values and in our time only means "tame, adaptable, conventional," at best "industrious, persevering, efficient and businesslike." Both could never forget, and again and again they emphasize the fact, that goodness in non-vulgar times meant something quite different from today, that goodness once upon a time signified "energy, bravery, daring, strength of character, power of endurance, power of attacking, power of overcoming," that it did *not* mean "harmlessness, absence of faults and vices, negative virtue, female virtue, commercial sharpness and cleverness, mediocrity."

True, Gobineau did not, like Nietzsche, hold Christianity openly responsible for this transvaluation of noble values into coward's values, but he nevertheless agrees with him as to the source of this evil by pointing with great emphasis to the influence of the later Semitic race. To the earlier Semite, the warrior-Semite, the Semite under his kings, he seems to have given full approval. This *Sémite-blanc primitif,* as he is called in the

Essay is, according to the author, even a near relation to his hero, the Aryan, and his actions, as those of unbroken conqueror tribes, found in Gobineau a natural and willing admirer. Unfortunately these early white Semites mixed their blood with lower races and thus degenerated. Through this mixture, the race of Shem fell forever from the high position it held in the ancient world; nay, it even became *le fond corrupteur* of this ancient world, and by its intermarriage with the pure and noble Aryan blood it ruined the race of Rome. Here it will be seen, we come across one of those deductions of Gobineau's which he—to satisfy his theory that every degeneration arises from the crossing of races— had to make, but which is nevertheless only a partial truth. For how, we may ask, could these insignificant Semitic tribes spoil the noble blood of a whole mighty empire, even supposing that some of them did intermarry with the Romans, which the Jews, as far as we know, never did to a great extent? And what, it might be asked, led the proud Romans to intermarry with such inferior beings?

This is, no doubt, a weak point in Gobineau's system: he overrates the physical effects of a race and neglects its spiritual influence; he overlooks the influence of ideas and values. Surely a race may influence the world directly by its blood; but yet more frequent and much more powerful is the indirect influence, the influence of ideas, and this is the influence which the Jews have exercised. It was by means of their ideas, not by means of their blood, that the Semitic race broke the Roman Empire. It was Christianity, that popular accentuation of Judaism, which among the slaves, women, and weaklings of Rome found such a ready acceptance, that slowly but surely undermined that unique and flourishing empire. It was Christianity that made the slaves equal to their masters, that, helped by decadent Pagan philosophy, poisoned the good conscience and healthy instincts of these masters, and finally led them to intermarry with slaves and barbarians. It was intermarriage with the non-race, with the people, that led to the ruin of Rome: it was the mixture of different classes much more than the mixtures of different races that produced that decadent and servile chaos of the later Roman Empire.

But apart from these minor shortcomings there are startling flashes of wisdom in the Essay, flashes which attest the unprejudiced and pagan attitude of Gobineau's mind, and further prove that Gobineau was a Nietzschean before Nietzsche. Gobineau sees the connection between later Semitism and Democracy, he sees that Democracy is the enemy of all government and all society: "All civilizations that assume democratic forms are speedily ruined," he says. In the question of slavery, he is likewise in agreement with Nietzsche: "Slavery," says our author, "like all human institutions, rests not only upon constraint but upon other conditions as well. ... There is no doubt that slavery sometimes has a legitimate basis, and we are almost justified in laying down that in this case it results quite as much from the consent of the slave as from the moral and physical predominance of the master."

But the real genius of Gobineau, the clear thought, flashes out—just as that of Schopenhauer in his *Parerga and Paralipomena*—when he forgets his system and speaks of what he has seen and felt.

Gobineau's "Philosophy of History," as we have seen, is to some extent forced and questionable, and even in its truer and indisputable parts it has been more lucidly developed by Friedrich Nietzsche; but when the theory of the Essay leaves Gobineau he becomes a true pioneer of thought. I am referring here to a science—or rather an art, which, after the collapse of wiredrawn metaphysics and idealist tomfooleries, will play the principal part in any further philosophy: the art of psychology, that is to say, the insight into the character of human beings and the subsequent valuation of this character.

It is in this that Gobineau, as a poet, excels. His psychology of the yellow race (Book III., cap. 4 and 5) is a masterpiece. His description of the purest and the noblest Aryan organization, that of the Brahmins, is of the greatest value even today and of special interest to Englishmen; and while perusing these eloquent chapters (Book III., cap. i and 2) we must not forget that it was penned fifty years before Meredith Townsend, in his "Asia and Europe," came to the same conclusions. All through the book we meet with observations on the habits and thoughts of mankind which charm us by their truth and insight

The Essay, as was to be expected, met with little success. Who in this specialized world could take an interest in a work that was based upon so many different sciences? Already the diplomatists, as we had seen, had ignored Gobineau's ideas by placing him amongst the *littérateurs* and professional Utopians, while the professional Utopians were not tempted to interest themselves in a man who had based his theories upon such an astounding series of facts. And those occupied with facts, the professional scientists, were then, as now, divided into a great number of clans, each busying itself with a certain set of facts, and, if honest, not over-much inclined to speak in public about a book which was beyond their comprehension. The specialization of our age, though of course better than an all-embracing dilettantism, is a danger to all truly comprehensive, philosophical works, which, even when noticed by men of science, are heartily recommended only to the colleagues of another speciality.

The archaeologist says that the book in question belongs to the department of anthropology, the anthropologist hands it over to the philologist, the philologist shifts the duty on to the Orientalist, the Orientalist to the theologian, the theologian recommends it to the earnest attention of the historian, while the historian completes the vicious circle by handing it back to the archaeologist. These conscientious men of science behave like a policeman whom, during my student days, I met one night in am obscure quarter of Berlin and with whom I struck up a friendship. I asked him why he did not arrest a certain drunkard who made such a terrible noise and would surely do harm to himself or others? "I never arrest a drunkard," he answered, "it means so much bother over a little thing: if the worst comes to the worst, all I do is to chase the fellow into another policeman's beat, and there the other policeman, you see, has the pleasure of running him in and giving evidence against him, and so on."

In our times, however, when a book is ignored or insufficiently spoken about in public, it is often taken seriously by a select circle; nay, it may even stir up, amongst a few, violent applause or condemnation. And that is what happened, at least with one man, in the case of Gobineau's Essay. It was his mighty friend and patron, Alexis de Tocqueville, the famous author of *La Démocratie en Amérique,* who was touched on the raw by what he called Gobineau's dangerous and pernicious doctrines.

The epistolary interchange between Tocqueville and Gobineau is all the more interesting as Tocqueville's answers are the typical objections of his and of our own age. Tocqueville was a typical Liberal representative of the nineteenth century—that is to say, a man whose opinions (whether he knows it or not) are based upon Christian prejudices. For Liberalism is a latent religion, Liberalism is crypto-Christianity, every Liberal is a

Nazarene priest in mufti. No doubt, Tocqueville was a very enlightened crypto-Christian, who could not or would not absolutely close his eyes to the danger of democracy and other unpalatable facts; but, being a Christian, his judgments on the one hand are very pessimistic as regards human nature and his proposals and remedies on the other are colored by a puerile optimism. The misgivings and doubts which Tocqueville has concerning democracy are many and grave, his fatalism and pessimism are as severe as or severer than Gobineau's; but he saves himself from Gobineau's conclusion by that peculiar and tenacious hopefulness, which is the outcome of the cowardice so characteristic of the Christian thinker. Desperately he clings to the most unsubstantiated assertions, all the more desperately as they are his "last straw," and he knows that giving up for a moment means the break-down of his whole system. Which of us has not met some philosophic Liberal, who, like Tocqueville, has the greatest contempt for his contemporaries, who takes a gloomy view about their future, who deplores their want of manliness, character, daring and independence, but who will never draw the right and straightforward conclusions from these facts? He will point out that the environment ought to be improved, or that education has been lacking, or that only the upper classes are spoilt and the people are "quite sound"; he will patiently wait for "evolution" or "progress" to better things, or for cooperative and socialistic reforms, nay, he will appeal to religion and a revival of morality and idealism—he will do anything, in short, rather than utter an honest yea or nay, rather than come to Gobineau's conclusion that no apple tree, by careful nursing, will produce grapes, that no education can get out of a man any qualities which are not in him, that base blood cannot be turned into noble blood by any "free" patent medicine, and that the present race of Europeans has, with very few exceptions, to be found in all nations and classes alike, become a countless horde of helots who are in many instances even useless helots. It is the shallow Christian Liberalism of the past century that comes out in these letters of Tocqueville to Gobineau, a Christian Liberalism which is, to be sure, carefully wrapped up in high-sounding principles and made palatable by the well-known exuberant phraseology of that numerous sect.

Having received the book on October 11th, 1853, M. de Tocqueville at once confesses that he has a great distrust of its principles and ideas because "it takes for granted," he says, "the fatality of constitution, and this fatality is applied not only to individuals but likewise to that collection of individuals called a race."

On November 17th, 1853, he repeats: "Your doctrine is a sort of fatalism, or, if you like, of predestination—which, of course, is different from the fatalism of St. Augustine, the Jansenists, and the Calvinists, inasmuch as yours is based more upon the deterioration of matter, or what you call race. This predestination seems to me very nearly related to pure materialism. It likewise tends to a great restriction of human liberty. And this, of course, is very bad," our author continues, "for how can anyone tell people who already live like slaves and barbarians, who are already prone to any sort of weakness and cowardice, that there is no hope for them, no possibility of perfection, of changing their habits and of improving their government?" "Don't you see," he concludes, "that from your doctrine naturally arise all the evils of inequality, pride, violence, tyranny, contempt of one's neighbor, and slavery in every form?"

All these arguments are highly typical of the Liberal. It is very significant that he at the outset tries to brand with the name of "materialist" a man who troubles about science, about race, about eugenics, about the body—for to the Christian (and our Liberal is a Christian) it is the soul alone that matters, at least so long as he is a real Liberal, and has not forgotten or adulterated his own principles. Tocqueville's complaint about Gobineau's restriction of human liberty and his reproach about a pure fatalism in Gobineau's views, is likewise entirely Christian, for the Christian is forced by his religion to believe in free will, and in the consequent perfectibility of every human soul, which, if perfected in the orthodox manner, becomes as good as anybody else's soul. In this belief, in this expectation, Tocqueville is a glorious optimist, an optimist, be it understood, for the future, for the kingdom to come, for the Messianic Empire, as promised by his priests, prophets and other prestidigitators. But when he begins to judge present conditions, and more still when he begins to act, his poisoned pessimistic and nihilistic nature and his entire disbelief in everything and everybody around him comes out most shamelessly. For the Christian, it must not be forgotten, has the "evil eye" for "the world," and is thus obliged to see evil in even the most healthy manifestations of human nature, which his anti-natural and anti-human morality forces him to condemn. What Tocqueville thinks of his contemporaries is really much worse than what Gobineau thinks, for Gobineau only complains of their weakness, adaptability, impotence, while Tocqueville despairs of their very nature, and like a true Christian all the more so, the more potent that nature is. Thus Gobineau despises but loves at the same time, while Tocqueville fears and loathes. But in spite of his loathing of mankind around him, Tocqueville, as a real Liberal, carefully avoids drawing any realistic conclusions from his observations. On the contrary, he who fears the people, wishes to do something for the people, he who despairs of their very nature, wishes them to live on in faith, love and hope for something better, which might possibly "turn up" (change of government, customs, etc, etc.) without being able to give a shadow of a practical proof why this should be better for them, how it should be brought about, and who should bring it about Between the Scylla of a senseless optimism and the Charybdis of an unjust pessimism he sails along, and if this Liberal Christian did not come to grief long ago through his want of balance and principle, it was not his merit, it was the absence of any efficient counter-current which kept his unstable barque afloat during the last century. *Quousque tandem?*

In a letter, dated July 30th, 1856, Tocqueville comes back to the charge that Gobineau's ideas are extremely pernicious and immoral. He likewise throws out the hint, and rightly, I think, that the system is hostile to the doctrine of his Church, and that no one, not even that "cynic" Mérimée, would dare to proclaim such views openly in modern France. This reproach is repeated in a more outspoken way in a letter of January 14th, 1857. Here Tocqueville writes: "The very essence of Christianity is the endeavour to make out of humanity a single family whose members should be equally capable of perfecting themselves and of becoming more and more similar to each other. How can this essence of Christianity be reconciled with a doctrine of history which postulates different and unequal races, whose powers of judgment and action are more or less limited, and whose original dispositions are something fixed, and thus hinders some of these races from attaining any sort of perfection? Christianity, certainly has tried to make out of all human beings brethren, and equal brethren. Your doctrine, however, considers them at the very best like cousins, whose father is in heaven. ... For you there are no other people in this world but the conquerors and the vanquished, masters and slaves, and that by the very right of birth. ... I therefore wish to point out to you

25

again that the perusal of your book has made me very doubtful about your faith, your religiosity."

It is astonishing—but in a way easily explained—that Gobineau denies with indignation the charge of not being a good Catholic. In one of his answers, which gives us a hint as to the origin and cause of the Essay, he tells Tocqueville that he has seen the revolution with his own eyes. On this occasion all the dirty blouses have produced such a disgust in him, have accentuated his ideas of justice and truth to such an extent that, if he had not been married, he would have been capable of becoming a monk, only in order to be as antagonistic to the spirit of revolution as possible. ... "Don't doubt my religion," he pleads most earnestly with Tocqueville. "If I say I am a Catholic, it is the truth. Of course I am not a perfect Catholic, which I regret, though some day I hope to be one, but at least I am a sincere Catholic, Catholic in heart and soul, and if I believed for a moment like you that my historical ideas were in opposition to the Catholic religion, I should give them up immediately."

Such were Gobineau's opinions on his religion in early life, opinions which no doubt became somewhat modified later on. But on the whole he really seems to have had, like several other Catholic free spirits, no idea or consciousness of his own want of orthodoxy. All his attention was concentrated upon the victorious heretics, upon our modern revolutionaries, and by fighting them to the utmost of his power it absolutely escaped him that he had abandoned his Church, a Church which, in spite of its pagan varnishing cannot deny certain moral principles and ideas—the equality of man, original sin, free will and others, upon which the whole of Christianity is founded. By fighting the heretics Gobineau had become a heretic himself, but a heretic after the fashion of the Renaissance, a heretic as many brilliant Popes had been before him, that is to say, a heretic from above. He had left his Church unconsciously, but rightly, for it must be stated here that no one who wishes honestly to fight the spirit of revolution can remain, or should remain within even the Catholic Church. The Catholic Church is indeed the most pagan of the Christian Churches; it is the most anti-Christian Church in existence; it is a Church that to a certain extent counteracts the baleful doctrines of true Christianity, for it is an aristocratic Church—but it is still a Church; it would cease to be a Church if it were to give up Christianity altogether: a non-Christian Church, like a plum cake without plums, would be an absurdity. Catholicism will always keep up Christianity, and with Christianity the spirit of revolution. Thus no true enemy of the revolution can remain even within the Catholic fold any more than Gobineau could. But the mere fact that Gobineau—at first, anyhow—still imagined himself to be a faithful son of his Church, will prove how naturally the spirit of an enlightened paganism arises in our midst, how inevitable is this grand aristocratic reaction against modern democracy, how healthy the whole movement is and how powerful it will one day become. It is a movement which has filled some minds with almost religious fervor, a very necessary fervor, by the bye, for democracy is itself the outcome of a religion and can only be fought by another religion. And it is a European movement, to be sure, just like its enemy, democracy; for Gobineau was by no means the only unconscious pagan of his age. In England we have had the similar and still more instructive case of Benjamin Disraeli. This great man, for whom Christianity was only another form of Judaism, likewise considered himself all his life as a true son of Semitism, as a pillar of his holy and ancestral creed, as a stalwart *defensor fidei* against the infidels—and all his life he had not the slightest suspicion that by fighting English Liberalism, Puritanism, Nonconformity, he was not fighting, as he thought, infidelity, *but faith*, that he was really fighting his own religion, or rather, the logical outcome of his religion.

Tocqueville's letter of January 24th, 1857, is the fitting coping-stone to this memorable correspondence. "Ever since I have known you," Tocqueville writes in an apparent fit of indignation, "I have found your temperament *essentiellement frondeur.* ... What end can be served by these political discussions between us? We belong to two different camps, camps that absolutely exclude each other. You consider the human race as consisting of big children; and, besides, these children are, according to you, degenerate and badly educated children. ... I am, like you, of the opinion that our present humanity is very badly educated, which fact is the principal cause of its miseries and weaknesses, but I sincerely hold that a better education could remedy the evil. At any rate, I do not consider myself as justified in renouncing this task of education forever. I believe that one can still lead the human race towards better things, and this by an appeal to its natural honesty and good sense. In short, I wish to treat men as grown-up beings —perhaps I am wrong in this. ... You, sir, on the other hand, profoundly despise our human kind; at least our special part of mankind; you consider our people not only in a state of momentous distress and submission, but incapable of ever again rising to the surface. Their very constitution, you think, condemns them to slavery. ... I do not allow myself such liberty of thought about my people and country, and I think that no one has any right to come to such desperate views concerning them. In my eyes, individuals and societies only become something through liberty. That liberty is more difficult to establish and to keep up in democratic societies like ours than in certain aristocratic societies that have preceded us, I have always admitted But that the establishment of democratic liberty is impossible, I shall never be courageous enough even to think. That any attempt in this direction must fail, and that there is absolutely no hope for its establishment—that is a thought with which I would ask God never to inspire me. No, no, I do not believe, and I do not wish to believe, that this human species which is at the head of the visible universe, has become that horde of bastards which you think it, a horde which consequently should be handed over without future hope of help to a small number of herdsmen or keepers, who after all are not better than we are and sometimes may be even worse. With your kind permission I beg to say that I have less confidence in you than in the goodness and justice of our Father in Heaven."

This letter breathes, if not wisdom, at least honesty. Gobineau's principle of race, as Tocqueville rightly sees, can never be "discussed" or "explained" or "taught," like that Socratic virtue, which proved its democratic origin by the very fact that it could be taught. Gobineau's "Virtue," his principle of race, cannot be transmitted in this easy Socratic way: it must be felt, and where it is not felt, explanations and discussions are useless. But in spite of Tocqueville and Christianity, it is felt and will be felt more and more, and one day the decision between the two different creeds, that of Tocqueville and that of Gobineau, will have to be made—a decision, not of Parliament, but of the battlefield: for the sons of the Europeans of today—unlike their fathers, who fought for markets—will again fight for ideas.

III

Gobineau did not listen to de Tocqueville. No man who wants to do anything in this world can or should listen to his friends. Like the treasure-seeker in the German fairy tale he must pursue his lonely way, regardless of all the warnings, mysterious voices, friendly admonitions, frightening prophecies, tempting offers, and fond entreaties that force themselves on his attention and seek to lead him astray. If he gives in for a moment, if he listens, if he turns to the right or the left —so the tale runs—he loses his treasure, his truth. Gobineau did not listen, and so he found the way to his truth.

But even the bravest have their hours of weakness and despair, and if the brave soldier lives to a certain age and has experienced all the meanness and vicissitudes of a hostile world, he too, begins to yearn for less solitude and more gratitude and may be tempted to make—what other and less heroic people do all their life long—a slight compromise. It was in his old age, when he was tired and worn out, that Gobineau made a compromise which, I think, in the interest of his work, he was perfectly justified in making. He had become a friend of Richard Wagner and allowed himself to be "discovered" by this man, who had not the slightest inkling of what Gobineau was driving at

It was a real abyss that separated Gobineau from Wagner. First of all Wagner had been a revolutionary, and Gobineau, the *gentilhomme,* the *honnête homme* of the ancient régime abhorred all kinds of revolutions and revolutionaries. He knew what to expect from revolutions; he knew what kind of people a revolution brings to the top; he knew that a revolution only causes a reaction, and that between reaction and revolution the highest interests of life suffer, and not only suffer, but are often crushed What had such a man to do with Wagner? True, Wagner was now an old man and had turned into a romanticist and a Christian. But such characteristics could likewise never please a man like Gobineau, who knew (or ought to have known) that an old revolutionary invariably becomes either reactionary or a Christian, and who likewise knew that revolution, romanticism and Christianity are only the three progressive stages of the same decadent ailment. Had not he seen it often enough? First, the revolutionary makes the world uglier and sicker than it ever was before, then the romanticist offers the "hashish" of his art to alleviate the torments of the sick, and when the patient's senses and intelligence are dulled and numbed the Christian steps in and offers his panacea of redemption to the "sinner," whose only sin is his stupidity. Wagner had been through all the three stages himself; he had been a revolutionary, a romanticist and a Christian, he thus knew the needs of his time by his own experience, and had some justification for posing as the principal adviser and physician, or rather quack doctor, to his age. What had Gobineau in common with this typical representative of a decadent and neurotic epoch?

"I call 'romantic' the sick, and 'classical' the healthy," said Goethe. Gobineau, like Goethe, belonged to the few healthy minds, the few "lucky strokes" of nature, of that most unlucky and unhealthy past century. He had been healthy enough to diagnose the sickness of his time, and could not possibly overlook the sickness of his new friend, Richard Wagner, and his Bayreuthian followers. The Germanization of Christianity by means of a theatrical art, the redemption of the world by vegetables, the improvement of the race by more love-matches and other fads of the actor genius, must certainly have caused many a smile to appear on the lips of the critical Count. On the other hand he, no doubt, was too much of an *homme du monde* to give his whole mind to his histrionic host and the crowd of wild enthusiasts around him. It is nevertheless on record that he invariably entered a sort of mild protest against some of the more popular ideas of the musical reformer. It was, for instance, in vain that Wagner, who of course, as a true son of his age, occupied himself with "social questions," tried to win over his new friend to Schopenhauer's philosophy of pity. To prefer in this world the poor to the rich, the fool to the wise, the sick to the healthy, was in Gobineau's opinion a great error. A brave and noble soul, he answered, is ready to help and give its best to the world in noble sacrifice by itself and quite independently of any philosophic teaching. To Christian resignation he opposed his pagan dignity, to Christian humility self respect, to tame forgiveness stoical forbearance or contempt, and to the passive and feminine virtues of faith, hope and love the antagonistic active and manly virtues of deed, daring and bravery in thought as well as in action.

And when it came to the equality of men he would not even listen. He likewise abhorred the "Teutonic" tendencies of Wagner, who in these days posed as Germany's truest protagonist and staunchest defender against the Jewish danger. Gobineau knew well enough that these Teutonic tendencies had caused in the past his *bête noire,* that mother of all modern revolutions, the German reformation. From his aristocratic point of view he could only see a heretic and a revolutionary in the modern German—and certainly he could never be persuaded by Wagner to believe in Germany's "great" reformer, Martin Luther. But he seems to have always been civil and tolerant toward his German acquaintance, his long travels, residences abroad and knowledge of mankind having no doubt taught him to wear that mask of bonhomie which the simple-minded are apt to mistake for affability and simplicity, but which is in reality nothing but cruel contempt There is a story related in the *Bayreuther Blätter*, according to which Wagner once praised the good influence of a well-brewed beer upon his favorite Luther and had asked Gobineau to join him in drinking the health of the famous miner's son. Gobineau is said to have winced a little, but after a while to have joined in with a smile, and the words: "Very well, let us drink the beer to the health of Martin Luther." It must have been a delightful scene. Gobineau drinking beer in the company of Germans to the health of a superstitious monk—does that not remind one of Louis XVI with the red cap of the revolution on his head giving friendly nods to his people below?

There is an article in the May-June number (1881) of the *Bayreuther Blätter*, entitled "Heroism and Christianity." It is a joint production of Montague and Capulet, of the Pagan and the Christian, of Gobineau and Richard Wagner. Gobineau wrote the article and Wagner added a preface of his own to it—and thus it became a most extraordinary document, reminding one of those Landsknecht-uniforms of the Middle Ages, of which one half was yellow and the other red, or perhaps, as in this case, one half black and the other white.

The black color fittingly represents the gloom of Gobineau's thought. He again repeats in this article his pessimistic views of the European peoples whose distinguishing features are sucked out by the ever-progressing vampire of democracy, a monster which their want of health and character is unable to resist. The views of the Essay are reiterated, but since his residence in Asia Gobineau has noticed another cloud upon the horizon of Europe; the yellow danger, the imminent Mongolian expansion. This danger he thinks is even more accentuated by the unconscious help it received from those "European door-keepers," the Slavonic peoples, who will in time be only too ready to hand over to their Asiatic cousins the keys of Europe. The gradual decadence of Europe—thus Gobineau concludes—was announced long ago in the Essay: the only mistake with which he had to reproach himself, is that from an optimism peculiar to youth he had thought the development of this decadence much slower than it really was and will turn out to be.

And now let us listen to the innocent, the "white," the Christian preface-writer who naturally lives in hope, in love, in faith, and in other clouds. In a very casual fashion, Wagner at first repeats Gobineau's ideas about the degeneration and decadence of mankind. He, like Gobineau, thinks that this degeneration was caused by the mixture of races which was brought about by an initial fault of the human race, inexperienced in its youth as it then was. This initial fault, it will be seen, has already a somewhat Semitic flavor: for by means of it the concept of "original sin" is smuggled into the system of Gobineau. But Wagner forgets or wishes to forget that Gobineau declares this fault to be absolutely fatal, ineradicable; for Gobineau, not being a theologian or a Teutonic metaphysician, preferred to stick to scientific observations, however disagreeable they might turn out to be. But Wagner knew what he was doing when he declared "decadence" to be a "fault" and a "sin." A sin, of course, allows of redemption; and by means of the redemption which our Christian has to offer, Gobineau's pessimism is turned into more hopeful channels. Man, no doubt, is a damnable sinner and a miserable decadent, but likewise a possible future hero—thus Wagner's secret thought runs. It is an astounding assumption, but what assumptions are impossible to pious souls, what benumbing of reason are they not capable of?

For our composer, who was now a Christian, was as such not allowed to lose hope in the sinner and the decadent, as did that gifted, though perhaps too gloomy, Gobineau. Wagner, therefore, in the latter half of this article, "Heroism and Christianity," expresses the firm belief, that out of the chaos of stupidity and impotence, which "our friend Gobineau" has laid bare, salvation is still possible. True, the blood of the most noble races has deteriorated, but even for the most humble race and individual there must be a way to hope and health. By means of that "only genuine Christian Sacrament, which consists in the symbolic consumption of the blood of Christ," a divine purification might be effected, and he, Wagner, would recommend this Sacrament as a sure antidote against the degeneration of mankind which Gobineau had described in such a masterly manner in his *Essay on the Inequality of Human Races*.

Rightly, M. Seillière,[1] the intelligent French critic, who unfortunately is not poet enough himself to appreciate to a proper degree either a Gobineau or a Nietzsche, says "Talk history to a mystic like Wagner! Gobineau's labor on such a man is lost entirely. This thick-skinned interpreter of his thinks that the only consequence of Gobineau's gloom and bitterness will be to inspire a certain wholesome shock to our thoughtless age, to shake that easy optimism in which we still indulge, and thus to prepare us gently for that holy path, that path of sighs and tears that leads to Golgotha and the Cross. Is it possible to love each other more and understand each other less than this prefacer and his author have done?"

No, it is not; but, nevertheless, to this hopeless misunderstanding on the part of Wagner, Gobineau

---

[1] Ernest Seillière: *Le Comte de Gobineau et l'Aryanisme Historique*: Paris, 1903 (p. 370).

35

owes his discovery: without his blind friend, Gobineau might have remained unknown to this very day. The whole world would have been poorer for it, but the loss would have been mostly felt by the Germans, with whom Gobineau has become a popular hero, a protagonist of the Empire, a name to conjure with for all the enemies of the Fatherland: Jews, Catholics, Poles, Latins, and other second-rate people. But this popularity of Gobineau in Germany—an irony as great as that of Gobineau's discovery by a romantic musician—is entirely due to a misunderstanding of Gobineau on the part of the Germans, a misunderstanding, however, which is to some extent caused by what I consider as one of the rare flaws in Gobineau's system itself.

The hatred of the French Revolution and the doctrine of the Equality of man had thrown Gobineau into such antagonism against everything around him that he finally began to hate France down to her very historical roots. He was tempted to see charlatanism, theatricality and exuberant phrase-making (which are the characteristics of a democratic age) everywhere even in that grand early history of the Latin races, and thus became very unjust, I think, to the whole of Graeco-Latin culture, and especially to the most flourishing ages of that culture, in Greece and Rome. Henceforth his ideal in history became the Germanic tribes of the Middle Ages, and their feudal institutions, which allowed a man to attach and defend his honor sword in hand—times, when a man was his own master still and not subjected to the law of *Polis* or *Urbs*. In *Polis* and *Urbs* the lawyers and phrasemongers would always prevail—among the warrior tribes of the Franks, the Normans, the Lombards, the glib tongue of sly plebeians had never to be feared, and a free and noble personality never stood in danger of being suppressed. Gobineau himself, isolated as he was amongst his plebeian surroundings, thought himself related to those ancient and noble tribes; he firmly believed in his descent from a Scandinavian and Germanic stock. He even wrote a book, "Ottar Jarl," in which the history of his ancestors is minutely described. This Ottar Jarl is a descendant of a Norwegian family of the ninth century, who, being a younger son, is disinherited from rural possessions according to law and consequently obliged to emigrate from Scandinavia. He becomes a pirate, descends upon the French coast, and there founds the feudal house of Gournay, the house from which Gobineau himself claimed descent. When our Count was French Minister in Stockholm, he one day made an excursion with some friends to those beautiful isles which, covered with pines, lie dotted in crystal waters all along the Swedish coast. Before a group of imposing ruins, Gobineau suddenly stopped and said: "I feel this is the place where I hail from"—a story which will set a good many people smiling. But it is a fact—which science, that satellite of poetical observation, may one day elucidate—that very sensitive people easily recognize the place where their ancestors have lived: there are Jews who at once feel at home in the South and among Orientals, and the French Count may have experienced a similar sensation when his foot had touched that Scandinavian spot.

Thus we need not deny that Count Gobineau had Norman blood in his veins, but the conclusion he draws from this fact, the veneration he feels for this blood, ought to be somewhat critically examined. It was modesty after all on the part of Gobineau, it seems to me, if he attributed his nobility of thought to his Norman and Germanic ancestry. For Gobineau was, above all, what these tribes never were, a man of daring thought. And the objection which I would raise to Gobineau's idealization and veneration of the ancient Germans is just this, that they were sadly lacking in all the higher elements of culture, sadly lacking in what Gobineau possessed—in ideas. In stating this I do not underrate the value of personal bravery and prowess as exhibited by these Franks, Lombards, and Normans, because these are virtues which our industrial age sadly lacks and urgently requires: but I do not consider these virtues alone sufficient. I am of the opinion that they only constitute a kind of barbarian greatness which can never be compared with that cultured greatness, that combination of great thought and great action which was the glory of Greece and Rome. Military prowess was possessed by such a race as the Huns, too; it was possessed, and is still possessed to some extent, by the Turks—but no one, I think, would set up Huns and Turks as model races for mankind. Where, I should like to ask the *manes* of Count Gobineau, are the ideas of his beloved Germanic tribes? Have they founded a religion like the Jews? Have they excelled in art, like the Assyrians, Babylonians, and Egyptians? In philosophy and tragedy like the Greeks, in government and law like the Romans? Have they bequeathed a holy or unholy book to the world—a book that could rival the Old Testament, the book of Manu, the tragedies of Sophocles, the manly history of Thucydides, the sweet poetry of Ovid and Horace? No, they have not. They have had no ideas, and, though poetically endowed like all youthful and martial peoples, this gift was never strong enough to withstand the onslaught of Oriental thought, and thus their song of the Nibelungs, their Beowulf, and even their Edda, have come down to us in a half-Christianized dress. They have had no ideas of their own to oppose to the Semitic idea: that is the reason, the only reason, why they were conquered and converted by the mere breath of a Christian missionary. It was the want of the inner Holy fire, the want of strong and burning passion, it was in short the poverty of the race which will put Count Gobineau's much-beloved Germanic tribes forever into the second rank, when compared for instance with that similar conqueror-tribe —the Arabs. The Arabs, too, were a martial people, and when they left their desert, they were as poor in earthly possessions as were the Franks and Normans; they had no art as yet and scarcely any written literature; but, when they had conquered the world, when they had gained their place in the sun, they at once proved that the germ of the great and the sublime was at least in them: they created that great Empire from the Tigris to the Guadalquivir in which art, science, and literature flourished, which kept the lamps of Hellenic thought burning in the midst of Christian darkness and which the Christianized Germanic tribes, the enemies of light, afterwards successfully extinguished. Rightly, therefore, and to this very day those historians, who though Christians are honest historians, regret the fall of Granada.

Why did Count Gobineau, universal historian that he was, fail to allude to Arabic civilization, fail to relate the story of the fall of Granada? It is a story which might well have appealed to him, as a poet, just as it has appealed to a colleague of his, to one who was more nearly related to the Arabs—Heinrich Heine. In November, 1491, Boabdil, the last king of the Moors, came out of Granada and gave the keys of the town to the victorious Catholic sovereigns, Ferdinand and Isabella. Then, with a few followers, he left for the south, but upon a rocky eminence which commanded a last view of Granada he checked his horse and, as his eyes for the last time wandered over the scenes of his departed greatness, his heart swelled and he burst into tears. "You do well," said his mother, when she saw him cry, "to weep like a woman for what you could not defend like a man." It was a Semitic mother who could speak these manly words to her son; words, no doubt, that caused a Semitic mother more pangs of pain than any other. Is it not almost certain that over his enthusiastic praise of the noble Germanic blood, Count Gobineau forgot that there was in the world a noble Semitic blood, a blood all the more important as it still exists amongst us almost in its racial purity?

IV

But happy that author whose writings have a decided weakness somewhere or contain a palpable untruth, for he is sure to be discovered! Unhappy that Homer who never nods, for he will nod forever, and no discoverer or disciple will awake him, and no posterity will rise up to do honor to his message. And thrice happy the author whose weaknesses are even misunderstood: *sic itur ad astra,* only thus and then is he sure to find the way to the heart of humanity.

Count Gobineau, as we have seen, had sung the praise of the noble Germanic blood, of a blood which, as he thought, ran in his own veins, and which he rightly judged to be different from and superior to that of other mortals. It was certainly a fault of his racial system that he forgot even to mention the noble Arabic blood, but this omission, after all, only slightly interferes with the value of his book as an original piece of work. But precisely by this flaw, by the neglect of the Semitic blood, by this praise of the noble Germanic blood, has he endeared himself to the heart of the Germans, who, once the question of race came to the foreground in European thought, were most eager to establish their claim to a noble past and a noble blood. For the Germans are people who live on thought and theories, people who consequently have to adapt themselves to any new theories that spring up on the intellectual horizon of our Continent. In this respect they are very unlike the "materialistic" Englishmen, who in their innermost heart have a contempt for "braininess," who think they can do without "ideas," who know for a certainty that they will "muddle through" somehow, for Providence, that just Providence, cannot—in their opinion—help having strong British propensities. The German rather looks down upon this British contempt of ideas, this blind trust in Providence: it is his glory to have acted differently, to have always helped Providence by his own thoughts—although I have my doubts whether Providence does not prefer the British modesty and non-interference to the German over-zeal and obtrusiveness. Be this as it may, one thing is quite certain: theories that arise anywhere in Europe are sure, sooner or later, to attract the attention of the Germans, and living by theories as they do, he has sooner or later to adapt himself to the new and victorious thought. Of late this new thought has not been very favorable to the Germans; it has become more and more difficult to adapt the old Teutonic ideals to the new theories—and Germany has consequently become somewhat embarrassed. Not for long, though—what could embarrass that gifted nation of "poets and thinkers " for long? The idea of "race," for instance, was certainly a very perplexing one for the Germans, who, after all, have troubled about race less than any nation in Europe, who have never had an aristocracy worthy of the name, like the French and English, like the Poles and Italians: but why should a thinking nation be embarrassed by a new idea, if this nation is at the same time also a poetical one? Let the poetical gift of this nation, let its powers of idealistic interpretation play round the "New Thought," and the thought is rendered harmless and ready for adaptation. If we cannot adapt ourselves to the new theories—thus the Germans reason—let us adapt the theories and their exponents for our own benefit, let us re-interpret them, let us poetize them, vaporize them, until ....

It is by means of this power of poetical interpretation, that the Germans have succeeded in making Gobineau a kind of national hero. No doubt this was a great feat of "poetic license," but the license was justified by success. Gobineau's name is uttered with the greatest respect all over the Fatherland, his books and letters have nearly all been translated: they have gone into many editions and are read all over the country, and Gobineau's "Renaissance"—five times translated into German—has even been on the répertoire of theaters. Many years ago, a Gobineau Society was formed in Germany; the ablest men of letters, scientists and politicians became members; to be a *Gobiniste* became a sort of patriotic duty—not to be a *Gobiniste* stamped one as an "enemy of the Empire." Gobineau has even been set up by these enthusiastic Teutonics as a sort of antipope against Nietzsche, and it has thus come about that the Frenchman is venerated in modern Germany with the same fervor as Nietzsche the German, is worshipped in France. But how was it done? What has Gobineau to do with modern Germany? How could the Germans appropriate him? The answer is: by means of their power of poetical interpretation. It is this German gift which has allowed the German nation, under the guidance of their princes and professors, to claim Gobineau's system for themselves and to apply it to their own history, past and present They have made use of Gobineau's weakness, his exaggerated praise of the German conqueror tribes, but they have misunderstood or "poetically interpreted" even this weakness, and have quite innocently transferred his praise of the Germanic past to the Germanic present, his praise of the

"Germanic hero" to the praise of the modern German citizen.

To Gobineau, modern Germany was as contemptible a country as modern France; for it was based, like France, upon a plebeian revolution, the Protestant Reformation, which he most heartily detested. And it was not only the Germany of the Reformation that Gobineau disliked; it was modern Germany as well; it was the Empire itself, that glory of the Teutomaniac, that roused his doubts and his displeasure. Can this cause wonder? How could a profound thinker like Gobineau overlook the flaw in this Empire, this powerful organization without aim, ideas or reason, this body without a soul, this incarnation of materialism on earth? How could a psychologist be deceived by that mask of foggy philosophy, romantic art and crazy idealism, behind which the modern German tries to hide his ignoble aspect? How could he be blinded by the "success" of such a motley crew, gained as this success was and is by the trampling down of every genuine individuality, of every valuable idea, of everything beautiful and noble? Thus even in the early days of the Empire, we see our Count in doubt about this modern Germany. "I understand," he writes to his friend, Professor Kellermann, of Tübingen, on August 18th, 1872, "the motives which have forced Germany into an excessive concentration of all her powers, but this very concentration is the surest way to paralyze all intellectual action, and thus your organization will cost you so much, not only financially, but also physically and morally, that I do not think anything good for the life of the whole or the parts can ensue from it." What a true prophet spoke here! And what deaf ears he found and still finds! Or, should I, as an excuse, say, what poetical ears? The warnings of this prophet are ignored by his audience, his conclusions from the past are falsified and misunderstood, and his message for the future—race—is misapplied by these intoxicated patriots to the present day, to themselves. For the modern Germans pretend that they are a race, that they are Gobineau's ideal Germanic race, and that their success in this world is due to their pure and noble blood. A brewer, when he grows wealthy and successful, desires a title and must be on the look-out for a pedigree.

To the honor of truth, however, it ought to be stated that it is not the true Gobineau who has become the god of the "cultured" modern Germans. After all, Gobineau was too much of an honest writer for this, too little of an idealist, too much of a man who never shirked facts and had uttered terrible truths, just as Stendhal, Mérimée, Nietzsche, and other brave Europeans had done. In order to make Gobineau palatable to the ordinary modern German, he had first to be remodeled and refashioned. It is a full-blown Englishman who has done Germany this service, an Englishman who has become Germanized, and who—just as converted Jews become more Christian than born Christians—has become more German, more idealistic, more of a poet than even the best German metaphysician. This man was Wagner's son-in-law, Mr. Houston Stewart Chamberlain.

Mr. Chamberlain's book, *The Foundations of the Nineteenth Century*,[2] is a double paean, a paean to modern Germany and to Christianity in its Protestant form, which latter, however, if I understand Mr. Chamberlain rightly, is still open to some improvement by the Teutonic genius, especially gifted as this genius is in the high realms of religion. And not only in religion, but in other spheres as well; for, according to Mr. Chamberlain,

---

[2] *The Foundations of the Nineteenth Century*, by Houston Stewart Chamberlain; transl. by John Lees (London, 1911). The page quotations are taken from this edition.

ever since the sixth century all men who have produced anything in politics, ideas, or art, without exception, belonged to the Germanic stock. Thus this stock (in which Mr. Chamberlain, for safety's sake, includes the Celts and the Slavs, but whose most gifted branch is the Teuton) has created all the great and good things in this world, while on the other hand everything bad or inferior is of Latin or Semitic origin. Great Latins and great Jews who appealed to Mr. Chamberlain's taste are of course allocated by him to the Germanic stock. Thus Christ, as is proved by Mr. Chamberlain, was only born in a Jewish milieu, but was a Jew neither by race nor spirit (Vol. I., p. 351). Thus the great Renaissance was never a creation of the fine Latin and Southern spirit, but a manifestation of the Germanic genius, which was racially predominant at that time in both northern and southern Italy. These ignoble Southerners, these slavish children of the "chaos of the peoples," with their "materialistic" Catholic Church governing them, would never have done anything without these pure-blooded idealistic Teutons who alone in this world have kept up the ideas of faith, race, nobility, and individuality. And as in the past so in the present: all true culture is Teutonic. For the Teuton is the artist of the modern world, he is "the only human being who can be compared with the Hellene—in him, too, the striking and specifically distinctive character is the simultaneous and equal development of knowledge, civilization and culture." (VoL II., p. 255.) As Lord Redesdale, who has written the preface to the- English translation, rightly puts it: "The leitmotiv which runs through the whole book is the assertion of the superiority of the Teutonic family to all the other races of the world."

Though Chamberlain's conclusions are very different from Gobineau's, it will on closer examination be seen that the root of Chamberlain's system is to be found in

Gobineau. Gobineau's is the idea of race, the idea of the pre-eminence of the Germanic stock, the idea of the rejuvenation of Rome by the invasion of the Germanic tribes, the idea of the manly and superior qualities of these tribes as opposed to Latin and Semitic inferiority: as also is Gobineau's the idea of the fraudulence and cowardice of the ancient Greeks and the little trust to be put in their historic narratives and the accounts of their victories. I feel quite certain that without Gobineau's epos, "The Decline and Fall of the Aryan," Chamberlain's "Rise and Progress of the Teuton" would never have been written. In place of Gobineau's gloomy and final vaticinations, of course, a "happy ending" had to be substituted, that "happy ending" which is so dear to our theatrical managers; for no true tragedy could be endured by our exhausted audiences, even were they composed of that flower of the nations, the Germans. It would have been folly for any of them to produce a true Gobineau before that decadent public, accustomed as it is to romantic optimism or nerve-racking brutalities. The adaptation of Gobineau to a more modern taste was therefore essential, and in justice to the adapter and popularizer, it should be added that he has done his work well He has suppressed the best thoughts of Gobineau, weakened the strong ones, accentuated the bad ones; dimmed, darkened and dulled the whole, and then added some ideas of his own which, though not in touch with truth, at least prove that our fortunate philosopher is in thorough touch with something else, to wit, his age. As a matter of fact, it is not difficult to please one's age if one belongs so closely to it as Mr. Chamberlain. *Quiconque ressemble au peuple, l'émeut*, as Goethe used to say.

In conformity with the spirit of the age, Chamberlain is a very religious and moral personality. No pagan, no Gobineau-gospel—and that in spite of

Goethe—could have any general success in Germany, where the upper classes hypocritically cling to the Church in the vain hope of keeping down, by means of Christianity, the atheistic and revolutionary middle and lower classes, and where these latter sincerely but unconsciously adhere to the essence of Christianity, its morality, which is that of submissive or revolutionary slaves. Even the Catholics of Germany have something crude, bigoted and low-churchy about them, which separate them entirely from their Catholic brethren, those semi-pagans of France, Italy, and even Ireland. There is no country in Europe more hopelessly Nazarene than Germany; and Chamberlain, by baptizing that over-healthy pagan Gobineau and also otherwise watering down some of his ideas, at once appealed to those countless thousands for whom water is everything, and truth, other than religious or moral, too intoxicating. Mr. Chamberlain, however, did not only become a mere Nazarene, but a German Nazarene— that is to say, a Jew-hater. Gobineau, too, had hated Semitism, but Gobineau's hatred of Semitism was of a very different kind. Gobineau's was an honest Antisemitism, it was, like Nietzsche's, an historical Antisemitism: it had nothing whatever to do with modern Antisemitism, that movement born from fear, envy, and impotence. This is how Count Gobineau speaks of the modern Jews: "In no period has daring thought in the realm of philosophy been wanting in the Jew. Nothing has changed with him in this respect, and I could quote several learned men of Bagdad who, by the audacity of their reasoning, are entirely worthy of the most heterodox spirits that their race has ever produced The Jewish mind is, of its very nature, enquiring, and it is eager to extract from the wealth of this world the element of knowledge as well as the element of gold."— (*Les Religions et les Philosophies dans l'Asie Centrale*, p. 66.)

Gobineau's Antisemitism (this must be upheld even in the teeth of German Jewry, which on account of the Teutonic misrepresentation of our author still looks askance at him) has nothing whatever to do with modern Antisemitism, it is not the Antisemitism of people who are (as Nietzsche has baptized them) "step-motherly treated by nature" (*schlecht weggekommene*): it is an upright, a genuine, a gentlemanly Antisemitism, it is the Antisemitism of the aristocrat, who sees his very blood threatened by revolutionary religions. Both Nietzsche's and Gobineau's Antisemitism, therefore, included of course Christianity. Chamberlain, however, turns this Antisemitism of an *honnête homme* into the Antisemitism of the people and directs it, according to the "needs of the age," against the modern Jews to the exclusion of Christians. He likewise turns Gobineau's anti-classical and anti-Roman tendencies into modern channels, that is to say, against the modern Catholics, the Jesuits, and that Roman Church which is still such an eyesore to the German Protestant. All this, of course, was done in good faith, without the wish to deceive and entirely without bad conscience on the part of the author.

The *Foundations* had a wonderful success. All the leaders of thought from the German Emperor down to the humblest schoolmaster were overflowing with delight. The German Emperor had a copy of the book sent to every school, and all the schoolmasters of the Fatherland were busy—with the additional help of the cane—in impressing upon the minds and bodies of the German youths their heroic descent. What they had long suspected, but did not dare to think, was now proved beyond all doubt; they were a noble, a pure race. Just as Molière's *bourgeois gentilhomme* was astonished and delighted when he was told by someone that he wrote "prose," the *bourgeois allemand* was perhaps less astonished but even more charmed that he was himself "poetry" and "culture," that his very blood was heroic and holy, that he was a member of a race, as a matter of fact, of the noblest race on earth. And out of this race, so Chamberlain had assured him in his book, there would "blossom out a future and harmonious culture such as the world had never seen before, a culture incomparably more beautiful than any of which history has to tell, a culture in which men would really be better and happier than they are at present!" (See Author's Introduction, p. xcviii.) God was in His Heaven, all was right with the world, the triumph of the Teuton assured forever. Standing upright in his triumphal car, with flashing eyes and quivering nostrils, this grandson of Arminius, captain no more of barbarian hordes, but of industry and of "culture" was driven up the Capitoline Hill to receive an enormous, well-deserved laurel wreath for his square, capacious, cultured head. Only one little important figure was missing in this noisy procession. In order to check the hubris of the victorious conqueror, in order to restrain that pride which invariably comes before the fall, the Romans never forgot to employ a slave, who was seen standing next to the hero upon the quadriga and heard to whisper into his ear from time to time the warning, "Remember that thou, too, art mortal." This slave was wanting; but instead of the slave a herd of slavish and time-serving authors and critics assured the pure-blooded captain on the triumphal car that Chamberlain's book was the last word on the subject, and that in this gifted Englishman the Teuton Achilles had at last found a heaven-inspired Homer who could do justice to his character and noble achievements in past, present and future.

Of course, there was likewise a great deal of profound dissent, there was also, from the more cautious critics, a demand for a closer study of the question and the acquisition of more scientific facts. But the fitting and the only answer to Chamberlain's gospel has never been given, nor, so far as I know, even been suspected. And how could it have been suspected? How could it have been thought that this author, this member of a pure race, this man "glorying in the consciousness of his pure race" (Vol. I., p. 269), would produce a real bastard book, a book in which two wholly incompatible ideas had been "crossed," two ideas by nature mutually exclusive of one another had been "married" and mixed together—that of race and that of Christianity? Has there ever been an unholier alliance, and that committed by an enemy of mésalliances, of cross-breedings, of purposeless intermarriages?

Race is a matter of selection and exclusion, something hostile to, or at least regardless of, the outer world. Christianity is the religion of "love," that is to say, it has nothing exclusive, but something obtrusive about it, especially if it is remembered that this declaration of "love" came from the lower classes. Thus Christianity from its beginning, and through all the ages up to this very hour, has had one aim, and that is to be a universal religion, a religion to be offered to all, a religion which, if accepted by all, would make out of humanity one great family of equal brethren. It was on account of this very idea that the first Christians separated from the Jews and founded that all-embracing religion which today is called Christianity—for the Jews themselves, or rather the Jewish Christians (as may be read in the Acts and the Pauline epistles) still held fast to the belief that their creed was not for everybody, that the Messiah had been sent to them alone, and that not every stranger and outsider had a right to participate in the Salvation. The idea of race, of exclusiveness, of "the chosen people" still haunted these Jews even after they had become Christians, and over the question of race (not over the question *whether* the Messiah had come, but *to whom* He had come) Jews and Christians soon separated. Thus a modern Jew may pride himself on race, a modern nobleman, like Gobineau or Nietzsche, may pride himself on race; but never a true and modern Christian, least of all a German Christian. For the German Protestant Christian is again a *réchauffé* of the first Christian, he is (as Mr. Chamberlain himself sees) a Pauline Christian, that is to say, a rebel, a heretic, a democrat: just as the first Christians rebelled against the Jews, he—by means of his Reformation—has rebelled against the aristocracy of the Italian Renaissance, he owes his "Empire," his present position in Europe, to his rebellion. It is likewise he who—indirectly by the same reformation—instigated the French Revolution; it is he who has brought all the democratic values to the front in modern Europe; it is he who even today, with his four millions of Socialists, marches in front of all the European democracies. Only a few months ago (May 8th, 1912) the German Reichstag by a great majority asked the Government to bring in a Bill legalizing in their colonies marriages between whites and blacks. That was indeed German, democratic, and Christian; but such people should never talk about race, for race was, is, and should be, the Germans' greatest abhorrence, an abhorrence which, if genuine, everyone can understand, and even tolerate to a certain extent. What cannot and must not be tolerated is the confusion of these two contradictory values—Race and Christianity.

It will be seen that my description of the German as a "hopeless Nazarene" needs some correction, the "hopelessness" in him being really more accentuated than the Christianity. In plain English: the German is modern—neither fish nor flesh, neither oil nor water, neither a Christian nor an aristocrat. A real aristocrat *must* abhor the idea of Christianity, just as a good Christian ought to abhor the idea of race. But the bad Christians and the bad aristocrats have a less decided taste—they behave like that capricious prima donna, who woke up one morning with the idea, "Tea is good, chocolate is good, why not have both together?" and then ordered her maid to bring her a cup of tea and chocolate mixed. Mr. Chamberlain, with unconscious humor, frequently points in his great book to the dualistic nature of the German character—it is no doubt due to this dualistic nature of his that dualistic books, tea-and-chocolate books, like Mr. Chamberlain's, appeal to him so very strongly. Sixty-thousand copies of this "philosophic" production have now been sold in Germany. *Similia similibus.*

On the whole, however, Mr. Chamberlain himself— my sense of justice prompts me to state this—ought to be exempted from the blame attached to his German admirers and should not be accused of any want of consistency in his taste. Mr. Chamberlain has even a very pronounced judgment and has always protested against that astounding tendency of his readers to swallow everything, to muddle everything, and to digest for instance even such antagonistic natures, as Gobineau and himself. On several occasions, and with great eloquence, Mr. Chamberlain has stated[3] that he has nothing to do with Gobineau and that his name should never be mentioned in the same breath even with that of the French Count, who was a man of quite different stamp. It would be rash to conclude from this protest that he has the intention of deceiving his public, that he wishes to pose as an original genius, that he wishes to impress upon mankind the fact that he is not an epigone and popularizer, but a creative spirit. This would be a

---

[3] See amongst others his *Wehr und Gegenwehr* (München, 1912), pp. 12-15.

great injustice to Mr. Chamberlain, who, it must be repeated, is, if nothing better, at least an honest man. The only conclusion to which his extraordinary and angry protest can lead us, is again a very honorable, though a negative one, namely, that Mr. Chamberlain does not belong to the numerous and disagreeable class of snobs. For a snob is a man who tries to get into touch with people above his station, and who, having gained access to the charmed circle, boasts of his distinguished acquaintances: there have even been snobs, who have accused themselves of having stolen silver spoons from a lord's table, only in order to let other people know they "have been there." But Mr. Chamberlain is quite a different man—he too, has been at a lord's table, but he never boasts about it, for he does not know that "he was there." And there was plenty of beautiful plate upon the table, but Mr. Chamberlain again did not know that it was silver. And the lord, who had lived in Oriental countries and had imbibed Eastern munificence with the air, had asked Mr. Chamberlain to help himself freely to everything on the table with the inclusion even of some of the valuable plate. Mr. Chamberlain consequently pocketed many silver spoons, but he considered them just ordinary spoons and did not attribute to them any special value. And then, when he came home, he procured plenty of shiny brass spoons (which look like gold), and partly with the lord's fine old silver and partly with his own shiny brass he feeds his numerous "Aryan" public, which is not very expert in matters artistic and much prefers Mr. Chamberlain's brass spoons to the count's old silver. It were only to be wished that Gobineau could return from Walhalla and assist once, as the guest of the evening, at such a grand "Aryan" dinner. No doubt he would experience a kind of satisfaction for having been a true though pessimistic prophet of the future of the Aryan. But, good heavens, how sorry he would have been for having wasted his silver spoons!

V

In Oriental towns, towards evening, when the talk and the bustle of the market is at its loudest, a voice from above is suddenly heard, ringing out into the crystal air over housetops and bazaars, over gardens and fountains, over rivers and coffee-houses, a voice that drowns with its clear and metallic force the noisy talk of the vulgar crowd in the market place below. It is the voice of the Muezzin who from the top of the minaret calls the faithful to prayer. Let us listen to him. Let us forget the literary market place below with its Jewish and Christian, French and German dealers in modern ideas, let us no longer heed that loud, crowded, and alas! so empty shopland, where the honest merchants are not intelligent, where the intelligent merchants are not honest, and where the crowds of sellers and buyers are neither one nor the other. Let us listen to the voice from above, let us listen to the Muezzin, let us listen to Gobineau's own words and ideas.

In light, sweet, and joyful tones this voice rings out of the pages of Gobineau's *Les Religions et les Philosophies dans l'Asie Centrale*. The first chapter of this book on the moral and religious character of the Asiatics, has justly become famous, and, with its lucid power of argument, will come as a surprise to many intelligent Europeans, accustomed as they are to look down upon all Asiatics as inferior beings. Gobineau is able to undermine many of their prejudices, for some of the so-called Asiatic vices are only vices in the eyes of the simple-minded European, and really turn out to be virtues, if only seen in the proper light. Thus, that dreaded Asiatic hypocrisy (a practice so common in Central Asia that it has received the special name of *Ketman*) is, according to our exploring ambassador, only a mask put on by the more profound Oriental mind in order to keep truth away from inferior or vulgar souls. Gobineau compares this behaviour of the modern Asiatic with that of the Greek philosophers, who likewise taught that all truth of a superior kind should be enveloped in mystery, for it was not reasonable to throw higher wisdom before inferior and unworthy beings. But while thus paying a high compliment to the intelligence and profundity of the Asiatic, Gobineau does not forget that drawback which every high development of the poetical and psychological faculties must bring in its train. It is this superabundance of thought which makes the Asiatic as much of a fantastic dreamer as a superabundance of common sense makes his European brother a dry matter-of-fact creature. And it is this crowd of ideas and theories, which constantly chase and supplant each other in the mind of the Asiatic, that are the cause and source of his political weakness. This over-intelligence, as it might be called, isolates our Asiatic from his fellows to such an extent that collective action (based as it always must be upon uniformity of sentiment in a large number of people) becomes almost an impossibility among the gifted Asiatic races. As a consolation it might be conceded to the Asiatic that fools find it much easier to combine, first because they are obliged to do so on account of their weakness, and then because no individuality of their own makes them shrink from too close a contact with their brethren. In Asia, Count Gobineau tells us, with an ironical side-glance at Europe, fools are the greatest exception.

But the best part of the book, and the greater part of it, is dedicated to the history of the Babists, a Persian sect founded shortly before Gobineau came to Persia, by

a young and spirited Persian who was called "The Bab."
It is a strange tale that our author has here to tell, a
story which seems to us more than familiar, reminding
us as it does of the common religious bonds of Asia and
Europe, of the holy tales of our own gospel. Was it the
intention of Count Gobineau—and this is a question
that will easily occur to a critic who is accustomed to
look for the meaning between the lines—to write a
parody on the ancient document of the Christian faith?
I do not think so for a moment, for Gobineau had, like
many Catholics, even free-thinking Catholics, a sort of
shyness about touching upon religion in too outspoken a
manner. If there is parody, it is entirely unconscious, but
parody undoubtedly there is. There is the Saviour, the
"Bab," that is to say, "the only door by which one can
reach the knowledge of God," a quiet, studious, patient,
and somewhat mystical youth, *une âme douce et un peu
rêveuse,*, as Gobineau describes him. He has quite a
number of interesting, though hardly novel, ideas in his
head: how to bring man happiness in this world, how to
unite under one ethical roof the Jew, the Christian, and
the Moslem, how to emancipate and enlighten the fair
sex, likewise how to be good and charitable though rich,
and how to be just and forgiving though dealing with
criminals and enemies. There was a faint flavor of
Buddhistic sweetness, I think, in this attractive
personality, who by his charming and persuasive manner
easily converted all those who came into contact with
him. But these new converts, less Buddhistic, of course,
and more impulsive than the Master, tried to strengthen
peaceful persuasion by other means. They openly
accused the authorities of immorality and corruption,
they ran about the streets looting, rioting and
threatening and insulting the mullahs (clergy), and thus
finally forced the Government to intervene between
them and their accusers—an intervention that caused a

bloody revolution in two provinces and was only suppressed with the greatest difficulty. The Savior, as seems to be the habit of Saviors, had promised to bring peace and happiness, but had in reality brought the sword—a sword, which, once unsheathed, naturally begins now to threaten himself and his two most faithful followers. And thus more and more the story begins to remind us of Asia, never-changing Asia. Those in authority, again wrongly assuming that the execution of the Savior would suppress a rebellion—have decided to do away with him. A sham action is brought against him, he is searchingly questioned by the judges, who are bent upon his ruin, he is asked for miracles by the Mullahs, who doubt his gift and his inspiration, but he, according to his followers, confounds them all. Well, however, though he stands the test, he is nevertheless condemned to death by his persecutors, frightened as these are about the progress of the rebellion.

The day of execution has come. From early morning till late in the evening the Bab and his two disciples are conducted, under the weight of their chains, through the town of Tabriz, the infuriated mob screaming and shaking their fists at them, striking the defenseless victims in the face amid screams of laughter at every successful blow. Then one of the disciples, as the result of all the pain and shame heaped upon him, gives way, and throwing himself on to the ground, begins to weep most bitterly. The captain of the guard promises him freedom if he will curse the Bab. And he curses the Bab. Then the captain of the guard asks him to spit into the Bab's face. And he spits into his face, and is then set free; but only in order to repent and commit afterwards, like Judas, a sort of expiatory suicide.

Then the other follower, a rich citizen of the town of Tabriz, is worked upon to give up the Bab; with truly fiendish cleverness his young wife and his children are fetched from the bazaar, they are confronted with him and they implore him to abjure his creed, to live again happily with them as before; but the man simply turns his head and remains firm, only asking as a favor to be executed before his Savior. The sun begins to set; the two are about to suffer the extreme penalty, and when in front of a large crowd they both hang side by side over the wall of the citadel, waiting to be shot, the faithful disciple is heard saying to the Bab: "Master, art thou satisfied with me?"... O Asia, there thou art once more with thy fanatics, thy dreamers, thy rebels, with thy martyrs, who willingly shed their blood for "truth," and thy Saviors who triumphantly wear the crown of thorns! There thou art once more, thou continent of eternal recurrences, putting to shame thy little sister Europe with her innocent belief in progress!

But still there is "progress," and the progress lies with the narrator who this time tells the holy story. It is related in a cold and skeptical manner, very accurately to be sure, but not without touches of irony and Voltairian wit, by a man who decidedly has some doubts about all Saviors and all enthusiasts, by a man who knows from his own experience that it is more difficult to live for truth than to die for it, by a man who has a silent smile even for self-sacrifice; for he knows that self-sacrifice comes most easily to those whose self does not matter much, to those who sacrifice little with their "selves." A *grand seigneur* is relating this extraordinary story, a man who is freethinking without being unprincipled, gay without being foolish, warm-hearted without being gushing, and cool without being phlegmatic or platitudinarian. It is an important contribution to literature: the first narrative of a holy movement, by an unholy and sober pen. It is a decided improvement upon a very holy book: it is a gospel written by a gentleman.

But let no one believe that this refined gentleman always preserves his refinement of manner. True, the tenor of the Count's literary work cannot be compared to that of the more passionate Nietzsche, whose mighty curses on civilization run into eighteen volumes and whose only prototypes in literature—prototypes standing, though, for the opposite ideal—are the ancient Jewish prophets. But let no one be mistaken by this outward appearance of more grace, repose, and restraint: at bottom, it must be repeated again and again, Gobineau and Nietzsche are men of the same stamp, and the French Count can raise his voice to the same dangerous pitch as the German, or rather anti-German philosopher. And on these rare occasions, we entirely miss that "Greek Harmony," that "golden mean," which is so dear to the Philistine worshippers of classical antiquity, we look absolutely in vain for that "sweetness and light," which a gifted, though Victorian, author once so urgently recommended to his public; true, there is light, but only for those who can see; true, there is sweetness, but only for people with healthy and not over-fastidious tongues. Listen only how our Count describes his own time, hear what he thinks of his contemporaries, see in what colors this master-author paints the picture of what he considers the universal slavery:

> Have a look at the world around you. Do you recognize its supreme barbarism—not a youthful, bold, courageous, picturesque, happy barbarism, but a savagery that is ugly, treacherous, repellent, ill-humored, that will kill all and create nothing? At any rate, admire its size, which is indeed enormous; admire the beautiful arrangement of its tripartite division; at its head, the motley tribe of the babblers! They lead everywhere, carry the keys, coin phrases, weep on finding themselves deceived, declare that they would never have imagined. ... Here now are the fools! They are everywhere, in front, at the side, in the rear; they run about,

bustle and grow excited, their sole business being to prevent anything from becoming ordered or decided before they are in a settled state themselves. But what is the use of their becoming settled? Hardly has one of their companies declared itself satisfied than other hungry swarms come up at a run to start the whole process afresh.

And finally, here are the beasts. The babblers have let them loose. .... You ask me what I make of this pandemonium. I interpret it for what it is—stupefaction, destruction and death. ...

Would you wish to spare this rabble, if you held in your hands a sure means of destroying it? That is your business! As for me, lend me for a moment the thunderbolts of Jupiter and you shall see! But I shall only destroy so much as is necessary of the irresponsible herd of beasts. ... It is not fit to discern anything; I do not attribute to it a soul, and it is not the herd's fault if it cannot be controlled. Nor do I wish to go in for any violent measures against the fools! I do not declare to you that they are the salt of the earth, but they assuredly are the pickle. We can, if need be, put up with them, and if we hang a few of them occasionally, the rest can be employed, if not in honorable, at any rate in useful occupations. Besides, it must be admitted, our planet produces them naturally without waiting much to be asked! The world, whatever we may say or do, could not succeed in getting rid of them, nor perhaps even in dispensing with them.

As to the babblers, I should be merciless. They are the vainglorious and criminal authors, the sole and detestable initiators of universal degeneration, and the rain of my fiery bolts would ruthlessly pour down upon their perverse heads. No, such a crew does not deserve to live: nay, this croaking vermin cannot live and let the world live in orderly fashion by its side. The great flourishing epochs of Humanity were those when such reptiles did not crawl upon the steps of power. Away with them!

Would anyone believe that a passage of such honest indignation—against the people, if you please, not against the "ruling classes"—was penned in the middle of that mob-petting nineteenth century? In the midst of the century of revolutionary slaves? In the midst of the era of romanticism, sentimentality, brutality, eccentricity, and idealism? Still it was written, written, of course, without reaching the long ears of that democratic age, but written nevertheless for a juster posterity—and the passage is found in what should be considered as one of the finest books of Gobineau, a novel published by him in 1874 in Stockholm, called the *Pléiades*.

While the Essay, and that in spite of its good points, will always have to be considered as a youthful production, the man Gobineau comes out best and fully developed in the book of his advanced years, the *Pléiades*. There is no more discussion here as in the Essay about color and nobility, Gobineau has modified to a certain extent that scientific idea of his younger days about a fine Aryan race that had fallen readymade from heaven, and was only spoiled by the blood of inferior stocks. The artist has here got the better of the philosopher and his system, and, although the system was upheld by Gobineau till the end, it does not interfere in the least with this novel. And for this reason some of the Count's dark pessimism has become latent, there is hope in the book, for Gobineau has discovered a clearing in the dismal forest of democracy, he has noticed that there is some nobility left on earth in spite of all popular laws, all fine literature, and all "spread of education." True, these higher qualities are only possessed by a very few individuals, who have managed to keep themselves, though with great difficulty, afloat after the universal shipwreck of aristocratic civilization. But what does it matter? They are still there; Gobineau has detected them, he rejoices over the brilliant discovery, and what is more, he gives us in this novel the bright portraits of these men, standing out from the dark background of universal slavery around them. There are men and women to be met here, who, like certain stars in the nocturnal sky, brilliantly outshine the millions of minor luminous bodies around them, men and women of light and brightness, who greet each other with flashing eyes over the heads of their poorer surroundings, men and women, who belong to the greater stars on the human firmament, who belong—hence the title of the book—to the *Pléiades*.

In the first pages of the novel we are introduced to some of the *Pléiades*, three travelers, a Frenchman, a German, and an Englishman, who begin their tale with the announcement: "We are three calenders, sons of kings." Gobineau, the admirer of the Orient, is imitating here the tales of "Thousand and One Nights," in which the Arabian storyteller regularly begins with, "I am the son of a king." These magical words—thus Gobineau explains—indicate that "the hero is endowed with special gifts, with rare qualities, which make him entirely different from the ordinary crowd of people around him." "I am the son of a king," however, Gobineau takes care to add, does *not* mean that he is really the son of a king, and that his father was not a merchant, artist, soldier, ironmonger, or stationmaster; it only signifies one thing: "I am—no matter where I come from—of a generous and courageous temperament, and I am a stranger to most of those influences which generally move and interest other human beings around me. My taste is not that of everybody—I have my own feelings on all subjects; I do not love or hate according to the leaders and criticism of the papers. The independence of my ideas, the absolute liberty of my opinions, are the certain indications and privileges of my noble origin. ..." And where do these extraordinary qualities come from? Through the mouth of one of the other travellers Gobineau gives the answer. "They arise from a sort of mysterious and native combination: it is a union in one individuality, of those noble, or, if you will, divine qualities, which his ancestors long ago possessed to the fullest degree, qualities which the unwholesome and undignified alliances with inferior beings may have suppressed, or may have only disguised for some time, but which nevertheless did not die entirely, but suddenly developed and blossomed out again in these after-born, the sons of the kings." The French traveller adds to this: "Thus there exist in the world of today a number of men, women and children, and that in all nations alike, whose personality is composed of the most precious atoms of their most precious ancestors, and who form an aristocracy of perhaps no more than 3,500 people in the whole world."

But how shall they make themselves heard? How is this aristocracy, submerged and nearly drowned as it is, to rise again to the top? How can they survive in an age like the present? Are not those few aristocrats, discovered by Gobineau in all classes of the population, much too isolated to be able to withstand the torrent of vulgarity around them? And how can they know one another, how can they hold out a helping hand to one another? Is not the aristocratic nature by itself adverse to that "combination" and "union" which has rightly become the panacea of all the weak, of all the democrats? Does it not rather prefer to stand alone? Does it not even rejoice in standing alone? Is there not a certain mixture of shyness and pride in the aristocrat, which forbids him to address others, to ask others for help, to complain to others, or even to open his heart to others? And is the aristocrat's shyness not justified, has he not been taught by hundreds of shameful experiences how he will be misunderstood, or what is worse, what fine specimens of humanity will understand him or pretend to understand him? Can he forget that it was the "Swine" that rushed first into Nietzsche's garden? Is he not in his innermost heart sure of the sad fate that he lives in a desert, of the sad fate that he *has* to live in a desert, and that his only companions there, if not swine, will be asses and camels?

Gobineau has an answer to all these questions, he knows a way out of our difficulties, he proves that—though not shirking any of the terrible facts of our wild present-day life—he is able to master this life, he is able to be a true guide through the wilderness of this life. It is through the mouth of the German Prince John Theodor that he gives a lesson to those isolated beings, whose strength among the uncounted numbers of weak people is in danger of becoming broken, or "adapted to the environment"—a lesson, though, which is not a social, a Christian, or an altruistic one. For the German Prince has the audacity to recommend to those aristocrats: "Look after yourself, see that you do not lose yourself, don't trouble about anything but the welfare of your own souls." But, perhaps, this after all is a Christian lesson, for is it not likewise one of the imperative demands of the Christian religion to look after one's soul? And it is this that the Prince recommends:

> I consider the honest man, the man who feels in himself a soul, has more than ever the imperious duty of recoiling back upon himself. This is peculiarly the work of times such as ours. All that society loses does not disappear, but takes refuge in individual lives. The whole is small, wretched, shameful, repulsive. The isolated being soars up and expands, and, as in Egyptian ruins, in the midst of a heap of rubbish, misshapen and unrecognizable debris, crumbled and shattered buildings, often difficult to restore, there survive and rise up towards heaven some giants, some obelisks, whose height maintains the noblest idea, perhaps an idea superior to what was formerly the temple or the town now razed forever; so nowadays men who are isolated, but at the bottom more noteworthy, more deserving of our admiration than were their precursors, help to keep up the notion of what the noblest and loftiest of God's creatures should be ... To work at ourselves, to raise what is good in us, to subdue

what is evil, to stifle or at least to shelve our worst instincts —this is henceforth our duty, the only duty that is of any avail!

There is a Christian ring about this passage, is there not? Yet it cannot be Christian, and it is not Christian, for the very reason that Gobineau practiced what he preached, which the Christian, at least if there is a shade of healthy instinct left in him, never does. And Gobineau practiced what he preached, though he, as an aristocratic writer, as a leader of humanity, had no need to do so, though he had full liberty to claim exceptional rights on account of his exceptional duties.

It is the duty only of the Christian—as a democrat— to live up to his principles. This duty, however, the Christian carefully avoids, and all the more carefully, the more of a Christian he is. A Bismarck, who "edits" a foreign telegram, causes a bloody war through it, and with all this humbly goes to Communion; a Tolstoi, who preaches the abolition of private property, but hands his own over to his wife—who recommends strict chastity in his *Kreuzersonata,* but begets a child himself a year after its publication—that is Christian, those (and many other discordant celebrities with them), were the true Christians, the great Christians of the nineteenth century. But the non-Nazarene noblemen of that time, such as Gobineau and Nietzsche, though at full liberty to live a hypocritical life, never did live it, nor were they obliged to live it, nor could they have lived it, for the purity of their character and intelligence would not have allowed to them what it apparently allows to all pious folk. Not to them was it granted to go through life making concessions right and left, not theirs the strength to live a life of contradiction and despair, not theirs the weakness never to approach, never to criticize Christian values; but not theirs either that religion of the Redeemer who apparently redeemeth His faithful servants of any serious thoughts on an unprincipled existence, not theirs the religion of the Comforter, who comforteth them through all the discomforts of a bad conscience, so that they live honored and idolized by all human kind to an old age!

There is no doubt that Gobineau's life in the midst of these comfortable great and small Christians was not a very enviable one. Nietzsche, as is well-known, went mad over the solitude of such an honest life in the midst of vile and stupid surroundings, and of Count Gobineau we know—if we could not read it between the lines of his writings—that he was only too frequently near the abyss of despair. "The principal thought of great minds is not to break," our author used to remark frequently, an opinion doubly significant, in the mouth of such a joyful, witty, spirited companion, such as according to the testimony of all contemporaries, German and French alike, Count Gobineau usually was. In Stockholm, especially, he seems to have suffered. He went there alone, his wife stayed away from the northern climate for reasons of health, and during his whole sojourn he apparently experienced only little desire to mix with the world at large. His lodgings were in a very quiet, and not even fashionable street, his whole mode of life was so simple that his colleagues of other nations frequently scoffed at it; the bell outside his chambers is said to have consisted of a hare's foot, and when this was rung, the Count's only companion and servant, a Syrian Christian, appeared and asked the visitor into a drawing-room, whose furniture was as old-fashioned and "out of season" as the ideas of its proprietor. Honoré Michon—this was the name of the servant—became Count Gobineau's dragoman, when he went to Persia; he hated Europe as heartily as did his master, but he loved his master more than he hated Europe, and was so devoted to him that he would never leave him afterwards; he would have gone to the North Pole—so the talk in diplomatic circles ran—if France had stood in need of a representative there and had singled out Gobineau as her Ambassador. Gobineau was likewise heartily attached to him and left the whole management of his modest establishment to the tender care of the Syrian, whose principal task was to look after two green parrots. But while ordinary minds are broken or "converted" by such uncongenial surroundings as two parrots and an exotic servant undoubtedly are, the sterner characters, as Gobineau rightly suggests in the *Pléiades*, are elevated and spurred on by adverse circumstances, and thus we owe to the solitude of Count Gobineau not only his best novel, but also that other book of his upon which his fame principally rests, *The Renaissance*.

It was only natural that the artistic imagination of a Gobineau willingly turned back to that golden time of the post-Christian era, to that only time of the Christian era which was no longer Christian, to that time when Christianity lay vanquished and broken in the very heart of Christianity, in Rome itself; to the time of the Renaissance. In his predilection for the Italian Revival, Gobineau only proved once more his intimate and genuine relationship to that best school of European thought, to those few eminent poets and critics, who had all hated the Semitic infection around them, who had all abhorred the Christian revolutionary spirit, who had all turned their backs upon the slaves and their clamorous desires for liberty and equality. In the age of the Renaissance it had been—so they all saw with deep envy—*their* turn; it was the age of liberty for them, for the best, the intelligent, the daring, the brave, the proud, the beautiful—the age for an enlightened aristocracy of birth and spirit. There was liberty then, because there was no equality, for where there is liberty there can be no equality, and where there is equality there can be no liberty. Liberty is the requirement of the few, equality the wish of the many—and Gobineau's age, having declared for the many, had driven its most valuable, its only useful members into despair, madness, suicide, or at least into isolation. No wonder, those few isolated beings—a Goethe, a Stendhal, a Nietzsche, a Gobineau, and even a Heine—turned their saddened eyes back to the opposite age, to the age of freedom for them, the generous, loving, free-spirited and brave; to the age, when Kings, Popes and Statesmen were not yet servants of the mob and of the State, but masters of the State, of their own individualities, of their own wishes, and above all had wishes and desires, that corresponded to those of the great artists and writers of their time. Noble Renaissance, to what depth of despair and darkness has the world "progressed" since then!

It was left to this late-born son of the Renaissance, this pagan by heart and intelligence, this super-Christian *gentilhomme*—it was left to Gobineau to give us in the following pages a true historical and poetical picture of the Renaissance, such as none of his or our own contemporaries have been able to present to the world. Himself a scholar, a poet, a sculptor, and likewise an ambassador, he was so nearly related to that glorious Italian age and its versatile genius, to a Michael Angelo and a Leonardo da Vinci, that an insight into the period and into the character of its leading spirits came to him naturally and instinctively. And thus here, over the head of four centuries, one lonely but kindred spirit speaks to his equals, to his true and only, but alas, departed brethren. He understands them, with their fears and their hopes, their loves and their hatreds, their virtues and their vices—he rightly diagnoses what ruined them, he rightly divines what had elevated them. Justice itself speaks out of the pages of the book, and that highest kind of justice, an innocent, childlike, a poet's justice, a justice that is high above moral prejudices. The clear and benevolent sun of Gobineau's thought shines upon weak and strong, upon Christians and Nobles, upon Protestants and Catholics, upon populace and artists, upon saints and criminals alike, and wherever its rays fall, they warm, they adorn, and they enlighten. A man like Luther, with whom Gobineau could hardly have had any sympathy, is brought nearer to our understanding, nay, to our heart; he too, that great destructive spirit, that great unconscious evildoer, could not have acted otherwise. A man like Savonarola, that monster of morality, that Puritan of the renascence, that "Bab" translated into European and Nazarene, is appreciated by our poet, a little too much, one would even think, especially when this moralist is said to have influenced the great Michael Angelo, whose morality was certainly of a different and higher order. And not only the moral and revolutionary heroes, the rebels and the Protestants, open their hearts to the magical key of the Count's genius, but likewise their enemies, the Catholics, the faithful sons of the ancient Church, the opponents and repressors of the Reformation. There is Charles V and his son, Philip II, stem and unbending both, typical representatives of law and order, men, who, though rightly considering the "Calvinistic and Lutheran abomination as a cancer in the flank of the Church," proceed to cure that cancer with fire and iron; favoring the Jesuitical order, re-establishing the medieval inquisition, re-introducing the Christian faith upon the Papal chair, and thus committing more murders and atrocities than that "monster" Caesar Borgia himself.

And murders and atrocities, which Gobineau in his innermost heart utterly condemns, for, as he is careful to inform us, these crimes of the Reformation and the counter-Reformation were, compared with those of Caesar Borgia, absolutely senseless, because they were religious crimes. There is not the slightest doubt that Count Gobineau's sympathies, in spite of his great tolerance and his poetical benevolence towards even the religious people of the period, are entirely on the side of the pagans, of the Popes and their artists, on the side of a Julius II and Caesar Borgia, of a Machiavelli, and Michael Angelo. Nor is the reason for this far to seek: his book is written in favor of the Master-Morality, and Gobineau's secret endeavor is to throw suspicion upon the prevailing and all-powerful Morality of his good and brave, though neurotic, feminine, and prosaic contemporaries. In a manner that will frighten many readers even today, Gobineau's deep, manly persuasion of "one right and duty for me, one right and duty for you" rings out of an audacious scene, that scene, where Pope Alexander VI defends his son Caesar Borgia before his sister Lucrezia, whose husband, Don Alphonso d'Aragon, Caesar Borgia has just strangled:—

> He is not a monster, my daughter, but a ruler who could not enter his destined sphere but at the price of the most sustained and sometimes the most pitiless effort. Listen to me, Lucrezia, and don't raise your hands to heaven. ... I am trying to awaken in you what I know to be true, clear-cut and powerful sentiments. .... My daughter, you are as beautiful as Pride, you are Strength itself! Hence I will speak to you. ... Know then that for that kind of persons whom fate summons to dominate others, the ordinary rules of life are reversed and duty becomes quite different. Good and evil are lifted to another, to a higher region, to a different plane. The virtues that may be applauded in an ordinary woman would in you become vices, merely because they would only be sources of error and ruin. Now the great law of this world is, not to do this or that, to avoid one thing and run after another: it is to live, to enlarge and develop one's most active and lofty qualities, in such a way that from any sphere we can always hew ourselves out a way to one that is wider, nobler, more elevated. Never forget that. Walk straight on. Do only what pleases you, but only do it, if it likewise serves you.

> Leave to the small minds, the rabble of underlings, all slackness and scruple. There is only one consideration worthy of you—the elevation of the house of Borgia and yourself.

But Caesar Borgia failed: the story of his ghastly death is vividly told in one of the scenes of the "Renaissance." And, with Caesar Borgia, failed the whole of the Renascence: through the quarrel between that *par nobile fratrum,* the Church and the Reformation (of which the less noble was the Reformation), art, life, health, beauty, everything good and noble and great was again banished from the world for centuries. "Thou hast conquered again, O Galilaean!" But hast Thou really conquered? Hast Thou really succeeded in eradicating out of all human breasts the yearning after something higher, nobler, and stronger, hast thou really extinguished in all human hearts the desire for joy, for light, for wisdom, and for beauty? Is the Renascence quite as dead as Thou wishest and as Thou thinkest, Thou humble and pale Galilaean, Thou enemy of rosy cheeks and proud necks? No, no, it is not dead, and it was never as dead as Thou hadst hoped and desired, and how little dead it was, is proved by the following beautiful pages of the French nobleman, who rightly lets his Michael Angelo predict an eternal life for that grand age, in spite of Thy triumph and Thy premature exaltation. "We are bequeathing," thus run the last words of the aged Michael Angelo, "We are bequeathing a great legacy, great examples. ... The earth is richer than it was before our coming. What is to disappear will not disappear altogether. ... The fields can rest and remain fallow for awhile: the seed is in the clods. The fog may spread and the grey and watery sky become covered with mist and rain, but the sun is above. ... Who knows what will come again?"

OSCAR LEVY, London, 1913.

71

INTRODUCTION TO GOBINEAU'S "INEQUALITY OF HUMAN RACES"

Though many people have accused this age of irreligion, there is at least one point of similarity between modern Europe and that pre-Christian Era to which our present religion is due. Just as in ancient Palestine, there are living amongst us two kinds of prophets—the prophets of evil and disaster, and those of bliss, or, as Europe likes to call it, of "progress." As in Palestine of old the public usually sides with the lighter, the optimistic, the more comfortable sort of people, with the prophets of bliss, while Time and Fate invariably decide in favor of the sterner and gloomier individuals, the prophets of evil. In the world today as well as in Palestine of old, the prophets of bliss are the false prophets; the prophets of evil, today as of yore, are the true ones. Such a true prophet was Count Arthur de Gobineau.

Even his friends—those few friends whom he gained at the end of his life—still thought him unduly pessimistic. Old Wagner, who introduced him to the German public, thought of brightening his gloom by a little Christian faith, hope, and charity, in order to make the pill more palatable to that great public, which he, the great Stage-manager, knew so well. Other Germans —Chamberlain, Schemann, and the Gobineau school— poured a great deal of water into his wine, sweetened it with patriotic syrups, adulterated it with their own pleasant inventions, which were all too readily swallowed by a gullible and credulous generation. But stern old Gobineau knew the world better than his young and cheerful offspring. He had seen through all that boisterous gaiety of the age, all its breathless labor, all its technical advancement, all its materialistic progress, and had diagnosed, behind it that muddle of moral values which our forefathers have bequeathed to us and which in our generation has only become a greater muddle still. The catastrophe which Gobineau had prophesied to an Aristocracy which had forgotten its tradition, to a Democracy which had no root in reality, to a Christianity which he thought entirely inefficient, is now upon us.

Under the stress of the present misfortunes, we frequently hear that all our previous opinions need revision, that we have to forget many things and to learn afresh still more, that we must try to build up our civilization on a safer basis, that we must reconsider and re-construct the values received from former ages. It is therefore our duty, I think, to turn back to those prophets who accused our forefathers of being on the road to destruction, all the more so as these prophets were likewise true poets who tried as such to point out the right road, endeavouring to remedy, as far as their insight went, the evil of their time. This is the best, and I trust a perfectly satisfactory, reason for the translation of "The Inequality of Human Races."

This book, written as early as 1853, is no doubt a youthful and somewhat bewildering performance, but it gives us the basis of Gobineau's creed, his belief in Race and Aristocracy as the first condition of civilization, his disbelief in the influence of environment, his distrust in the efficacy of religion and morality. The latter kind of skepticism brings him into relationship with Nietzsche, who has even accentuated Count Gobineau's suspicions and who has branded our morality as Slave-Morality, and consequently as harmful to good government. What a Europe without Masters, but with plenty of Half-masters and Slaves, was driving at, Gobineau foresaw as well as Nietzsche.

I sincerely hope that no intelligent reader will overlook this skeptical attitude of Gobineau towards religion, because that is a point of great importance at the present time, when our faith will certainly thrive again on a misfortune, which, by the propagation of slave-values, it indirectly has caused. It is this skepticism against the Church and its Semitic values, which separates a Gobineau from Disraeli, to whom otherwise —in his rejection of Buckle, Darwin, and their science, in his praise of Race and Aristocracy, and in his prophecy of evil—he is so nearly related. Disraeli still believed in a Church based upon a revival of the old principles; Gobineau, like Nietzsche, had no hope whatever in this respect. It is the great merit of both Nietzsche and Gobineau, that they were not, like Disraeli, trying to revive a corpse, but that they frankly acknowledged, the one that the corpse was dead, the other that it was positively poisoning the air. The occasional bows which Gobineau makes to the Church cannot, I repeat, mislead any serious critics of his work, especially if they likewise consult his later books. Both Spinoza and Montaigne had the same laudable habit, and they did not mean it either. For the first business of a great freethinker is not to be mistaken for a little one; his greatest misfortune is to be "understood" by the wrong class of people, and thus an occasional bow to the old and venerable Power—apart from the safety which it procures—protects him from an offensive handshake with enthusiastic and unbalanced disciples and apostles.

OSCAR LEVY
Geneva, *July* 1915

FROM THE AUTHOR'S DEDICATION
(1854)[4]

TO HIS MAJESTY GEORGE V, KING OF HANOVER

The great events—the bloody wars, the revolutions, and the breaking up of laws—which have been rife for so many years in the States of Europe, are apt to turn men's minds to the study of political problems. While the vulgar consider merely immediate results, and heap all their praise and blame on the little electric spark that marks the contact with their own interests, the more serious thinker will seek to discover the hidden causes of these terrible upheavals. He will descend, lamp in hand, by the obscure paths of philosophy and history; and in the analysis of the human heart or the careful search among the annals of the past he will try to gain the master-key to the enigma which has so long baffled the imagination of man.

Like every one else, I have felt all the prickings of curiosity to which our restless modern world gives rise. But when I tried to study, as completely as I could, the forces underlying this world, I found the horizon of my inquiry growing wider and wider. I had to push further and further into the past, and, forced by analogy almost in spite of myself, to lift my eyes further and further into the future. It seemed that I should aspire to know not merely the immediate causes of the plagues that are supposed to chasten us, but also to trace the more

---

[4] This dedication and the following preface apply to the whole work, of which the present volume contains the first book. The remaining books are occupied by a detailed examination of the civilizations mentioned at the end of this volume, and it is of these as well as the present book that the author is thinking, in his preface, when speaking of his imitators. A few passages in the dedication that relate exclusively to these books have been omitted.—Tr.

remote reasons for those social evils which the most meagre knowledge of history will show to have prevailed, in exactly the same form, among all the nations that ever lived, as well as those which survive today—evils that in all likelihood will exist among nations yet unborn.

Further, the present age, I thought, offered peculiar facilities for such an inquiry. While its very restlessness urges us on to a kind of historical chemistry, it also makes our labors easier. The thick mists, the profound darkness that from time immemorial veiled the beginnings of civilizations different from our own, now lift and dissolve under the sun of science. An analytic method of marvellous delicacy has made a Rome, unknown to Livy, rise before us under the hands of Niebuhr, and has unravelled for us the truths that lay hid among the legendary tales of early Greece. In another quarter of the world, the Germanic peoples, so long misunderstood, appear to us now as great and majestic as they were thought barbarous by the writers of the Later Empire. Egypt opens its subterranean tombs, translates its hieroglyphs, and reveals the age of its pyramids. Assyria lays bare its palaces with their endless inscriptions, which had till yesterday been buried beneath their own ruins. The Iran of Zoroaster has held no secrets from the searching eyes of Burnouf, and the Vedas of early India take us back to events not far from the dawn of creation. From all these conquests together, so important in themselves, we gain a larger and truer understanding of Homer, Herodotus, and especially of the first chapters of the Bible, that deep well of truth, whose riches we can only begin to appreciate when we go down into it with a fully enlightened mind.

These sudden and unexpected discoveries are naturally not always beyond the reach of criticism. They are far from giving us complete lists of dynasties, or an unbroken sequence of reigns and events. In spite, however, of the fragmentary nature of their results, many of them are admirable for my present purpose, and far more fruitful than the most accurate chronological tables would be. I welcome, most of all, the revelation of manners and customs, of the very portraits and costumes, of vanished peoples. We know the condition of their art. Their whole life, public and private, physical and moral, is unrolled before us, and it becomes possible to reconstruct, with the aid of the most authentic materials, that which constitutes the personality of races and mainly determines their value.

With such a treasury of knowledge, new or newly understood, to draw upon, no one can claim any longer to explain the complicated play of social forces, the causes of the rise and decay of nations, in the light of the purely abstract and hypothetical arguments supplied by a skeptical philosophy. Since we have now an abundance of positive facts crowding upon us from all sides, rising from every sepulcher, and lying ready to every seeker's hand, we may no longer, like the theorists of the Revolution, form a collection of imaginary beings out of clouds, and amuse ourselves by moving these chimeras about like marionettes, in a political environment manufactured to suit them. The reality is now too pressing, too well known; and it forbids games like these, which are always unseasonable, and sometimes impious. There is only one tribunal competent to decide rationally upon the general characteristics of man, and that is history—a severe judge, I confess, and one to whom we may well fear to appeal in an age so wretched as our own.

Not that the past is itself without stain. It includes everything, and so may well have many faults, and more than one shameful dereliction of duty, to confess. The men of today might even be justified in flourishing in its face some new merits of their own. But suppose, as an answer to their charges, that the past suddenly called up the gigantic shades of the heroic ages, what would they say then? If it reproached them with having compromised the names of religious faith, political honor, and moral duty, what would they answer? If it told them that they are no longer fit for anything but to work out the knowledge of which the principles had already been recognized and laid down by itself; that the virtue of the ancients has become a laughing-stock, that energy has passed from man to steam, that the light of poetry is out, that its great prophets are no more, and that what men call their interests are confined to the most pitiful tasks of daily life;—how could they defend themselves?

They could merely reply that not every beautiful thing is dead which has been swallowed up in silence; it may be only sleeping. All ages, they might say, have beheld periods of transition, when life grapples with suffering and in the end arises victorious and splendid. Just as Chaldæa in its dotage was succeeded by the young and vigorous Persia, tottering Greece by virile Rome, and the degenerate rule of Augustulus by the kingdoms of the noble Teutonic princes, so the races of modern times will regain their lost youth.

This was a hope I myself cherished for a brief moment, and I should like to have at once flung back in the teeth of History its accusations and gloomy forebodings, had I not been suddenly struck with the devastating thought, that in my hurry I was putting forward something that was absolutely without proof. I began to look about for proofs, and so, in my sympathy for the living, was more and more driven to plumb to their depths the secrets of the dead.

Then, passing from one induction to another, I was gradually penetrated by the conviction that the racial question overshadows all other problems of history, that it holds the key to them all, and that the inequality of the races from whose fusion a people is formed is enough to explain the whole course of its destiny. Every one must have had some inkling of this colossal truth, for every one must have seen how certain agglomerations of men have descended on some country, and utterly transformed its way of life; how they have shown themselves able to strike out a new vein of activity where, before their coming, all had been sunk in torpor. Thus, to take an example, a new era of power was opened for Great Britain by the Anglo-Saxon invasion, thanks to a decree of Providence, which by sending to this island some of the peoples governed by the sword of your Majesty's illustrious ancestors, was to bring two branches of the same nation under the scepter of a single house—a house that can trace its glorious title to the dim sources of the heroic nation itself.

Recognizing that both strong and weak races exist, I preferred to examine the former, to analyze their qualities, and especially to follow them back to their origins. By this method I convinced myself at last that everything great, noble, and fruitful in the works of man on this earth, in science, art, and civilization, derives from a single starting-point, is the development of a single germ and the result of a single thought; it belongs to one family alone, the different branches of which have reigned in all the civilized countries of the universe.

THE INEQUALITY OF HUMAN RACES

CHAPTER I

THE MORTAL DISEASE OF CIVILIZATIONS AND SOCIETIES PROCEEDS FROM GENERAL CAUSES COMMON TO THEM ALL

The fall of civilizations is the most striking, and, at the same time, the most obscure, of all the phenomena of history. It is a calamity that strikes fear into the soul, and yet has always something so mysterious and so vast in reserve, that the thinker is never weary of looking at it, of studying it, of groping for its secrets. No doubt the birth and growth of peoples offer a very remarkable subject for the observer; the successive development of societies, their gains, their conquests, their triumphs, have something that vividly takes the imagination and holds it captive. But all these events, however great one may think them, seem to be easy of explanation; one accepts them as the mere outcome of the intellectual gifts of man. Once we recognize these gifts, we are not astonished at their results; they explain, by the bare fact of their existence, the great stream of being whose source they are. So, on this score, there need be no difficulty or hesitation. But when we see that after a time of strength and glory all human societies come to their decline and fall—all, I say, not this or that; when we see in what awful silence the earth shows us, scattered on its surface, the wrecks of the civilizations that have preceded our own—not merely the famous civilizations, but also many others, of which we know nothing but the names, and some, that lie as skeletons of stone in deep world-old forests, and have not left us even this shadow of a memory; when the mind returns to our modern States, reflects on their extreme youth, and confesses that they are a growth of yesterday, and that some of them are already toppling to their fall: then at last we recognize, not without a certain philosophic shudder, that the words of the prophets on the instability of mortal things apply with the same rigor to civilizations as to peoples, to peoples as to States, to States as to individuals; and we are forced to affirm that every assemblage of men, however ingenious the network of social relations that protects it, acquires on the very day of its birth, hidden among the elements of its life, the seed of an inevitable death.

But what is this seed, this principle of death? Is it uniform, as its results are, and do all civilizations perish from the same cause?

At first sight we are tempted to answer in the negative; for we have seen the fall of many empires, Assyria, Egypt, Greece, Rome, amid the clash of events that had no likeness one to the other. Yet, if we pierce below the surface, we soon find that this very necessity of coming to an end, that weighs imperiously on all societies without exception, presupposes such a general cause, which, though hidden, cannot be explained away. When we start from this fixed principle of natural death —a principle unaffected by all the cases of violent death, —we see that all civilizations, after they have lasted some time, betray to the observer some little symptoms of uneasiness, which are difficult to define, but not less difficult to deny; these are of a like nature in all times and all places. We may admit one obvious point of difference between the fall of States and that of civilizations, when we see the same kind of culture sometimes persisting in a country under foreign rule and weathering every storm of calamity, at other times being destroyed or changed by the slightest breath of a contrary wind; but we are, in the end, more and more driven to the idea that the principle of death which can be seen at the base of all societies is not only inherent in their life, but also uniform and the same for all.

To the elucidation of this great fact I have devoted the studies of which I here give the results.

We moderns are the first to have recognized that every assemblage of men, together with the kind of culture it produces, is doomed to perish. Former ages did not believe this. Among the early Asiatics, the religious consciousness, moved by the spectacle of great political catastrophes, as if by some apparition from another world, attributed them to the anger of heaven smiting a nation for its sins; they were, it was thought, a chastisement meet to bring to repentance the criminals yet unpunished. The Jews, misinterpreting the meaning of the Covenant, supposed that their Empire would never come to an end. Rome, at the very moment when she was nearing the precipice, did not doubt that her own empire was eternal.[5] But the knowledge of later generations has increased with experience; and just as no one doubts of the mortal state of humanity, because all the men who preceded us are dead, so we firmly believe that the days of peoples are numbered, however great the number may be; for all those who held dominion before us have now fallen out of the race. The wisdom of the ancients yields little that throws light on our subject, except one fundamental axiom, the recognition of the finger of God in the conduct of this world; to this firm and ultimate principle we must adhere, accepting it in the full sense in which it is understood by the Catholic Church. It is certain that no civilization falls to the ground unless God wills it; and when we apply to the mortal state of all societies the sacred formula used by the ancient priesthoods to explain some striking catastrophes, which they wrongly considered as isolated facts, we are asserting a truth of the first importance, which should govern the search for all the truths of this

---

[5] Amédée Thierry, *La Gaule sous l'administration romaine*, vol. i, p. 244.

world. Add, if you will, that all societies perish because they are sinful—and I will agree with you; this merely sets up a true parallel to the case of individuals, finding in sin the germ of destruction. In this regard, there is no objection to saying that human societies share the fate of their members; they contract the stain from them, and come to a like end. This is to reason merely by the light of nature. But when we have once admitted and pondered these two truths, we shall find no further help, I repeat, in the wisdom of the ancients.

That wisdom tells us nothing definite as to the ways in which the Divine will moves in order to compass the death of peoples; it is, on the contrary, driven to consider these ways as essentially mysterious. It is seized with a pious terror at the sight of ruins, and admits too easily that the fallen peoples could not have been thus shaken, struck down, and hurled into the gulf, except by the aid of miracles. I can readily believe that certain events have had a miraculous element, so far as this is stated by Scripture; but where, as is usually the case, the formal testimony of Scripture is wanting, we may legitimately hold the ancient opinion to be incomplete and unenlightened. We may, in fact, take the opposite view, and recognize that the heavy hand of God is laid without ceasing on our societies, as the effect of a decision pronounced before the rise of the first people; and that the blow falls according to rule and foreknowledge, by virtue of fixed edicts, inscribed in the code of the universe by the side of other laws which, in their rigid severity, govern organic and inorganic nature alike.

We may justly reproach the philosophy of the early sacred writers with a lack of experience; and so, we may say, they explain a mystery merely by enunciating a theological truth which, however certain, is itself another mystery. They have not pushed their inquiries so far as to observe the facts of the natural world. But at least one cannot accuse them of misunderstanding the greatness of the problem and scratching for solutions at the surface of the ground. In fact, they have been content to state the question in lofty language; and if they have not solved it, or even thrown light upon it, at least they have not made it a breeder of errors. This puts them far above the rationalistic schools and all their works.

The great minds of Athens and Rome formulated the theory, accepted by later ages, that States, civilizations, and peoples, are destroyed only by luxury, effeminacy, misgovernment, fanaticism, and the corruption of morals. These causes, taken singly or together, were declared to be responsible for the fall of human societies; the natural corollary being that in the absence of these causes there can be no solvent whatever. The final conclusion is that societies, more fortunate than men, die only a violent death; and if a nation can be imagined as escaping the destructive forces I have mentioned, there is no reason why it should not last as long as the earth itself. When the ancients invented this theory, they did not see where it was leading them; they regarded it merely as a buttress for their ethical notions, to establish which was, as we know, the sole aim of their historical method. In their narrative of events, they were so taken up with the idea of bringing out the admirable influence of virtue, and the deplorable effects of vice and crime, that anything which marred the harmony of this excellent moral picture had little interest for them, and so was generally forgotten or set aside. This method was not only false and petty, but also had very often a different result from that intended by its authors; for it applied the terms "virtue" and "vice" in an arbitrary way, as the needs of the moment dictated. Yet, to a certain extent, the theory is excused by the stern and noble sentiment that lay at the base of it; and if the genius of Plutarch and Tacitus has built mere romances and libels on this foundation, at any rate the libels are generous, and the romances sublime.

I wish I could show myself as indulgent to the use that the authors of the eighteenth century have made of the theory. But there is too great a difference between their masters and themselves. The former had even a quixotic devotion to the maintenance of the social order; the latter were eager for novelty and furiously bent on destruction. The ancients made their false ideas bear a noble progeny; the moderns have produced only monstrous abortions. Their theory has furnished them with arms against all principles of government, which they have reproached in turn with tyranny, fanaticism, and corruption. The Voltairean way of "preventing the ruin of society" is to destroy religion, law, industry, and commerce, under the pretext that religion is another name for fanaticism, law for despotism, industry and commerce for luxury and corruption. Where so many errors reign, I certainly agree that we have "bad government."

I have not the least desire to write a polemic; my object is merely to show how an idea common to Thucydides and the Abbé Raynal can produce quite opposite results. It makes for conservatism in the one, for an anarchic cynicism in the other—and is an error in both. The causes usually given for the fall of nations are not necessarily the real causes; and though I willingly admit that they may come to the surface in the death-agony of a people, I deny that they have enough power, enough destructive energy, to draw on, by themselves, the irremediable catastrophe.

CHAPTER II

FANATICISM, LUXURY, CORRUPTION OF MORALS, AND IRRELIGION DO NOT NECESSARILY LEAD TO THE FALL OF SOCIETIES

I must first explain what I understand by a "society." I do not mean the more or less extended sphere within which, in some form or other, a distinct sovereignty is exercised. The Athenian democracy is not a "society" in our sense, any more than the Kingdom of Magadha, the empire of Pontus, or the Caliphate of Egypt in the time of the Fatimites. They are fragments of societies, which, no doubt, change, coalesce, or break up according to the natural laws that I am investigating; but their existence or death does not imply the existence or death of a society. Their formation is usually a mere transitory phenomenon, having but a limited or indirect influence on the civilization in which they arise. What I mean by a "society" is an assemblage of men moved by similar ideas and the same instincts; their political unity may be more or less imperfect, but their social unity must be complete. Thus Egypt, Assyria, Greece, India, and China were, or still are, the theater where distinct and separate societies have played out their own destinies, save when these have been brought for a time into conjunction by political troubles. As I shall speak of the parts only when my argument applies to the whole, I shall use the words "nation" or "people" either in the wide or the narrow sense, without any room for ambiguity. I return now to my main subject, which is to show that fanaticism, luxury, corruption of morals, and irreligion do not necessarily bring about the ruin of nations.

All these phenomena have been found in a highly developed state, either in isolation or together, among peoples which were actually the better for them—or at any rate not the worse.

The Aztec Empire in America seems to have existed mainly "for the greater glory" of fanaticism. I cannot imagine anything more fanatical than a society like that of the Aztecs, which rested on a religious foundation, continually watered by the blood of human sacrifice. It has been denied,[6] perhaps with some truth, that the ancient peoples of Europe ever practiced ritual murder on victims who were regarded as innocent, with the exception of shipwrecked sailors and prisoners of war. But for the ancient Mexicans one victim was as good as another. With a ferocity recognized by a modern physiologist[7] as characteristic of the races of the New World, they massacred their fellow citizens on their altars, without pity, without flinching, and without discrimination. This did not prevent their being a powerful, industrious, and wealthy people, which would certainly for many ages have gone on flourishing, reigning, and throat-cutting, had not the genius of Hernando Cortés and the courage of his companions stepped in to put an end to the monstrous existence of such an Empire. Thus fanaticism does not cause the fall of States.

Luxury and effeminacy have no better claims than fanaticism. Their effects are to be seen only in the upper classes; and though they assumed different forms in the ancient world, among the Greeks, the Persians, and the Romans, I doubt whether they were ever brought to a greater pitch of refinement than at the present day, in France, Germany, England, and Russia—especially in the last two. And it is just these two, England and Russia,

---

6 By C.F. Weber, *Lucani Pharsalia* (Leipzig, 1828), vol. i, pp. 122-3, *note.*

7 Prichard, "Natural History of Man." Dr. Martius is still more explicit. *Cf.* Martius and Spix, *Reise in Brasilian*, vol. i, pp. 379-80.

that, of all the States of modern Europe, seem to be gifted with a peculiar vitality. Again, in the Middle Ages, the Venetians, the Genoese, and the Pisans crowded their shops with the treasures of the whole world; they displayed them in their palaces, and carried them over every sea. But they were certainly none the weaker for that. Thus luxury and effeminacy are in no way the necessary causes of weakness and ruin.

Again, the corruption of morals, however terrible a scourge it may be, is not always an agent of destruction. If it were, the military power and commercial prosperity of a nation would have to vary directly with the purity of its morals; but this is by no means the case. The curious idea that the early Romans had all the virtues[8] has now been rightly given up by most people. We no longer see anything very edifying in the patricians of the early Republic, who treated their wives like slaves, their children like cattle, and their creditors like wild beasts. If there were still any advocates to plead their unrighteous cause by arguing from an assumed "variation in the moral standard of different ages," it would not be very hard to show how flimsy such an argument is. In all ages the misuse of power has excited equal indignation. If the rape of Lucrece did not bring about the expulsion of the kings, if the tribunate[9] was not established owing to the attempt of Appius Claudius, at any rate the real causes that lay behind these two great revolutions, by cloaking themselves under such pretexts, reveal the state of public morality at the time. No, we cannot account

---

[8] Balzac, *Lettre à madame la duchesse de Montausier.*

[9] The power of the Tribunate was revived after Appius' decemvirate in 450 B.C., but the office had been founded more than forty years before. On the other hand, consular tribunes were first elected after 450 (in 445); but the consular tribunate could hardly be described as a "great revolution." The author may be confusing the two tribunates.—Tr.

for the greater vigor of all early peoples by alleging their greater virtue. From the beginning of history, there has been no human society, however small, that has not contained the germ of every vice. And yet, however burdened with this load of depravity, the nations seem to march on very comfortably, and often, in fact, to owe their greatness to their detestable customs. The Spartans enjoyed a long life and the admiration of men merely owing to their laws, which were those of a robber-state. Was the fall of the Phoenicians due to the corruption that gnawed their vitals and was disseminated by them over the whole world? Not at all; on the contrary, this corruption was the main instrument of their power and glory. From the day when they first touched the shores of the Greek islands,[10] and went their way, cheating their customers, robbing their hosts, abducting women for the slave-market, stealing in one place to sell in another —from that day, it is true, their reputation fell not unreasonably low; but they did not prosper any the less for that, and they hold a place in history which is quite unaffected by all the stories of their greed and treachery.

Far from admitting the superior moral character of early societies, I have no doubt that nations, as they grow older and so draw nearer their fall, present a far more satisfactory appearance from the censor's point of view. Customs become less rigid, rough edges become softened, the path of life is made easier, the rights existing between man and man have had time to become better defined and understood, and so the theories of social justice have reached, little by little, a higher degree of delicacy. At the time when the Greeks overthrew the Empire of Darius, or when the Goths entered Rome, there were probably far more honest men in Athens, Babylon, and the imperial city than in the

---

[10] *Cp.* Homer, "Odyssey," xv, 415 *sqq.*

glorious days of Harmodius, Cyrus the Great, and Valerius Publicola.

We need not go back to those distant epochs, but may judge them by ourselves. Paris is certainly one of the places on this earth where civilization has touched its highest point, and where the contrast with primitive ages is most marked; and yet you will find a large number of religious and learned people admitting that in no place and time were there so many examples of practical virtue, of sincere piety, of saintly lives governed by a fine sense of duty, as are to be met today in the great modern city. The ideals of goodness are as high now as they ever were in the loftiest minds of the seventeenth century; and they have laid aside the bitterness, the strain of sternness and savagery—I was almost saying, of pedantry—that sometimes colored them in that age. And so, as a set-off to the frightful perversities of the modern spirit, we find, in the very temple where that spirit has set up the high altar of its power, a striking contrast, which never appeared to former centuries in the same consoling light as it has to our own.

I do not even believe that there is a lack of great men in periods of corruption and decadence; and by "great men" I mean those most richly endowed with energy of character and the masculine virtues. If I look at the list of the Roman Emperors (most of them, by the way, as high above their subjects in merit as they were in rank) I find names like Trajan, Antoninus Pius, Septimius Severus, and Jovian; and below the throne, even among the city mob, I see with admiration all the great theologians, the great martyrs, the apostles of the primitive Church, to say nothing of the virtuous Pagans. Strong, brave, and active spirits filled the camps and the Italian towns; and one may doubt whether in the time of Cincinnatus, Rome held, in proportion, so many men of eminence in all the walks of practical life. The testimony of the facts is conclusive.

Thus men of strong character, men of talent and energy, so far from being unknown to human societies in the time of their decadence and old age, are actually to be found in greater abundance than in the days when an empire is young. Further, the ordinary level of morality is higher in the later period than in the earlier. It is not generally true to say that in States on the point of death the corruption of morals is any more virulent than in those just born. It is equally doubtful whether this corruption brings about their fall; for some States, far from dying of their perversity, have lived and grown fat on it. One may go further, and show that moral degradation is not necessarily a mortal disease at all; for, as against the other maladies of society, it has the advantage of being curable; and the cure is sometimes very rapid.

In fact, the morals of any particular people are in continual ebb and flow throughout its history. To go no further afield than our own France, we may say that, in the fifth and sixth centuries, the conquered race of the Gallo-Romans were certainly better than their conquerors from a moral point of view. Taken individually, they were not always their inferiors even in courage and the military virtues.[11] In the following centuries, when the two races had begun to intermingle, they seem to have deteriorated; and we have no reason to be very proud of the picture that was presented by our dear country about the eighth and ninth centuries. But in the eleventh, twelfth, and thirteenth, a great change came over the scene. Society had succeeded in harmonizing its most discordant elements, and the state

---

[11] Augustin Thierry, *Récits des temps mérovingiens*; see especially the story of Mummolus.

of morals was reasonably good. The ideas of the time were not favorable to the little casuistries that keep a man from the right path even when he wishes to walk in it. The fourteenth and fifteenth centuries were times of terrible conflict and perversity. Brigandage reigned supreme. It was a period of decadence in the strictest sense of the word; and the decadence was shown in a thousand ways. In view of the debauchery, the tyranny, and the massacres of that age, of the complete withering of all the finer feelings in every section of the State—in the nobles who plundered their villeins, in the citizens who sold their country to England, in a clergy that was false to its professions—one might have thought that the whole society was about to crash to the ground and bury its shame deep under its own ruins. ... The crash never came. The society continued to live; it devised remedies, it beat back its foes, it emerged from the dark cloud. The sixteenth century was far more reputable than its predecessor, in spite of its orgies of blood, which were a pale reflection of those of the preceding age. St. Bartholomew's day is not such a shameful memory as the massacre of the Armagnacs. Finally, the French people passed from this semi-barbarous twilight into the pure splendor of day, the age of Fénelon, Bossuet, and the Montausier. Thus, up to Louis XIV, our history shows a series of rapid changes from good to evil, from evil to good; while the real vitality of the nation has little to do with its moral condition. I have touched lightly on the larger curves of change; to trace the multitude of lesser changes within these would require many pages. To speak even of what we have all but seen with our own eyes, is it not clear that in every decade since 1787 the standard of morality has varied enormously? I conclude that the corruption of morals is a fleeting and unstable phenomenon; it becomes sometimes worse and sometimes better, and so cannot be considered as necessarily causing the ruin of societies.

I must examine here an argument, put forward in our time, which never entered people's heads in the eighteenth century; but as it fits in admirably with the subject of the preceding paragraph, I could not find a better place in which to speak of it. Many people have come to think that the end of a society is at hand when its religious ideas tend to weaken and disappear. They see a kind of connection between the open profession of the doctrines of Zeno and Epicurus at Athens and Rome, with the consequent abandonment (according to them) of the national cults, and the fall of the two republics. They fail to notice that these are virtually the only examples that can be given of such a coincidence. The Persian Empire at the time of its fall was wholly under the sway of the Magi. Tyre, Carthage, Judaea, the Aztec and Peruvian monarchies were struck down while fanatically clinging to their altars. Thus it cannot be maintained that all the peoples whose existence as a nation is being destroyed are at that moment expiating the sin they committed in deserting the faith of their fathers. Further, even the two examples that go to support the theory seem to prove much more than they really do. I deny absolutely that the ancient cults were ever given up in Rome or Athens, until the day when they were supplanted in the hearts of all men by the victorious religion of Christ. In other words, I believe that there has never been a real breach of continuity in the religious beliefs of any nation on this earth. The outward form or inner meaning of the creed may have changed; but we shall always find some Gallic Teutates making way for the Roman Jupiter, Jupiter for the Christian God, without any interval of unbelief, in exactly the same way as the dead give up their inheritance to the living. Hence, as there has never been a nation of which one could say that it had no faith at all, we have no right to assume that "the lack of faith causes the destruction of States."

I quite see the grounds on which such a view is based. Its defenders will tell us of "the notorious fact" that a little before the time of Pericles at Athens, and about the age of the Scipios at Rome the upper classes became more and more prone, first to reason about their religion, then to doubt it, and finally to give up all faith in it, and to take pride in being atheists. Little by little, we shall be told, the habit of atheism spread, until there was no one with any pretensions to intellect at all who did not defy one augur to pass another without smiling.

This opinion has a grain of truth, but is largely false. Say, if you will, that Aspasia, at the end of her little suppers, and Laelius, in the company of his friends, made a virtue of mocking at the sacred beliefs of their country; no one will contradict you. But they would not have been allowed to vent their ideas too publicly; and yet they lived at the two most brilliant periods of Greek and Roman history. The imprudent conduct of his mistress all but cost Pericles himself very dear; we remember the tears he shed in open court, tears which would not of themselves have secured the acquittal of the fair infidel. Think, too, of the official language held by contemporary poets, how Sophocles and Aristophanes succeeded Æschylus as the stern champions of outraged deity. The whole nation believed in its gods, regarded Socrates as a revolutionary and a criminal, and wished to see Anaxagoras brought to trial and condemned. ... What of the later ages? Did the impious theories of the philosophers succeed at any time in reaching the masses? Not for a single day. Skepticism remained a luxury of the fashionable world and of that world alone. One may call it useless to speak of the thoughts of the plain citizens, the country folk, and the slaves, who had no influence in the government, and could not impose their ideas on their rulers. They had, however, a very real influence; and the proof is that until paganism was at its last gasp, their temples and shrines had to be kept going, and their acolytes to be paid. The most eminent and enlightened men, the most fervent in their unbelief, had not only to accept the public honor of wearing the priestly robe, but to undertake the most disagreeable duties of the cult—they who were accustomed to turn over, day and night, *manu diurna, manu nocturna,* the pages of Lucretius. Not only did they go through these rites on ceremonial occasions, but they used their scanty hours of leisure, hours snatched with difficulty from the life-and-death game of politics, in composing treatises on augury. I am referring to the great Julius.[12] Well, all the emperors after him had to hold the office of high-priest, even Constantine. He, certainly, had far stronger reason than all his predecessors for shaking off a yoke so degrading to his honor as a Christian prince; yet he was forced by public opinion, that blazed up for the last time before being extinguished forever, to come to terms with the old national religion. Thus it was not the faith of the plain citizens, the country folk, and the slaves that was of small account; it was the theories of the men of culture that mattered nothing. They protested in vain, in the name of reason and good sense, against the absurdities

---

[12] Caesar, the democrat and skeptic, knew how to hold language contrary to his opinions when it was necessary. His funeral oration on his aunt is very curious: "On the mother's side," he said, "Julia was descended from kings; on her father's, from the immortal gods: for the Marcian Reges, whose name her mother bore, were sprung from Ancus Marcius, while Venus is the ancestress of the Julii, the clan to which belongs the family of the Caesars. Thus in our blood is mingled at the same time the sanctity of kings, who are the mightiest of men, and the awful majesty of the gods, who hold kings themselves in their power" (Suetonius, "Julius," p. 6). Nothing could be more monarchical; and also, for an atheist, nothing could be more religious.

of paganism; the mass of the people neither would nor could give up one belief before they had been provided with another. They proved once more the great truth that it is affirmation, not negation, which is of service in the business of this world. So strongly did men feel this truth in the third century that there was a religious reaction among the higher classes. The reaction was serious and general, and lasted till the world definitely passed into the arms of the Church. In fact, the supremacy of philosophy reached its highest point under the Antonines and began to decline soon after their death. I need not here go deeply into this question, however interesting it may be for the historian of ideas; it will be enough for me to show that the revolution gained ground as the years went on, and to bring out its immediate cause.

The older the Roman world became, the greater was the part played by the army. From the emperor, who invariably came from the ranks, down to the pettiest officer in his Praetorian guard and the prefect of the most unimportant district, every official had begun his career on the parade-ground, under the vine-staff of the centurion; in other words they had all sprung from the mass of the people, of whose unquenchable piety I have already spoken. When they had scaled the heights of office, they found confronting them, to their intense annoyance and dismay, the ancient aristocracy of the municipalities, the local senators, who took pleasure in regarding them as upstarts, and would gladly have turned them to ridicule if they had dared. Thus the real masters of the State and the once predominant families were at daggers drawn. The commanders of the army were believers and fanatics—Maximin, for example, and Galerius, and a hundred others. The senators and decurions still found their chief delight in the literature of the skeptics; but as they actually lived at court, that is to say among soldiers, they were forced to adopt a way of speaking and an official set of opinions which should not put them to any risk. Gradually an atmosphere of devotion spread through the Empire; and this led the philosophers themselves, with Euhemerus at their head, to invent systems of reconciling the theories of the rationalists with the State religion—a movement in which the Emperor Julian was the most powerful spirit. There is no reason to give much praise to this renaissance of pagan piety, for it caused most of the persecutions under which our martyrs have suffered. The masses, whose religious feelings had been wounded by the atheistic sects, had bided their time so long as they were ruled by the upper classes. But as soon as the empire had become democratic, and the pride of these classes had been brought low, then the populace determined to have their revenge. They made a mistake, however, in their victims, and cut the throats of the Christians, whom they took for philosophers, and accused of impiety. What a difference there was between this and an earlier age! The really skeptical pagan was King Agrippa, who wished to hear St. Paul merely out of curiosity.[13] He listened to him, disputed with him, took him for a madman, but did not dream of punishing him for thinking differently from himself. Another example is the historian Tacitus, who was full of contempt for the new sectaries, but blamed Nero for his cruelty in persecuting them. Agrippa and Tacitus were the real unbelievers. Diocletian was a politician ruled by the clamours of his people; Decius and Aurelian were fanatics like their subjects.

Even when the Roman Government had definitely gone over to Christianity, what a task it was to bring the different peoples into the bosom of the Church! In

---

[13] Acts xxvi, 24, 28, 31.

Greece there was a series of terrible struggles, in the Universities as well as in the small towns and villages. The bishops had everywhere such difficulty in ousting the little local divinities that very often the victory was due less to argument and conversion than to time, patience, and diplomacy. The clergy were forced to make use of pious frauds, and their ingenuity replaced the deities of wood, meadow, and fountain, by saints, martyrs, and virgins. Thus the feelings of reverence continued without a break; for some time they were directed to the wrong objects, but they at last found the right road. ... But what am I saying? Can we be so certain that even in France there are not to be found to this day a few places where the tenacity of some odd superstition still gives trouble to the parish priest? In Catholic Brittany, in the eighteenth century, a bishop had a long struggle with a village-people that clung to the worship of a stone idol. In vain was the gross image thrown into the water; its fanatical admirers always fished it out again, and the help of a company of infantry was needed to break it to pieces. We see from this what a long life paganism had—and still has. I conclude that there is no good reason for holding that Rome and Athens were for a single day without religion.

Since then, a nation has never, either in ancient or modern times, given up one faith before being duly provided with another, it is impossible to claim that the ruin of nations follows from their irreligion.

I have now shown that fanaticism, luxury, and the corruption of morals have not necessarily any power of destruction, and that irreligion has no political reality at all; it remains to discuss the influence of bad government, which is well worth a chapter to itself.

CHAPTER III

THE RELATIVE MERIT OF GOVERNMENTS HAS NO INFLUENCE ON THE LENGTH OF A NATION'S LIFE

I know the difficulty of my present task. That I should even venture to touch on it will seem a kind of paradox to many of my readers. People are convinced, and rightly convinced, that the good administration of good laws has a direct and powerful influence on the health of a people; and this conviction is so strong, that they attribute to such administration the mere fact that a human society goes on living at all. Here they are wrong.

They would be right, of course, if it were true that nations could exist only in a state of well being; but we know that, like individuals, they can often go on for a long time, carrying within them the seeds of some fell disease, which may suddenly break out in a virulent form. If nations invariably died of their sufferings, not one would survive the first years of its growth; for it is precisely in those years that, they show the worst administration, the worst laws, and the greatest disorder. But in this respect they are the exact opposite of the human organism. The greatest enemy that the latter has to fear, especially in infancy, is a continuous series of illnesses—we know beforehand that there is no resisting these; to a society, however, such a series does no harm at all, and history gives us abundant proof that the body politic is always being cured of the longest, the most terrible and devastating attacks of disease, of which the worst forms are ill-conceived laws and an oppressive or negligent administration.[14]

We will first try to make clear in what a "bad government" consists.

It is a malady that seems to take many forms. It would be impossible even to enumerate them all, for they are multiplied to infinity by the differences in the constitutions of peoples, and in the place and time of their existence. But if we group these forms under four main headings, there are very few varieties that will not be included.

A government is bad when it is set up by a foreign Power. Athens experienced this kind of government under the Thirty Tyrants; they were driven out, and the national spirit, far from dying under their oppressive rule, was tempered by it to a greater hardness.

A government is bad when it is based on conquest, pure and simple. In the fourteenth century practically the whole of France passed under the yoke of England. It emerged stronger than before, and entered on a career of great brilliance. China was overrun and conquered by hordes of Mongols; it managed to expel them beyond its borders, after sapping their vitality in a most extraordinary way. Since that time China has fallen into a new servitude; but although the Manchus have already enjoyed more than a century of sovereignty, they are on the eve of suffering the same fate as the Mongols, and have passed through a similar period of weakness.

A government is especially bad when the principle on which it rests becomes vitiated, and ceases to operate in the healthy and vigorous way it did at first. This was the condition of the Spanish monarchy. It was based on

---

[14] The reader will understand that I am not speaking of the political existence of a center of sovereignty, but of the life of a whole society, or the span of a whole civilization. The distinction drawn at the beginning of chap. ii must be applied here.

the military spirit and the idea of social freedom; towards the end of Philip II's reign it forgot its origin and began to degenerate. There has never been a country where all theories of conduct had become more obsolete, where the executive was more feeble and discredited, where the organization of the church itself was so open to criticism. Agriculture and industry, like everything else, were struck down and all but buried in the morass where the nation was decaying. ... But is Spain dead? Not at all. The country of which so many despaired has given Europe the glorious example of a desperate resistance to the fortune of our arms; and at the present moment it is perhaps in Spain, of all the modern States, that the feeling of nationality is most intense.

Finally, a government is bad when, by the very nature of its institutions, it gives color to an antagonism between the supreme power and the mass of the people, or between different classes of society. Thus, in the Middle Ages, we see the kings of England and France engaged in a struggle with their great vassals, and the peasants flying at the throats of their overlords. In Germany, too, the first effects of the new freedom of thought were the civil wars of the Hussites, the Anabaptists, and all the other sectaries. A little before that, Italy was in such distress through the division of the supreme power, and the quarrel over the fragments between the Emperor, the Pope, the nobles, and the communes, that the masses, not knowing whom to obey, often ended by obeying nobody. Did this cause the ruin of the whole society? Not at all. Its civilization was never more brilliant, its industry more productive, its influence abroad more incontestable.

I can well believe that sometimes, in the midst of these storms, a wise and potent law-giver came, like a sunbeam, to shed the light of his beneficence on the peoples he ruled. The light remained only for a short space; and just as its absence had not caused death, so its presence did not bring life. For this, the times of prosperity would have had to be frequent and of long duration. But upright princes were rare in that age, and are rare in all ages. Even the best of them have their detractors, and the happiest pictures are full of shadow. Do all historians alike regard the time of King William III as an era of prosperity for England? Do they all admire Louis XIV, the Great, without reserve? On the contrary; the critics are all at their posts, and their arrows know where to find their mark. And yet these are, on the whole, the best regulated and most fruitful periods in the history of ourselves and our neighbors. Good governments are so thinly sown on the soil of the ages, and even when they spring up, are so withered by criticism; political science, the highest and most intricate of all sciences, is so incommensurate with the weakness of man, that we cannot sincerely claim that nations perish from being ill-governed. Thank heaven they have the power of soon becoming accustomed to their sufferings, which, in their worst forms, are infinitely, preferable to anarchy. The most superficial study of history will be enough to show that however bad may be the government that is draining away the life-blood of a people, it is often better than many of the administrations that have gone before.

CHAPTER IV

THE MEANING OF THE WORD "DEGENERATION"; THE MIXTURE OF RACIAL ELEMENTS; HOW SOCIETIES ARE FORMED AND BROKEN UP

However little the spirit of the foregoing pages may have been understood, no one will conclude from them that I attach no importance to the maladies of the social organism, and that, for me, bad government, fanaticism, and irreligion are mere unmeaning accidents. On the contrary I quite agree with the ordinary view, that it is a lamentable thing to see a society being gradually undermined by these fell diseases, and that no amount of care and trouble would be wasted if a remedy could only be found. I merely add that if these poisonous blossoms of disunion are not grafted on a stronger principle of destruction, if they are not the consequences of a hidden plague more terrible still, we may rest assured that their ravages will not be fatal and that after a time of suffering more or less drawn out, the society will emerge from their toils, perhaps with strength and youth renewed.

The examples I have brought forward seem to me conclusive, though their number might be indefinitely increased. Through some such reasoning as this the ordinary opinions of men have at last come to contain an instinctive perception of the truth. It is being dimly seen that one ought not to have given such a preponderant importance to evils which were after all merely derivative, and that the true causes of the life and death of peoples should have been sought elsewhere, and been drawn from a deeper well. Men have begun to look at the inner constitution of a society, by itself, quite apart from all circumstances of health or disease. They have shown themselves ready to admit that no external cause could lay the hand of death on any society, so long as a certain destructive principle, inherent in it from the first, born from its womb and nourished on its entrails, had not reached its full maturity; on the other hand, so soon as this destructive principle had come into existence, the society was doomed to certain death, even though it had the best of all possible governments—in exactly the same way as a spent horse will fall dead on a concrete road.

A great step in advance was made, I admit, when the question was considered from this point of view, which was anyhow much more philosophic than the one taken up before. Bichat,[15] as we know, did not seek to discover the great mystery of existence by studying the human subject from the outside; the key to the riddle, he saw, lay within. Those who followed the same method, in our own subject, were travelling on the only road that really led to discoveries. Unfortunately, this excellent idea of theirs was the result of mere instinct; its logical implications were not carried very far, and it was shattered on the first difficulty. "Yes," they cried, "the cause of destruction lies hidden in the very vitals of the social organism; but what *is* this cause?" *"Degeneration,"* was the answer; "nations die when they are composed of elements that have *degenerated."* The answer was excellent, etymologically and otherwise. It only remained to define the meaning of "nation that has degenerated." This was the rock on which they foundered; a *degenerate people* meant, they said, "A people which through bad government, misuse of wealth, fanaticism, or irreligion, had lost the characteristic virtues of its ancestors." What a fall is there! Thus a

---

[15] The celebrated physiologist (1771-1802), and author of *L'Anatomie générale.* —Tr.

people dies of its endemic diseases because it is degenerate, and is degenerate because it dies. This circular argument merely proves that the science of social anatomy is in its infancy. I quite agree that societies perish because they are degenerate, and for no other reason. This is the evil condition that makes them wholly unable to withstand the shock of the disasters that close in upon them; and when they can no longer endure the blows of adverse fortune, and have no power to raise their heads when the scourge has passed, then we have the sublime spectacle of a nation in agony. If it perish, it is because it has no longer the same vigor as it had of old in battling with the dangers of life; in a word, because it is *degenerate.* I repeat, the term is excellent; but we must explain it a little better, and give it a definite meaning. How and why is a nation's vigor lost? How does it degenerate? These are the questions which we must try to answer. Up to the present, men have been content with finding the word, without unveiling the reality that lies behind. This further step I shall now attempt to take.

The word *degenerate,* when applied to a people, means (as it ought to mean) that the people has no longer the same intrinsic value as it had before, because it has no longer the same blood in its veins, continual adulterations having gradually affected the quality of that blood. In other words, though the nation bears the name given by its founders, the name no longer connotes the same race; in fact, the man of a decadent time, the *degenerate* man properly so called, is a different being, from the racial point of view, from the heroes of the great ages. I agree that he still keeps something of their essence; but the more he degenerates the more attenuated does this "something" become. The heterogeneous elements that henceforth prevail in him give him quite a different nationality—a very original one, no doubt, but such originality is not to be envied. He is only a very distant kinsman of those he still calls his ancestors. He, and his civilization with him, will certainly die on the day when the primordial race-unit is so broken up and swamped by the influx of foreign elements, that its effective qualities have no longer a sufficient freedom of action. It will not, of course, absolutely disappear, but it will in practice be so beaten down and enfeebled, that its power will be felt less and less as time goes on. It is at this point that all the results of degeneration will appear, and the process may be considered complete.

If I manage to prove this proposition, I shall have given a meaning to the word "degeneration." By showing how the essential quality of a nation gradually alters, I shift the responsibility for its decadence, which thus becomes, in a way, less shameful, for it weighs no longer on the sons, but on the nephews, then on the cousins, then on collaterals more or less removed. And when I have shown by examples that great peoples, at the moment of their death, have only a very small and insignificant share in the blood of the founders, into whose inheritance they come, I shall thereby have explained clearly enough how it is possible for civilizations to fall—the reason being that they are no longer in the same hands. At the same time I shall be touching on a problem which is much more dangerous than that which I have tried to solve in the preceding chapters. This problem is: "Are there serious and ultimate differences of value between human races; and can these differences be estimated? "

I will begin at once to develop the series of arguments that touch the first point; they will indirectly settle the second also.

To put my ideas into a clearer and more easily intelligible form I may compare a nation to a human body, which, according to the physiologists, is constantly renewing all its parts; the work of transformation that goes on is incessant, and after a certain number of years the body retains hardly any of its former elements. Thus, in the old man, there are no traces of the man of middle age, in the adult no traces of the youth, nor in the youth of the child; the personal identity in all these stages is kept purely by the succession of inner and outer forms, each an imperfect copy of the last. Yet I will admit one difference between a nation and a human body; in the former there is no question of the "forms" being preserved, for these are destroyed and disappear with enormous rapidity. I will take a people, or better, a tribe, at the moment when, yielding to a definite vital instinct, it provides itself with laws and begins to play a part in the world. By the mere fact of its wants and powers increasing, it inevitably finds itself in contact with other similar associations, and by war or peaceful measures succeeds in incorporating them with itself.

Not all human families can reach this first step; but it is a step that every tribe must take if it is to rank one day as a nation. Even if a certain number of races, themselves perhaps not very far advanced on the ladder of civilization, have passed through this stage, we cannot properly regard this as a general rule.

Indeed, the human species seems to have a very great difficulty in raising itself above a rudimentary type of organization; the transition to a more complex state is made only by those groups of tribes, that are eminently gifted. I may cite, in support of this, the actual condition of a large number of communities spread throughout the world. These backward tribes, especially the Polynesian negroes, the Samoyedes and others in the far north, and the majority of the African races, have never been able to shake themselves free from their impotence; they live side by side in complete independence of each other.

The stronger massacre the weaker, the weaker try to move as far away as possible from the stronger. This sums up the political ideas of these embryo societies, which have lived on in their imperfect state, without possibility of improvement, as long as the human race itself. It may be said that these miserable savages are a very small part of the earth's population. Granted; but we must take account of all the similar peoples who have lived and disappeared. Their number is incalculable, and certainly includes the vast majority of the pure-blooded yellow and black races.

If then we are driven to admit that for a very large number of human beings it has been, and always will be, impossible to take even the first step towards civilization; if, again, we consider that these peoples are scattered over the whole face of the earth under the most varying conditions of climate and environment, that they live indifferently in the tropics, in the temperate zones, and in the Arctic circle, by sea, lake, and river, in the depths of the forest, in the grassy plains, in the arid deserts, we must conclude that a part of mankind, is in its own nature stricken with a paralysis, which makes it forever unable to take even the first step towards civilization, since it cannot overcome the natural repugnance, felt by men and animals alike, to a crossing of blood.

Leaving these tribes, that are incapable of civilization, on one side, we come, in our journey upwards, to those which understand that if they wish to increase their power and prosperity, they are absolutely compelled, either by war or peaceful measures, to draw their neighbors within their sphere of influence. War is undoubtedly the simpler way of doing this. Accordingly, they go to war. But when the campaign is finished, and the craving for destruction is satisfied, some prisoners are left over; these prisoners become slaves, and as slaves, work for their masters. We have class distinctions at once, and an industrial system: the tribe has become a little people. This is a higher rung on the ladder of civilization, and is not necessarily passed by all the tribes which have been able to reach it; many remain at this stage in cheerful stagnation.

But there are others, more imaginative and energetic, whose ideas soar beyond mere brigandage. They manage to conquer a great territory, and assume rights of ownership not only over the inhabitants, but also over their land. From this moment a real nation has been formed. The two races often continue for a time to live side by side without mingling; and yet, as they become indispensable to each other, as a community of work and interest is gradually built up, as the pride and rancor of conquest begin to ebb away, as those below naturally tend to rise to the level of their masters, while the masters have a thousand reasons for allowing, or even for promoting, such a tendency, the mixture of blood finally takes place, the two races cease to be associated with distinct tribes, and become more and more fused into a single whole.

The spirit of isolation is, however, so innate in the human race, that even those who have reached this advanced stage of crossing refuse in many cases to take a step further. There are some peoples who are, as we know positively, of mixed origin, but who keep their feeling for the clan to an extraordinary degree. The Arabs, for example, do more than merely spring from different branches of the Semitic stock; they belong at one and the same time to the so-called families of Shem and Ham, not to speak of a vast number of local strains that are intermingled with these. Nevertheless, their attachment to the tribe, as a separate unit, is one of the most striking features of their national character and their political history. In fact, it has been thought possible to attribute their expulsion from Spain not only to the actual breaking up of their power there, but also, to a large extent, to their being continually divided into smaller and mutually antagonistic groups, in the struggles for promotion among the Arab families at the petty courts of Valentia, Toledo, Cordova, and Grenada.[16]

We may say the same about the majority of such peoples. Further, where the tribal separation has broken down, a national feeling takes its place, and acts with a similar vigor, which a community of religion is not enough to destroy. This is the case among the Arabs and the Turks, the Persians and the Jews, the Parsees and the Hindus, the Nestorians of Syria and the Kurds. We find it also in European Turkey, and can trace its course in Hungary, among the Magyars, the Saxons, the Wallachians, and the Croats. I know, from what I have seen with my own eyes, that in certain parts of France, the country where races are mingled more than perhaps anywhere else, there are little communities to be found to this day, who feel a repugnance to marrying outside their own village.

I think I am right in concluding from these examples, which cover all countries and ages, including our own, that the human race in all its branches has a secret repulsion from the crossing of blood, a repulsion which in many of the branches is invincible, and in others is only conquered to a slight extent. Even those who most completely shake off the yoke of this idea cannot get rid of the few last traces of it; yet such

---

[16] This attachment of the Arab tribes to their racial unity shows itself sometimes in a very curious manner. A traveller (M. Fulgence Fresnel, I think) says that at Djiddah, where morals are very lax, the same Bedouin girl who will sell her favors for the smallest piece of money would think herself dishonored if she contracted a legal marriage with the Turk or European to whom she contemptuously lends herself.

peoples are the only members of our species who can be civilized at all.

Thus mankind lives in obedience to two laws, one of repulsion, the other of attraction; these act with different force on different peoples. The first is fully respected only by those races which can never raise themselves above the elementary completeness of the tribal life, while the power of the second, on the contrary, is the more absolute, as the racial units on which it is exercised are more capable of development.

Here especially I must be concrete. I have just taken the example of a people in embryo, whose state is like that of a single family. I have given them the qualities which will allow them to pass into the state of a nation. Well, suppose they have become a nation. History does not tell me what the elements were that constituted the original group; all I know is that these elements fitted it for the transformation which I have made it undergo. Now that it has grown, it has only two possibilities. One or other of two destinies is inevitable. It will either conquer or be conquered.

I will give it the better part, and assume that it will conquer. It will at the same time rule, administer, and civilize. It will not go through its provinces, sowing a useless harvest of fire and massacre. Monuments, customs, and institutions will be alike sacred. It will change what it can usefully modify, and replace it by something better. Weakness in its hands will become strength. It will behave in such a way that, in the words of Scripture, it will be magnified in the sight of men.

I do not know if the same thought has already struck the reader; but in the picture which I am presenting—and which in certain features is that of the Hindus, the Egyptians, the Persians and the Macedonians—two facts appear to me to stand out. The first is that a nation, which itself lacks vigor and power, is suddenly called upon to share a new and a better destiny—that of the strong masters into whose hands it has fallen; this was the case with the Anglo-Saxons, when they had been subdued by the Normans. The second fact is that a picked race of men, a sovereign people, with the usual strong propensities of such a people to cross its blood with another's, finds itself henceforth in close contact with a race whose inferiority is shown, not only by defeat, but also by the lack of the attributes that may be seen in the conquerors. From the very day when the conquest is accomplished and the fusion begins, there appears a noticeable change of quality in the blood of the masters. If there were no other modifying influence at work, then—at the end of a number of years, which would vary according to the number of peoples that composed the original stock—we should be confronted with a new race, less powerful certainly than the better of its two ancestors, but still of considerable strength. It would have developed special qualities resulting from the actual mixture, and unknown to the communities from which it sprang. But the case is not generally so simple as this, and the intermingling of blood is not confined for long to the two constituent peoples;

The empire I have just been imagining is a powerful one and its power is used to control its neighbors. I assume that there will be new conquests; and, every time, a current of fresh blood will be mingled with the main stream. Henceforth, as the nation grows, whether by war or treaty, its racial character changes more and more. It is rich, commercial, and civilized. The needs and the pleasures of other peoples find ample satisfaction in its capitals, its great towns, and its ports; while its myriad attractions cause many foreigners to make it their home. After a short time, we might truly say that a distinction of castes takes the place of the original distinction of races.

I am willing to grant that the people of whom I am speaking is strengthened in its exclusive notions by the most formal commands of religion, and that some dreadful penalty lurks in the background, to awe the disobedient. But since the people is civilized, its character is soft and tolerant, even to the contempt of its faith. Its oracles will speak in vain; there will be births outside the caste-limits. Every day new distinctions will have to be drawn, new classifications invented; the number of social grades will be increased, and it will be almost impossible to know where one is, amid the infinite variety of the subdivisions, that change from province to province, from canton to canton, from village to village. In fact, the condition will be that of the Hindu countries. It is only, however, the Brahman who has shown himself so tenacious of his ideas of separation; the foreign peoples he civilized have never fastened these cramping fetters on their shoulders, or any rate have long since shaken them off. In all the States that have made any advance in intellectual culture, the process has not been checked for a single moment by those desperate shifts to which the law-givers of the Aryavarta were put, in their desire to reconcile the prescriptions of the Code of Manu with the irresistible march of events. In every other place where there were really any castes at all, they ceased to exist at the moment when the chance of making a fortune, and of becoming famous by useful discoveries or social talents, became open to the whole world, without distinction of origin. But also, from that same day, the nation that was originally the active, conquering, and civilizing power began to disappear; its blood became merged in that of all the tributaries which it had attracted to its own stream.

Generally the dominating peoples begin by being far fewer in number than those they conquer; while, on the other hand, certain races that form the basis of the population in immense districts are extremely prolific—the Celts, for example, and the Slavs. This is yet another reason for the rapid disappearance of the conquering races. Again, their greater activity and the more personal part they take in the affairs of the State make them the chief mark for attack after a disastrous battle, a proscription, or a revolution. Thus, while by their very genius for civilization they collect round them the different elements in which they are to be absorbed, they are the victims, first of their original smallness of number, and then of a host of secondary causes which combine together for their destruction.

It is fairly obvious that the time when the disappearance takes place will vary considerably, according to circumstances. Yet it does finally come to pass, and is everywhere quite complete, long before the end of the civilization which the victorious race is supposed to be animating. A people may often go on living and working, and even growing in power, after the active, generating force of its life and glory has ceased to exist. Does this contradict what I have said above? Not at all; for while the blood of the civilizing race is gradually drained away by being parcelled out among the peoples that are conquered or annexed, the impulse originally given to these peoples still persists. The institutions which the dead master had invented, the laws he had prescribed, the customs he had initiated—all these live after him. No doubt the customs, laws, and institutions have quite forgotten the spirit that informed their youth; they survive in dishonored old age, every day more sapless and rotten. But so long as even their shadows remain, the building stands, the body seems to have a soul, the pale ghost walks. When the original impulse has worked itself out, the last word has been said. Nothing remains; the civilization is dead.

I think I now have all the data necessary for grappling with the problem of the life and death of nations; and I can say positively that a people will never die, if it remains eternally composed of the same national elements. If the empire of Darius had, at the battle of Arbela, been able to fill its ranks with Persians, that is to say with real Aryans; if the Romans of the later Empire had had a Senate and an army of the same stock as that which existed at the time of the Fabii, their dominion would never have come to an end. So long as they kept the same purity of blood, the Persians and Romans would have lived and reigned. In the long run, it might be said, a conqueror, more irresistible than they, would have appeared on the scene; and they would have fallen under a well-directed attack, or a long siege, or simply by the fortune of a single battle. Yes, a State might be overthrown in this way, but not a civilization or a social organism. Invasion and defeat are but the dark clouds that for a time blot out the day, and then pass over. Many examples might be brought forward in proof of this.

In modern times the Chinese have been twice conquered. They have always forced their conquerors to become assimilated to them, and to respect their customs; they gave much, and took hardly anything in return. They drove out the first invaders, and in time will do the same with the second.

The English are the masters of India, and yet their moral hold over their subjects is almost non-existent. They are themselves influenced in many ways by the local civilization, and cannot succeed in stamping their ideas on a people that fears its conquerors, but is only physically dominated by them. It keeps its soul erect, and its thoughts apart from theirs. The Hindu race has become a stranger to the race that governs it today, and its civilization does not obey the law that gives the battle to the strong. External forms, kingdoms, and empires have changed, and will change again; but the foundations on which they rest, and from which they spring, do not necessarily change with them. Though Hyderabad, Lahore, and Delhi are no longer capital cities, Hindu society none the less persists. A moment will come, in one way or another, when India will again live publicly, as she already does privately, under her own laws; and, by the help either of the races actually existing or of a hybrid proceeding from them, will assume again, in the full sense of the word, a political personality.

The hazard of war cannot destroy the life of a people. At most, it suspends its animation for a time, and in some ways shears it of its outward pomp. So long as the blood and institutions of a nation keep to a sufficient degree the impress of the original race, that nation exists. Whether, as in the case of the Chinese, its conqueror has, in a purely material sense, greater energy than itself; whether, like the Hindu, it is matched, in a long and arduous trial of patience, against a nation, such as the English, in all points its superior; in either case the thought of its certain destiny should bring consolation—one day it will be free. But if, like the Greeks, and the Romans of the later Empire, the people has been absolutely drained of its original blood, and the qualities conferred by the blood, then the day of its defeat will be the day of its death. It has used up the time that heaven granted at its birth, for it has completely changed its race, and with its race its nature. It is therefore degenerate.

In view of the preceding paragraph, we may regard as settled the vexed question as to what would have happened if the Carthaginians, instead of falling before the fortunes of Rome, had become masters of Italy. Inasmuch as they belonged to the Phoenician stock, a stock inferior in the citizen-virtues to the races that produced the soldiers of Scipio, a different issue of the battle of Zama could not have made any change in their destiny. If they had been lucky on one day, the next would have seen their luck recoil on their heads; or they might have been merged in the Italian race by victory, as they were by defeat. In any case the final result would have been exactly the same. The destiny of civilizations is not a matter of chance; it does not depend on the toss of a coin. It is only men who are killed by the sword; and when the most redoubtable, warlike, and successful nations have nothing but valor in their hearts, military science in their heads, and the laurels of victory in their hands, without any thought that rises above mere conquest, they always end merely by learning, and learning badly, from those they have conquered, how to live in time of peace. The annals of the Celts and the Nomadic hordes of Asia tell no other tale than this.

I have now given a meaning to the word *degeneration;* and so have been able to attack the problem of a nation's vitality. I must next proceed to prove what for the sake of clearness I have had to put forward as a mere hypothesis; namely, that there are real differences in the relative value of human races. The consequences of proving this will be considerable, and cover a wide field. But first I must lay a foundation of fact and argument capable of holding up such a vast building; and the foundation cannot be too complete. The question with which I have just been dealing was only the gateway of the temple.

CHAPTER V

RACIAL INEQUALITY IS NOT THE RESULT OF INSTITUTIONS

The idea of an original, clear-cut, and permanent inequality among the different races is one of the oldest and most widely held opinions in the world. We need not be surprised at this, when we consider the isolation of primitive tribes and communities, and how in the early ages they all used to "retire into their shell"; a great number have never left this stage. Except in quite modern times, this idea has been the basis of nearly all theories of government. Every people, great or small, has begun by making inequality its chief political motto. This is the origin of all systems of caste, of nobility, and of aristocracy, in so far as the last is founded on the right of birth. The law of primogeniture, which assumes the pre-eminence of the first born and his descendants, is merely a corollary of the same principle. With it go the repulsion felt for the foreigner and the superiority which every nation claims for itself with regard to its neighbors. As soon as the isolated groups have begun to intermingle and to become one people, they grow great and civilized, and look at each other in a more favorable light, as one finds the other useful. Then, and only then, do we see the absolute principle of the inequality, and hence the mutual hostility, of races questioned and undermined. Finally, when the majority of the citizens have mixed blood flowing in their veins, they erect into a universal and absolute truth what is only true for themselves, and feel it to be their duty to assert that all men are equal. They are also moved by praiseworthy dislike of oppression, a legitimate hatred towards the abuse of power; to all thinking men these cast an ugly shadow on the memory of races which have once been dominant, and which have never failed (for such is the way of the world) to justify to some extent many of the charges that have been brought against them. From mere declamation against tyranny, men go on to deny the natural causes of the superiority against which they are declaiming. The tyrant's power is, to them, not only misused, but usurped. They refuse, quite wrongly, to admit that certain qualities are by a fatal necessity the exclusive inheritance of such and such a stock. In fact, the more heterogeneous the elements of which a people is composed, the more complacently does it assert that the most different powers are, or can be, possessed in the same measure by every fraction of the human race, without exception. This theory is barely applicable to these hybrid philosophers themselves; but they extend it to cover all the generations which were, are, and ever shall be on the earth. They end one day by summing up their views in the words which, like the bag of Æolus, contain so many storms— "All men are brothers."[17]

This is the political axiom. Would you like to hear it in its scientific form? "All men," say the defenders of human equality, "are furnished with similar intellectual powers, of the same nature, of the same value, of the same compass." These are not perhaps their exact words, but they certainly give the right meaning. So the brain of the Huron Indian contains in an undeveloped form an intellect which is absolutely the same as that of the Englishman or the Frenchman! Why then, in the course

---

[17]   The man
        Of virtuous soul commands not, nor obeys;
        Power, like a desolating pestilence,
        Pollutes whate'er it touches; and obedience,
        Bane of all genius, virtue, freedom, truth,
        Makes slaves of men, and of the human frame
        A mechanized automaton.
                    Shelley, "Queen Mab."

of the ages, has he not invented printing or steam power? I should be quite justified in asking our Huron why, if he is equal to our European peoples, his tribe has never produced a Caesar or a Charlemagne among its warriors, and why his bards and sorcerers have, in some inexplicable way, neglected to become Homers and Galens. The difficulty is usually met by the blessed phrase, "the predominating influence of environment." According to this doctrine, an island will not see the same miracles of civilization as a continent, the same people will be different in the north from what it is in the south, forests will not allow of developments which are favored by open country. What else? the humidity of a marsh, I suppose, will produce a civilization which would inevitably have been stifled by the dryness of the Sahara! However ingenious these little hypotheses may be, the testimony of fact is against them. In spite of wind and rain, cold and heat, sterility and fruitfulness, the world has seen barbarism and civilization flourishing everywhere, one after the other, on the same soil. The brutish fellah is tanned by the same sun as scorched the powerful priest of Memphis; the learned professor of Berlin lectures under the same inclement sky that once beheld the wretched existence of the Finnish savage.

The curious point is that the theory of equality, which is held by the majority of men and so has permeated our customs and institutions, has not been powerful enough to overthrow the evidence against it; and those who are most convinced of its truth pay homage every day to its opposite. No one at any time refuses to admit that there are great differences between nations, and the ordinary speech of men, with a naive inconsistency, confesses the fact. In this it is merely imitating the practice of other ages which were not less convinced than we are—and for the same reason—of the absolute equality of races.

While clinging to the liberal dogma of human brotherhood, every nation has always managed to add to the names of others certain qualifications and epithets that suggest their unlikeness from itself. The Roman of Italy called the Græco-Roman a *Græculus*, or "little Greek," and gave him the monopoly of cowardice and empty chatter. He ridiculed the Carthaginian settler, and pretended to be able to pick him out among a thousand for his litigious character and his want of faith. The Alexandrians were held to be witty, insolent, and seditious. In the Middle Ages, the Anglo-Norman kings accused their French subjects of lightness and inconstancy. Today, every one talks of the "national characteristics" of the German, the Spaniard, the Englishman, and the Russian. I am not asking whether the judgments are true or not. My sole point is that they exist, and are adopted in ordinary speech. Thus, if on the one hand human societies are called equal, and on the other we find some of them frivolous, others serious; some avaricious, others thriftless; some passionately fond of fighting, others careful of their lives and energies;—it stands to reason that these differing nations must have destinies which are also absolutely different, and, in a word, unequal. The stronger will play the parts of kings and rulers in the tragedy of the world. The, weaker will be content with a more humble position.

I do not think that the usual idea of a national character for each people has yet been reconciled with the belief, which is just as widely held, that all peoples are equal. Yet the contradiction is striking and flagrant, and all the more serious because the most ardent democrats are the first to claim superiority for the Anglo-Saxons of North America over all the nations of the same continent. It is true that they ascribe the high position of their favorites merely to their political constitution. But, so far as I know, they do not deny that the countrymen of Penn and Washington, are, as a nation, peculiarly prone to set up liberal institutions in all their places of settlement, and, what is more, to keep them going. Is not this very tenacity a wonderful characteristic of this branch of the human race, and the more precious because most of the societies which have existed, or still exist, in the world seem to be without it?

I do not flatter myself that I shall be able to enjoy this inconsistency without opposition. The friends of equality will no doubt talk very loudly, at this point, about "the power of customs and institutions." They will tell me once more how powerfully the health and growth of a nation are influenced by "the essential quality of a government, taken by itself," or "the fact of despotism or liberty." But it is just at this point that I too shall oppose their arguments.

Political institutions have only two possible sources. They either come directly from the nation which has to live under them, or they are invented by a powerful people and imposed on all the States that fall within its sphere of influence.

There is no difficulty in the first hypothesis. A people obviously adapts its institutions to its wants and instincts; and will beware of laying down any rule which may thwart the one or the other. If, by some lack of skill or care, such a rule is laid down, the consequent feeling of discomfort leads the people to amend its laws, and put them into more perfect harmony with their express objects. In every autonomous State, the laws, we may say, always emanate from the people; not generally because it has a direct power of making them, but because, in order to be good laws, they must be based upon the people's point of view, and be such as it might have thought out for itself, if it had been better informed. If some wise lawgiver seems, at first sight, the sole source of some piece of legislation, a nearer view will show that his very wisdom has led him merely to give out the oracles that have been dictated by his nation. If he is a judicious man, like Lycurgus, he will prescribe nothing that the Dorian of Sparta could not accept. If he is a mere doctrinaire, like Draco, he will draw up a code that will soon be amended or repealed by the Ionian of Athens, who, like all the children of Adam, is incapable of living for long under laws that are foreign to the natural tendencies of his real self. The entrance of a man of genius into this great business of law-making is merely a special manifestation of the enlightened will of the people; if the laws simply fulfilled the fantastic dreams of one individual, they could not rule any people for long. We cannot admit that the institutions thus invented and moulded by a race of men make that race what it is. They are effects, not causes. Their influence is, of course, very great; they preserve the special genius of the nation, they mark out the road on which it is to travel, the end at which it must aim. To a certain extent, they are the hothouse where its instincts develop, the armory that furnishes its best weapons for action. But they do not create their creator; and though they may be a powerful element in his success by helping on the growth of his innate qualities, they will fail miserably whenever they attempt to alter these, or to extend them beyond their natural limits. In a word, they cannot achieve the impossible.

Ill-fitting institutions, however, together with their consequences, have played a great part in the world. When Charles I, by the evil counsels of the Earl of Strafford, wished to force absolute monarchy on the English, the King and his minister were walking on the blood-stained morass of political theory. When the Calvinists dreamed of bringing the French under a government that was at once aristocratic and republican, they were just as far away from the right road.

When the Regent[18] tried to join hands with the nobles who were conquered in 1652, and to carry on the government by intrigue, as the co-adjutor and his friends had desired,[19] her efforts pleased nobody, and offended equally the nobility, the clergy, the Parliament, and the Third Estate. Only a few tax-farmers were pleased. But when Ferdinand the Catholic promulgated against the Moors of Spain his terrible, though necessary, measures of destruction; when Napoleon re-established religion in France, flattered the military spirit, and organized his power in such a way as to protect his subjects while coercing them, both these sovereigns, having studied and understood the special character of their people, were building their house upon a rock. In fact, bad institutions are those which, however well they look on paper, are not in harmony with the national qualities or caprices, and so do not suit a particular State, though they might be very successful in the neighboring country. They would bring only anarchy and disorder, even if they were taken from the statute-book of the angels. On the contrary, other institutions are good for the opposite reason, though they might be condemned, from a particular point of view or even absolutely, by the political philosopher or the moralist. The Spartans were small in number, of high courage, ambitious, and violent. Ill-fitting laws might have turned them into a mere set

---

[18] Anne of Austria, mother of Louis XIV.—Tr.

[19] The Comte de Saint-Priest, in an excellent article in the *Revue des Deux Mondes*, has rightly shown that the party crushed by Cardinal Richelieu had nothing in common with feudalism or the great aristocratic methods of government. Montmorency, Cinq-Mars, and Marillac tried to overthrow the State merely in order to obtain favor and office for themselves. The great Cardinal was quite innocent of the "murder of the French nobility," with which he has been so often reproached.

of pettifogging knaves; Lycurgus made them a nation of heroic brigands.

There is no doubt about it. As the people is born before the laws, the laws take after the people; and receive from it the stamp which they are afterwards to impress in their turn. The changes made in institutions by the lapse of time are a great proof of what I say.

I have already mentioned that as nations become greater, more powerful, and more civilized, their blood loses its purity and their instincts are gradually altered. As a result, it becomes impossible for them to live happily under the laws that suited their ancestors. New generations have new customs and tendencies, and profound changes in the institutions are not slow to follow. These are more frequent and far-reaching in proportion as the race itself is changed; while they are rarer, and more gradual, so long as the people is more nearly akin to the first founders of the State. In England, where modifications of the stock have been slower and, up to now, less varied than in any other European country, we still see the institutions of the fourteenth and fifteenth centuries forming the base of the social structure. We find there, almost in its first vigor, the communal organization of the Plantagenets and the Tudors, the same method of giving the nobility a share in the government, the same gradations of rank in this nobility, the same respect for old families tempered with the same love of low-born merit. Since James I, however, and especially since the Union under Queen Anne, the English blood has been more and more prone to mingle with that of the Scotch and Irish, while other nations have also helped, by imperceptible degrees, to modify its purity. The result is that innovations have been more frequent in our time than ever before, though they have always remained fairly faithful to the spirit of the original constitution.

In France, intermixture of race has been far more common and varied. In some cases, by a sudden turn of the wheel, power has even passed from one race to another. Further, on the social side, there have been complete changes rather than modifications, and these were more or less far-reaching, as the groups that successively held the chief power were more or less different. While the north of France was the preponderating element in national politics, feudalism—or rather a degenerate parody of feudalism—maintained itself with fair success; and the municipal spirit followed its fortunes. After the expulsion of the English, in the fifteenth century, and the restoration of national independence under Charles VII, the central provinces, which had taken the chief part in this revolution and were far less Germanic in race than the districts beyond the Loire, naturally saw their Gallo-Roman blood predominant in the camp and the council-chamber. They combined the taste for military life and foreign conquest—the heritage of the Celtic race—with the love of authority that was innate in their Roman blood; and they turned the current of national feeling in this direction. During the sixteenth century they largely prepared the ground on which, in 1599, the Aquitanian supporters of Henry IV, less Celtic though still more Roman than themselves, laid the foundation stone of another and greater edifice of absolute power. When Paris, whose population is certainly a museum of the most varied ethnological specimens, had finally gained dominion over the rest of France owing to the centralizing policy favored by the Southern character, it had no longer any reason to love, respect, or understand any particular tendency or tradition. This great capital, this Tower of Babel, broke with the past—the past of Flanders, Poitou, and Languedoc—and dragged the whole of France into ceaseless experiments with doctrines that were quite out of harmony with its ancient customs.

We cannot therefore admit that institutions make peoples what they are in cases where the peoples themselves have invented the institutions. But may we say the same of the second hypothesis, which deals with cases where a nation receives its code from the hands of foreigners powerful enough to enforce their will, whether the people like it or not?

There are a few cases of such attempts; but I confess I cannot find any which have been carried out on a great scale by governments of real political genius in ancient or modern times. Their wisdom has never been used to change the actual foundations of any great national system. The Romans were too clever to try such dangerous experiments. Alexander the Great had never done so; and the successors of Augustus, like the conqueror of Darius, were content to rule over a vast mosaic of nations, all of which clung to their own customs, habits, laws, and methods of government. So long as they and their fellow-subjects remained racially the same, they were controlled by their rulers only in matters of taxation and military defense.

There is, however, one point that must not be passed over. Many of the peoples subdued by the Romans had certain features in their codes so outrageous that their existence could not be tolerated by Roman sentiment; for example, the human sacrifices of the Druids, which were visited with the severest penalties. Well, the Romans, for all their power, never "succeeded in completely stamping out these barbarous rites. In Narbonese Gaul the victory was easy, as the native population had been almost entirely replaced by Roman colonists. But in the center, where the tribes were wilder, the resistance was more obstinate; and in the Breton Peninsula, where settlers from England in the fourth century brought back the ancient customs with the ancient blood, the people continued, from mere feelings of patriotism and love of tradition, to cut men's throats on their altars as often as they dared. The strictest supervision did not succeed in taking the sacred knife and torch out of their hands. Every revolt began by restoring this terrible feature of the national cult; and Christianity, still panting with rage after its victory over an immoral polytheism, hurled itself with shuddering horror against the still more hideous superstitions of the Armorici. It destroyed them only after a long struggle; for as late as the seventeenth century shipwrecked sailors were massacred and wrecks plundered in all the parishes on the seaboard where the Cymric blood had kept its purity. These barbarous customs were in accordance with the irresistible instincts of a race which had not yet become sufficiently mixed, and so had seen no reason to change its ways.

It is, however, in modern times especially that we find examples of institutions imposed by a conqueror and not accepted by his subjects. Intolerance is one of the chief notes of European civilization. Conscious of its own power and greatness, it finds itself confronted either by different civilizations or by peoples in a state of barbarism. It treats both kinds with equal contempt; and as it sees obstacles to its own progress in everything that is different from itself, it is apt to demand a complete change in its subjects' point of view. The Spaniards, however, the English, the Dutch, and even the French, did not venture to push their innovating tendencies too far, when the conquered peoples were at all considerable in number. In this they copied the moderation that was forced on the conquerors of antiquity. The East, and North and West Africa, show clear proof that the most enlightened nations cannot set up institutions unsuited to the character of their subjects. I have already mentioned that British India lives its ancient life, under its own immemorial laws. The Javanese have lost all political independence, but are very far from accepting any institutions like those of the Netherlands. They continue to live bound as they lived free; and since the sixteenth century, when Europe first turned her face towards the East, we cannot find the least trace of any moral influence exerted by her, even in the case of the peoples she has most completely conquered.

Not all these, however, have been so numerous as to force self-control on their European masters. In some cases the persuasive tongue has been backed by the stern argument of the sword. The order has gone forth to abolish existing customs, and put in their place others which the masters knew to be good and useful. Has the attempt ever succeeded?

America provides us with the richest field for gathering answers to this question. In the South, the Spaniards reigned without check, and to what end? They uprooted the ancient empires, but brought no light. They founded no race like themselves.

In the North the methods were different, but the results just as negative. In fact, they have been still more unfruitful, still more disastrous from the point of view of humanity. The Spanish Indians, are, at any rate, extremely prolific,[20] and have even transformed the blood of their conquerors, who have now dropped to their level. But the Redskins of the United States have withered at the touch of the Anglo-Saxon energy. The few who remain are growing less every day; and those few are as uncivilized, and as incapable of civilization, as their forefathers.

---

[20] A. von Humboldt, *Examen critique de l'histoire de la géographie du nouveau continent,* vol. ii, pp. 129-30.

In Oceania, the facts point to the same conclusions; the natives are dying out everywhere. We sometimes manage to take away their arms, and prevent them from doing harm; but we do not change their nature. Wherever the European rules, they drink brandy instead of eating each other. This is the only new custom which our active minds have been quite successful in imposing; it does not mark a great step in advance.

There are in the world two Governments formed on European models by peoples different from us in race; one in the Sandwich Islands, the other at San Domingo. A short sketch of these two Governments will be enough to show the impotence of all attempts to set up institutions which are not suggested by the national character.

In the Sandwich Islands the representative system is to be seen in all its majesty. There is a House of Lords, a House of Commons, an executive Ministry, a reigning King; nothing is wanting. But all this is mere ornament. The real motive power that keeps the machine going is a body of Protestant missionaries. Without them, King, Lords, and Commons would not know which way to turn, and would soon cease to turn at all. To the missionaries alone belongs the credit of furnishing the ideas, of putting them into a palatable form, and imposing them on the people; they do this either by the influence they exert on their neophytes, or, in the last resort, by threats. Even so, I rather think that if the missionaries had nothing but King and Parliament to work with, they might struggle for a time with the stupidity of their scholars, but would be forced in the end to take themselves a large and prominent part in the management of affairs. This would show their hand too obviously; and so they avoid it by appointing a ministry that consists simply of men of European race. The whole business is thus a matter of agreement between the

Protestant mission and its nominees; the rest is merely for show.

As to the King, Kamehameha III, he appears to be a prince of considerable parts. He has given up tattooing his face, and although he has not yet converted all the courtiers to his views, he already experiences the well-earned satisfaction of seeing nothing on their faces and cheeks but chaste designs, traced in thin outline. The bulk of the nation, the landed nobility and the townspeople, cling, in this and other respects, to their old ideas. The European population of the Sandwich Islands is, however, swollen every day by new arrivals. There are many reasons for this. The short distance separating the Hawaiian Kingdom from California makes it a very interesting focus for the clear-sighted energy of the white race. Deserters from the whaling vessels or mutinous sailors are not the only colonists; merchants, speculators, adventurers of all kinds, flock to the islands, build houses, and settle down. The native race is gradually tending to mix with the invaders and disappear. I am not sure that the present representative and independent system of administration will not soon give place to an ordinary government of delegates, controlled by some great power. But of this I am certain, that the institutions that are brought in will end by establishing themselves firmly, and the first day of their triumph will necessarily be the last for the natives.

At San Domingo the independence is complete. There are no missionaries to exert a veiled and absolute power, no foreign ministry to carry out European ideas; everything is left to the inspiration of the people itself. Its Spanish part consists of mulattoes, of whom I need say nothing. They seem to imitate, well or badly, all that is most easily grasped in our civilization. They tend, like all hybrids, to identify themselves with the more creditable of the races to which they belong. Thus they are capable, to a certain extent, of reproducing our customs. It is not among them that we must study the question in its essence. Let us cross the mountains that separate the Republic of San Domingo from the State of Haiti.

We find a society of which the institutions are not only parallel to our own, but are derived from the latest pronouncements of our political wisdom. All that the most enlightened liberalism has proclaimed for the last sixty years in the deliberative assemblies of Europe, all that has been written by the most enthusiastic champions of man's dignity and independence, all the declarations of rights and principles—these have all found their echo on the banks of the Artibonite. Nothing African has remained in the statute law. All memories of the land of Ham have been officially expunged from men's minds. The State language has never shown a trace of African influence. The institutions, as I said before, are completely European. Let us consider how they harmonize with the manners of the people.

We are in a different world at once. The manners are as depraved, brutal, and savage as in Dahomey or among the Fellatahs.[21] There is the same barbaric love of finery coupled with the same indifference to form. Beauty consists in color, and so long as a garment is of flaming red and edged with tinsel, the owner does not trouble about its being largely in holes. The question of cleanliness never enters anyone's head. If you wish to approach a high official in this country, you find yourself being introduced to a gigantic negro lying on his back, on a wooden bench. His head is enveloped in a torn and dirty handkerchief, surmounted by a cocked hat, all over gold lace. An immense sword hangs from his shapeless

---

[21] See the articles of Gustave d'Alaux in the *Revue des deux Mondes.*

body. His embroidered coat lacks the final perfection of a waistcoat. Our general's feet are cased in carpet slippers. Do you wish to question him, to penetrate his mind, and learn the nature of the ideas he is revolving there? You will find him as uncultured as a savage, and his bestial self-satisfaction is only equalled by his profound and incurable laziness. If he deigns to open his mouth, he will roll you out all the commonplaces which the newspapers have been inflicting on us for the last half-century. The barbarian knows them all by heart. He has other interests, of course, and very different interests; but no other ideas. He speaks like Baron Holbach, argues like Monsieur de Grimm, and has ultimately no serious preoccupation except chewing tobacco, drinking alcohol, disemboweling his enemies, and conciliating his sorcerers. The rest of the time he sleeps.

The State is divided among two factions. These are separated from each other by a certain incompatibility, not of political theory, but of skin. The mulattoes are on one side, the negroes on the other. The former have certainly more intelligence and are more open to ideas. As I have already remarked in the case of San Domingo, the European blood has modified the African character. If these men were set in the midst of a large white population, and so had good models constantly before their eyes, they might become quite useful citizens. Unfortunately the negroes are for the time being superior in strength and numbers. Although their racial memory of Africa has its origin, in many cases, as far back as their grandfathers, they are still completely under the sway of African ideals. Their greatest pleasure is idleness; their most cogent argument is murder. The most intense hatred has always existed between the two parties in the island. The history of Haiti, of democratic Haiti, is merely a long series of massacres; massacres of mulattoes by negroes, or of negroes by mulattoes, according as the one or the other held the reins of power. The constitution, however enlightened it may pretend to be, has no influence whatever. It sleeps harmlessly upon the paper on which it is written. The power that reigns unchecked is the true spirit of these peoples. According to the natural law already mentioned, the black race, belonging as it does to a branch of the human family that is incapable of civilization, cherishes the deepest feelings of repulsion towards all the others. Thus we see the negroes of Haiti violently driving out the whites and forbidding them to enter their territory. They would like to exclude even the mulattoes; and they aim at their extermination. Hatred of the foreigner is the mainspring of local politics. Owing, further, to the innate laziness of the race, agriculture is abolished, industry is not even mentioned, commerce becomes less every day. The hideous increase of misery prevents the growth of population, which is actually being diminished by the continual wars, revolts, and military executions. The inevitable result is not far off. A country of which the fertility and natural resources used to enrich generation after generation of planters will become a desert; and the wild goat will roam alone over the fruitful plains, the magnificent valleys, the sublime mountains, of the Queen of the Antilles.[22]

Let us suppose for a moment that the peoples of this unhappy island could manage to live in accordance with the spirit of their several races. In such a case they would not be influenced, and so (of course) overshadowed by foreign theories, but would found their society in free

---

[22] The colony of San Domingo, before its emancipation, was one of the places where the luxury and refinement of wealth had reached its highest point. It was, to a superior degree, what Havana has become through its commercial activity. The slaves are now free and have set their own house in order. This is the result!

obedience to their own instincts. A separation between the two colors would take place, more or less spontaneously, though certainly not without some acts of violence.

The mulattoes would settle on the seaboard, in order to keep continually in touch with Europeans. This is their chief wish. Under European direction they would become merchants (and especially money-brokers), lawyers, and physicians. They would tighten the links with the higher elements of their race by a continual crossing of blood; they would be gradually improved and lose their African character in the same proportion as their African blood.

The negroes would withdraw to the interior and form small societies like those of the runaway slaves in San Domingo itself, in Martinique, Jamaica, and especially in Cuba, where the size of the country and the depth of the forests baffle all pursuit. Amid the varied and tropical vegetation of the Antilles, the American negro would find the necessities of life yielded him in abundance and without labor by the fruitful earth. He would return quite freely to the despotic, patriarchal system that is naturally suited to those of his brethren on whom the conquering Muslims of Africa have not yet laid their yoke. The love of isolation would be at once the cause and the result of his institutions. Tribes would be formed, and become, at the end of a short time, foreign and hostile to each other. Local wars would constitute the sole political history of the different cantons; and the island, though it would be wild, thinly peopled, and ill-cultivated, would yet maintain a double population. This is now condemned to disappear, owing to the fatal influence wielded by laws and institutions that have no relation to the mind of the negro, his interests, and his wants.

The examples of San Domingo and the Sandwich Islands are conclusive. But I cannot leave this part of my subject without touching on a similar instance, of a peculiar character, which strongly supports my view. I cited first a State where the institutions, imposed by Protestant preachers, are a mere childish copy of the British system. I then spoke of a government, materially free, but spiritually bound by European theories; which it tries to carry out, with fatal consequences for the unhappy population. I will now bring forward an instance of quite a different kind; I mean the attempt of the Jesuits to civilize the natives of Paraguay.[23]

These missionaries have been universally praised for their fine courage and lofty intelligence. The bitterest enemies of the Order have not been able to withhold a warm tribute of admiration for them. If any institutions imposed on a nation from without ever had a chance of success, it was certainly those of the Jesuits, based as they were on a powerful religious sentiment, and supported by all the links of association that could be devised by an exact and subtle knowledge of human nature. The Fathers were persuaded, as so many others have been, that barbarism occupies the same place in the life of peoples as infancy does in the life of a man; and that the more rudeness and savagery a nation shows, the younger it really is.

In order, then, to bring their neophytes to the adult stage, they treated them like children, and gave them a despotic government, which was as unyielding in its real aims, as it was mild and gracious in its outward appearance. The savage tribes of America have, as a rule, democratic tendencies; monarchy and aristocracy are rarely seen among them, and then only in a very limited form. The natural character of the Guaranis, among

---

[23] Consult, on this subject, Prichard, d'Orbigny, A. von Humboldt, etc.

whom the Jesuits came, did not differ in this respect from that of the other tribes. Happily, however, their intelligence was relatively higher, and their ferocity perhaps a little less, than was the case with most of their neighbors; they had, too, in some degree, the power of conceiving new needs. About a hundred and twenty thousand souls were collected together in the mission villages, under the control of the Fathers. All that experience, unremitting study, and the living spirit of charity had taught the Jesuits, was now drawn upon; they made untiring efforts to secure a quick, though lasting, success. In spite of all their care, they found that their absolute power was not sufficient to keep their scholars on the right road, and they had frequent proofs of the want of solidity in the whole structure.

The proof was complete, when in an evil hour the edict of the Count of Aranda ended the reign of piety and intelligence in Paraguay. The Guaranis, deprived of their spiritual guides, refused to trust the laymen set over them by the Crown of Spain. They showed no attachment to their new institutions. They felt once more the call of the savage life, and today, with the exception of thirty-seven straggling little villages on the banks of the Parana, the Paraguay, and the Uruguay—villages in which the population is, no doubt, partly hybrid—the rest of the tribes have returned to the woods, and live there in just as wild a state as the western tribes of the same stock, Guaranis and Cirionos. I do not say that they keep all the old customs in their original form, but at any rate their present ones show an attempt to revive the ancient practices, and are directly descended from them; for no human race can be unfaithful to its instincts, and leave the path that has been marked out for it by God. We may believe that if the Jesuits had continued to direct their missions in Paraguay, their efforts would, in the course of time, have had better results. I admit it; but, in accordance with our universal law, this could only have happened on one condition—that a series of European settlements should have been gradually made in the country under the protection of the Jesuits. These settlers would have mingled with the natives, have first modified and then completely changed their blood. A State would have arisen, bearing perhaps a native name and boasting that it had sprung from the soil; but it would actually have been as European as its own institutions.

This is the end of my argument as to the relation between institutions and races.

CHAPTER VI

NATIONS, WHETHER PROGRESSING OR STAGNATING, ARE INDEPENDENT OF THE REGIONS IN WHICH THEY LIVE

I must now consider whether the development of peoples is affected (as many writers have asserted) by climate, soil, or geographical situation. And although I have briefly touched on this point in speaking of environment, I should be leaving a real gap in my theory if I did not discuss it more thoroughly.

Suppose that a nation lives in a temperate climate, which is not hot enough to sap its energies, or cold enough to make the soil unproductive; that its territory contains large rivers, wide roads suitable for traffic, plains and valleys capable of varied cultivation, and mountains filled with rich veins of ore—we are usually led to believe that a nation so favored by nature will be quick to leave the stage of barbarism, and will pass, with no difficulty, to that of civilization.[24] We are just as ready to admit, as a corollary, that the tribes which are burnt by the sun or numbed by the eternal ice will be much more liable to remain in a savage state, living as they do on nothing but barren rocks. It goes without saying, that on this hypothesis, mankind is capable of perfection only by the help of material nature, and that its value and greatness exist potentially outside itself. This view may seem attractive at first sight, but it has no support whatever from the facts of observation.

Nowhere is the soil more fertile, the climate milder, than in certain parts of America. There is an abundance of great rivers. The gulfs, the bays, the harbors, are large,

---

[24] Compare Carus, *Über ungleiche Befähigung der verschiedenen Menschheitstämme für höhere geistige Entwickelung* (Leipzig, 1849), p. 96 *et passim*.

deep, magnificent, and innumerable. Precious metals can be dug out almost at the surface of the ground. The vegetable world yields in abundance, and almost of its own accord, the necessaries of life in the most varied forms; while the animals, most of which are good for food, are a still more valuable source of wealth. And yet the greater part of this happy land has been occupied, for centuries, by peoples who have not succeeded, to the slightest extent, in exploiting their treasures.

Some have started on the road to improvement. In more than one place we come upon an attenuated kind of culture, a rudimentary attempt to extract the minerals. The traveller may still, to his surprise, find a few useful arts being practiced with a certain ingenuity. But all these efforts are very humble and uncoordinated; they are certainly not the beginnings of any definite civilization. In the vast territory between Lake Erie and the Gulf of Mexico, the River Missouri and the Rocky Mountains,[25] there certainly existed, in remote ages, a nation which has left remarkable traces of its presence. The remains of buildings, the inscriptions engraved on

---

[25] Prichard, "Natural History of Man," sec. 37. *See also* Squier, "Observations on the Aboriginal Monuments of the Mississippi Valley."

rocks, the tumuli,[26] the mummies, show that it had reached an advanced state of mental culture. But there is nothing to prove a very close kinship between this mysterious people and the tribes that now wander over its tombs. Suppose, if you will, that there was some relation between them, whether by way of blood or of slavery, and that thus the natives of today did learn from the ancient lords of the country, the first rudiments of the arts they practice so imperfectly; this only makes us wonder the more that they should have found it impossible to carry any further what they had been taught. In fact, this would supply one more reason for my belief that not every people would be capable of civilization, even if it chose the most favored spot on earth as its settlement.

Indeed, civilization is quite independent of climate and soil, and their adaptability to man's wants. India and Egypt are both countries which have had to be

---

[26] The special construction of these tumuli and the numerous instruments and utensils they contain are occupying the attention of many eminent American antiquaries. It is impossible to doubt the great age of these monuments. Squier is perfectly right in finding a proof of this in the mere fact that the skeletons discovered in the tumuli fall to pieces when brought into the slightest contact with the air, although the conditions for their preservation are excellent, so far as the quality of the soil is concerned. On the other hand, the bodies which lay buried under the cromlechs of Brittany, and which are at least 1800 years old, are perfectly firm. Hence we may easily imagine that there is no relation between these ancient inhabitants of the land and the tribes of the present day— the Lenni-Lenapes and others. I must not end this note without praising the industry and resource shown by American scholars in the study of the antiquities of their continent. Finding their labors greatly hindered by the extreme brittleness of the skulls they had exhumed, they discovered, after many abortive attempts, a way of pouring a preparation of bitumen into the bodies, which solidifies at once and keeps the bones from crumbling. This delicate process, which requires infinite care and quickness, seems, as a rule, to be entirely successful.

artificially fertilized;[27] yet they are famous centers of human culture and development. In China, certain regions are naturally fertile; but others have needed great labor to fit them for cultivation. Chinese history begins with the conquest of the rivers. The first benefits conferred by the ancient Emperors were the opening of canals and the draining of marshes. In the country between the Euphrates and the Tigris, that beheld the splendor of the first Assyrian empire, and is the majestic scene of our most sacred recollections—in this region, where wheat is said to grow of its own accord,[28] the soil is naturally so unproductive that vast works of irrigation, carried out in the teeth of every difficulty, have been needed to make it a fit abode for man. Now that the canals are destroyed or filled up, sterility has resumed its ancient reign. I am therefore inclined to believe that nature did not favor these regions as much as we are apt to think. But I will not discuss the point. I will grant, if you like, that China, Egypt, India, and Assyria, contained all the conditions of prosperity, and were eminently suited for the founding of powerful empires and the development of great civilizations. But, we must also admit, these conditions were of such a kind that, in order to receive any benefit from them the inhabitants must have reached beforehand, by other means, a high stage of social culture. Thus, for the commerce to be able to make use of the great waterways, manufactures, or at any rate agriculture, must have already existed; again, neighboring peoples would not have been

---

[27] Ancient India required a vast amount of clearing on the part of the first white settlers. *See* Lassen, *Indische Altertumskunde*, vol. i. As to Egypt, compare Bunsen, *Agyptens Stelle in dey Weltgeschichte*, as to the fertilization of the Fayoum, a vast work executed by the early kings.

[28] "They say that it spontaneously produces wheat, barley, beans, and sesame, and all the edible plants that grow in the plains" (Syncellus).

144

attracted to these great centers before towns and markets had grown up and prospered. Thus the great natural advantages of China, India, and Assyria, imply not only a considerable mental power on the part of the nations that profited by them, but even a civilization going back beyond the day when these advantages began to be exploited. We will now leave these specially favored regions, and consider others.

When the Phoenicians, in the course of their migration, left Tylos, or some other island in the southeast, and settled in a portion of Syria, what did they find in their new home? A desert and rocky coast, forming a narrow strip of land between the sea and a range of cliffs that seemed to be cursed with everlasting barrenness. There was no room for expansion in such a place, for the girdle of mountains was unbroken on all sides. And yet this wretched country, which should have been a prison, became, thanks to the industry of its inhabitants, a crown studded with temples and palaces. The Phoenicians, who seemed forever condemned to be a set of fish-eating barbarians, or at most a miserable crew of pirates, were, as a fact, pirates on a grand scale; they were also clever and enterprising merchants, bold and lucky speculators. "Yes," it may be objected, "necessity is the mother of invention; if the founders of Tyre and Sidon had settled in the plains of Damascus, they would have been content to live by agriculture, and would probably have never become a famous nation. Misery sharpened their wits, and awakened their genius."

Then why does it not awaken the genius of all the tribes of Africa, America, and Oceania, who find themselves in a similar condition? The Kabyles of Morocco are an ancient race; they have certainly had a long time for reflection, and, what is more striking still, have had every reason to imitate the customs of their betters; why then have they never thought of a more fruitful way of alleviating their wretchedness than mere brigandage on the high seas? Why, in the Indian archipelago, which seems created for trade, and in the Pacific islands, where intercommunication is so easy, are nearly all the commercial advantages in the hands of foreigners—Chinese, Malays, and Arabs? And where half-caste natives or other mixed races have been able to share in these advantages, why has the trade at once fallen off? Why is the internal exchange of commodities carried on more and more by elementary methods of barter? The fact is, that for a commercial state to be established on any coast or island, something more is necessary than an open sea, and the pressure exerted by the barrenness of the land—something more, even, than the lessons learned from the experience of others; the native of the coast or the island must be gifted with the special talent that alone can lead him to profit by the tools that lie to his hand, and alone can point him the road to success.

It is not enough to show that a nation's value in the scale of civilization does not come from the fertility—or, to be more precise, the infertility—of the country where it happens to live. I must also prove that this value is quite independent of all the material conditions of environment. For example, the Armenians, shut up in their mountains—the same mountains where, for generations, so many other peoples have lived and died in barbarism—had already reached a high stage of civilization in a very remote age. Yet their country was almost entirely cut off from others; it had no communication with the sea, and could boast of no great fertility.

The Jews were in a similar position. They were surrounded by tribes speaking the dialects of a language cognate with their own, and for the most part closely connected with them in race; yet they outdistanced all these tribes. They became warriors, farmers, and traders. Their method of government was extremely complicated; it was a mixture of monarchy and theocracy, of patriarchal and democratic rule (this last being represented by the assemblies and the prophets), all in a curious equilibrium. Under this government they lived through long ages of prosperity and glory, and by a scientific system of emigration they conquered the difficulties that were put in the way of their expansion by the narrow limits of their territory. And what kind of territory was it? Modern travelers know what an amount of organized effort was required from the Israelite farmers, in order to keep up its artificial fertility. Since the chosen race ceased to dwell in the mountains and the plains of Palestine, the well where Jacob's flocks came down to drink has been filled up with sand, Naboth's vineyard has been invaded by the desert, and the bramble flourishes in the place where stood the palace of Ahab. And what did the Jews become, in this miserable corner of the earth? They became a people that succeeded in everything it undertook, a free, strong, and intelligent people, and one which, before it lost, sword in hand, the name of an independent nation, had given as many learned men to the world as it had merchants.[29]

The Greeks themselves could not wholly congratulate themselves on their geographical position. Their country was a wretched one, for the most part. Arcadia was beloved of shepherds, Bœotia claimed to be dear to Demeter and Triptolemus; but Arcadia and Bœotia play a very minor part in Greek history. The rich and brilliant Corinth itself, favored by Plutus and Aphrodite, is in this respect only in the second rank. To which city belongs the chief glory? To Athens, where the

---

[29] Salvador, *Histoire des Juifs.*

fields and olive-groves were perpetually covered with grey dust, and where statues and books were the main articles of commerce; to Sparta also, a city buried in a narrow valley, at the foot of a mass of rocks which Victory had to cross to find her out.

And what of the miserable quarter of Latium that was chosen for the foundation of Rome? The little river Tiber, on whose banks it lay, flowed down to an almost unknown coast, that no Greek or Phoenician ship had ever touched, save by chance; was it through her situation that Rome became the mistress of the world? No sooner did the whole world lie at the feet of the Roman eagles, than the central government found that its capital was ill-placed; and the long series of insults to the eternal city began. The early emperors had their eyes turned towards Greece, and nearly always lived there. When Tiberius was in Italy he stayed at Capri, a point facing the two halves of the empire. His successors went to Antioch. Some of them, in view of the importance of Gaul, went as far north as Treves. Finally, an edict took away even the title of chief city from Rome and conferred it on Milan. If the Romans made some stir in the world, it was certainly in spite of the position of the district from which their first armies issued forth.

Coming down to modern history I am overwhelmed by the multitude of facts that support my theory. I see prosperity suddenly leaving the Mediterranean coasts, a clear proof that it was not inseparably attached to them. The great commercial cities of the Middle Ages grew up in places where no political philosopher of an earlier, time would have thought of founding them. Novgorod rose in the midst of an ice-bound land; Bremen on a coast almost as cold. The Hanseatic towns in the center of Germany were built in regions plunged, as it seemed, in immemorial slumber. Venice emerged from a deep gulf in the Adriatic. The balance of political power was shifted to places scarcely heard of before, but now gleaming with a new splendor. In France the whole strength was concentrated to the north of the Loire, almost beyond the Seine. Lyons, Toulouse, Narbonne, Marseilles, and Bordeaux fell from the high dignity to which they had been called by the Romans. It was Paris that became the important city, Paris, which was too far from the sea for purposes of trade, and which would soon prove too near to escape the invasions of the Norman pirates. In Italy, towns formerly of the lowest rank became greater than the city of the Popes. Ravenna rose from its marshes, Amalfi began its long career of power. Chance, I may remark, had no part in these changes, which can all be explained by the presence, at the given point, of a victorious or powerful race. In other words, a nation does not derive its value from its position; it never has and never will. On the contrary, it is the people which has always given—and always will give—to the land its moral, economic, and political value.

I add, for the sake of clearness, that I have no wish to deny the importance of geographical position for certain towns, whether they are trade-centers, ports, or capitals. The arguments that have been brought forward,[30] in the case of Constantinople and especially of Alexandria, are indisputable. There certainly exist different points which we may call "the keys of the earth." Thus we may imagine that when the isthmus of Panama is pierced, the power holding the town that is yet to be built on the hypothetical canal, might play a great part in the history of the world. But this part will be played well, badly, or even not at all, according to the intrinsic excellence of the people in question. Make Chagres into a large city, let the two seas meet under its

---

[30] M. Saint-Marc Girardin, in the *Revue des Deux Mondes.*

walls, and assume that you are free to fill it with what settlers you will. Your choice will finally determine the future of the new town. Suppose that Chagres is not exactly in the best position to develop all the advantages coming from the junction of the two oceans; then, if the race is really worthy of its high calling, it will remove to some other place where it may in perfect freedom work out its splendid destiny.[31]

---

[31] We may cite, on the subject treated in this chapter, the opinion of a learned historian, though it is rather truculent in tone:

"A large number of writers are convinced that the country makes the people; that the Bavarians or the Saxons were predestined by the nature of the soil to become what they are today; that Protestantism does not suit the South, nor Catholicism the North, and so on. Some of the people who interpret history in the light of their meagre knowledge, narrow sympathies, and limited intelligence would like to show that the nation of which we are speaking (the Jews) possessed such and such qualities—whether these gentlemen understand the nature of the qualities or not—merely from having lived in Palestine instead of India or Greece. But if these great scholars, who are so clever in proving everything, would condescend to reflect that the soil of the Holy Land has contained in its limited area very different peoples, with different ideas and religions, and that between these various peoples and their successors at the present day there have been infinite degrees of diversity, although the actual country has remained the same—they would then see how little influence is exerted by material conditions on a nation's character and civilization." Ewald, *Geschichte des Volkes Israel,* vol. i, p. 259.

CHAPTER VII

CHRISTIANITY NEITHER CREATES NOR CHANGES THE CAPACITY FOR CIVILIZATION

After my arguments on the subject of institutions and climates, I come to another, which I should really have put before all the rest; not that I think it stronger than they are, but because the facts on which it is based naturally command our reverence. If my conclusions in the preceding chapters are admitted, two points become increasingly evident: first, that most human races are forever incapable of civilization, so long as they remain unmixed; secondly, that such races are not only without the inner impulse necessary to start them on the path of improvement, but also that no external force, however energetic in other respects, is powerful enough to turn their congenital barrenness into fertility. Here we shall be asked, no doubt, whether the light of Christianity is to shine in vain on entire nations, and whether some peoples are doomed never to behold it at all.

Some writers have answered in the affirmative. They have not scrupled to contradict the promise of the Gospel, by denying the most characteristic feature of the new law, which is precisely that of being accessible to all men. Their view merely restates the old formula of the Hebrews, to which it returns by a little larger gate than that of the Old Covenant; but it returns all the same. I have no desire to follow the champions of this idea, which is condemned by the Church, nor have I the least difficulty in admitting that all human races are gifted with an equal capacity for being received into the bosom of the Christian Communion. Here there is no impediment arising from any original difference between races; for this purpose their inequalities are of no account. Religions and their followers are not, as has been assumed, distributed in zones over the surface of the earth. It is not true that Christianity must rule from this meridian to that, while from such and such a point Islam takes up the scepter, holding it only as far as a certain impassable frontier, and then having to deliver it into the hands of Buddhism or Brahmanism, while the fetishists of the tribe of Ham divide among themselves the rest of the world.

Christians are found in all latitudes and all climates. Statistics, inaccurate perhaps, but still approximately true, show us a vast number of them, Mongols wandering in the plains of Upper Asia, savages hunting on the tableland of the Cordilleras, Eskimos fishing in the ice of the Arctic circle, even Chinese and Japanese dying under the scourge of the persecutor. The least observation will show this, and will also prevent us from falling into the very common error of confusing the universal power of recognizing the truths of Christianity and following its precepts, with the very different faculty that leads one human race, and not another, to understand the earthly conditions of social improvement, and to be able to pass from one rung of the ladder to another, so as to reach finally the state which we call *civilization*. The rungs of this ladder are the measure of the inequality of human races.

It was held, quite wrongly, in the last century, that the doctrine of renunciation, a cornerstone of Christianity, was essentially opposed to social development; and that people to whom the highest virtue consists in despising the things here below, and in turning their eyes and hearts, without ceasing, towards the heavenly Jerusalem, will not do much to help the progress of this world. The very imperfection of man may serve to rebut such an argument. There has never been any serious reason to fear that he will renounce the joys of earth; and though the counsels of religion were expressly directed to this point, we may say that they were pulling against a current that they knew to be irresistible, and were merely demanding a great deal in order to obtain a very little. Further, the Christian precepts are a great aid to society; they plane away all roughness, they pour the oil of charity on all social relations, they condemn violence, force men to appeal to the sole authority of reason, and so gain for the spirit a plenitude of power which works in a thousand ways for the good of the flesh. Again, religion elevates the mind by the metaphysical and intellectual character of its dogmas, while through the purity of its moral ideal it tends to free the spirit from a host of corrosive vices and weaknesses, which are dangerous to material progress. Thus, as against the philosophers of the eighteenth century, we are right in calling Christianity a civilizing power—but only within certain limits; if we take the words in too wide a sense, we shall find ourselves drawn into a maze of error.

Christianity is a civilizing force in so far as it makes a man better minded and better mannered; yet it is only indirectly so, for it has no idea of applying this improvement in morals and intelligence to the perishable things of this world, and it is always content with the social conditions in which it finds its neophytes, however imperfect the conditions may be.. So long as it can pull out the noxious weeds that stifle the well-being of the soul, it is indifferent to everything else. It leaves all men as it finds them—the Chinese in his robes, the Eskimo in his furs, the first eating rice, and the second eating whale-blubber. It does not require them to change their way of life. If their state can be improved as a direct consequence of their conversion, then Christianity will certainly do its best to bring such an improvement about; but it will not try to alter a single custom, and certainly will not force any advance from one civilization to another, for it has not yet adopted one itself. It uses all civilizations and is above all. There are proofs in abundance, and I will speak of them in a moment; but I must first make the confession that I have never understood the ultra-modern doctrine which identifies the law of Christ and the interests of this world in such a way that it creates from their union a fictitious social order which it calls "Christian civilization."

There is certainly such a thing as a pagan civilization, just as there is a Brahman, Buddhist, or Jewish civilization. Societies have existed, and still exist, which are absolutely based on religion. Religion has given them their constitution, drawn up their laws, settled their civic duties, marked out their frontiers, and prescribed their foreign policy. Such societies have only been able to persist by placing themselves under a more or less strict theocracy. We can no more imagine their living without their rites and creeds than we can imagine the rites and creeds existing by themselves, without the people. The whole of antiquity was more or less in this condition. Roman statesmanship certainly invented the legal tolerance of creeds, and a decadent theology produced a vast system of fusion and assimilation of cults; but these belonged to the latest age of paganism, when the fruit was already rotten on the tree. While it was young and flourishing, there were as many Jupiters, Mercuries, and Venuses, as there were towns. The god was a jealous god, in a sense quite different from the jealousy of the Jewish God; he was still more exclusive, and recognized no one but his fellow-citizens in this world and the next. Every ancient civilization rose to greatness under the aegis of some divinity, of some particular cult. Religion and the State were united so closely and inseparably that the responsibility for all that happened was shared between them. We may speak, if we will, of "finding traces of the cult of the Tyrian Heracles in the public policy of Carthage"; but I think that we can really identify the effects of the doctrines taught by the priests with the policy of the suffetes and the trend of social development. Again, I have no doubt that the dog-headed Anubis, Isis Neith, and the Ibises taught the men of the Nile valley all that they knew and practiced. Christianity, however, acted in this respect quite differently from all preceding religions; this was its greatest innovation. Unlike them, it had no chosen people. It was addressed to the whole world, not only to the rich or the poor. From the first it received from the Holy Ghost the gift of tongues,[32] that it might speak to each man in the language of his country, and proclaim the Gospel by means of the ideas and images that each nation could best understand. It did not come to change the outward part of man, the material world; it taught him to despise this outward part, and was only concerned with his inner self. We read in a very ancient apocryphal book, "Let not the strong man boast of his strength, nor the rich man of his riches; but let him who will be glorified glorify himself in the Lord."[33] Strength, riches, worldly power, and the way of ambition—all these have no meaning for our law. No civilization whatever has excited its envy or contempt; and because of this rare impartiality, and the consequences that were to flow from it, the law could rightly call itself "Catholic," or universal. It does not belong exclusively to any civilization. It did not come to bless any one form of earthly existence; it rejects none, and would purify all.

The canonical books, the writings of the Fathers, the stories of the missionaries of all ages, are filled with

---

[32] Acts ii, 4, 8, 9-11.

[33] Apocryphal Gospels: "The Story of Joseph the Carpenter," chap. i.

proofs of this indifference to the outward forms of social life, and to social life itself. Provided that a man believes, and that none of his daily actions tend to transgress the ordinances of religion, nothing else matters. Of what importance is the shape of a Christian's house, the cut and material of his clothes, his system of government, the measure of tyranny or liberty in his public institutions? He may be a fisherman, a hunter, a ploughman, a sailor, a soldier—whatever you like. In all these different employments is there anything to prevent a man—to whatever nation he belong, English, Turkish, Siberian, American, Hottentot—from receiving the light of the Christian faith? Absolutely nothing; and when this result is attained, the rest counts for very little. The savage Galla can remain a Galla, and yet become as staunch a believer, as pure a "vessel of election," as the holiest prelate in Europe. It is here that Christianity shows its striking superiority to other religions, in its peculiar quality of *grace*. We must not take this away, in deference to a favorite idea of modern Europe, that something of material utility must be found everywhere, even in the holiest things.

During the eighteen centuries that the Church has existed, it has converted many nations. In all these it has allowed the political conditions to reign unchecked, just as it found them at first. It began by protesting to the world of antiquity that it did not wish to alter in the slightest degree the outward forms of society. It has been even reproached, on occasion, with an excess of tolerance in this respect; compare, for example, the attitude of the Jesuits towards the Chinese ceremonies. We do not, however, find that Christianity has ever given the world a unique type of civilization to which all believers had to belong. The Church adapts itself to everything, even to the mud-hut; and wherever there is a savage too stupid even to understand the use of shelter, you are sure to find a devoted missionary sitting beside him on the hard rock, and thinking of nothing but how to impress his soul with the ideas essential to salvation. Christianity is thus not a civilizing power in the ordinary sense of the word; it can be embraced by the most different races without stunting their growth, or making demands on them that they cannot fulfil.

I said above that Christianity elevates the soul by the sublimity of its dogmas, and enlarges the intellect by their subtlety. This is only true in so far as the soul and intellect to which it appeals are capable of being enlarged and elevated. Its mission is not "to bestow the gift of genius, or to provide ideas for those who are without them. Neither genius nor ideas are necessary for salvation. Indeed the Church has expressly declared that it prefers the weak and lowly to the strong. It gives only what it wishes to receive. It fertilizes but does not create. It supports but does not lift on high. It takes the man as he is, and merely helps him to walk. If he is lame, it does not ask him to run.

If I open the "Lives of the Saints," shall I find many wise men among them? Certainly not. The company of the blessed ones whose name and memory are honored by the Church consists mainly of those who were eminent for their virtue and devotion; but, though full of genius in all that concerned heaven, they had none for the things of earth. When I see St. Rosa of Lima honored equally with St. Bernard, the intercession of St. Zita valued no less than that of St. Teresa; when I see all the Anglo-Saxon saints, most of the Irish monks, the unsavory hermits of the Egyptian Thebaid, the legions of martyrs who sprang from the dregs of the people and whom a sudden flash of courage and devotion raised to shine eternally in glory—when I see all these venerated to the same extent as the cleverest apologists of dogma, as the wisest champions of the faith, then I find myself justified in my conclusion that Christianity is not a civilizing power, in the narrow and worldly sense of the phrase. Just as it merely asks of every man what he has himself received, so it asks nothing of any race but what it is capable of giving, and does not set it in a higher place among the civilized races of the earth than its natural powers give it a right to expect. Hence I absolutely deny the egalitarian argument which identifies the possibility of adopting the Christian faith with that of an unlimited intellectual growth. Most of the tribes of South America were received centuries ago into the bosom of the Church; but they have always remained savages, with no understanding of the European civilization unfolding itself before their eyes. I am not surprised that the Cherokees of North America have been largely converted by Methodist missionaries; but it would greatly astonish me if this tribe, while it remained pure in blood, ever managed to form one of the States of the American Union, or exert any influence in Congress. I find it quite natural also that the Danish Lutherans and the Moravians should have opened the eyes of the Eskimos to the light of faith; but I think it equally natural that their disciples should have remained in the social condition in which they had been stagnating for ages. Again, the Swedish Lapps are, as we might have expected, in the same state of barbarism as their ancestors, even though centuries have passed since the gospel first brought them the message of salvation. All these peoples may produce—perhaps have produced already—men conspicuous for their piety and the purity of their lives; but I do not expect to see learned theologians among them, or skillful soldiers, or clever mathematicians, or great artists. In other words they will forever exclude the select company of the fine spirits who clasp hands across the ages and continually renew the strength of the dominant races. Still less will those rare and mighty geniuses appear who are followed by their nations, in the paths they mark out for themselves, only if those nations are themselves able to understand them and go forward under their direction. Even as a matter of justice we must leave Christianity absolutely out of the present question. If all races are equally capable of receiving its benefits, it cannot have been sent to bring equality among men. Its kingdom, we may say, is in the most literal sense "not of this world."

Many people are accustomed to judge the merits of Christianity in the light of the prejudices natural to our age; and I fear that, in spite of what I have said above, they may have some difficulty in getting rid of their inaccurate ideas. Even if they agree on the whole with my conclusions, they may still believe that the scale is turned by the indirect action of religion on conduct, of conduct on institutions, of institutions on the whole social order. I cannot admit any such action. My opponents will assert that the personal influence of the missionaries, nay, their mere presence, will be enough to change appreciably the political condition of the converts and their ideas of material well-being. They will say, for example, that these apostles nearly always (though not invariably) come from a nation more advanced than that to which they are preaching; thus they will of their own accord, almost by instinct, change the merely human customs of their disciples, while they are reforming their morals. Suppose the missionaries have to do with savages, plunged in an abyss of wretchedness through their own ignorance. They will instruct them in useful arts and show them how men escape from famine by work on the land. After providing the necessary tools for this, they will go further, and teach them how to build better huts, to rear cattle, to control the water-supply—both in order to irrigate their fields, and to prevent inundations. Little by little they will manage to give them enough taste for matters of the intellect to make them use an alphabet, and perhaps, as the Cherokees have done,[34] invent one for themselves. Finally, if they are exceptionally successful, they will bring their cultivated disciples to imitate so exactly the customs of which the missionaries have told them, that they will possess, like the Cherokees and the Creeks on the south bank of the Arkansas, flocks of valuable sheep, and even a collection of black slaves to work on their plantations. They will be completely equipped for living on the land.

I have expressly chosen as examples the two races which are considered to be the most advanced of all. Yet, far from agreeing with the advocates of equality, I cannot imagine any more striking instances than these of the general incapacity of any race to adopt a way of life which it could not have found for itself.

These two peoples are the isolated remnant of many nations which have been driven out or annihilated by the whites. They are naturally on a different plane from the rest, since they are supposed to be descended from the ancient Alleghany race to which the great ruins found to the north of the Mississippi are attributed.[35] Here is already a great inconsistency in the arguments of those who assert that the Cherokees are the equals of the European races; for the first step in their proof is that these Alleghany tribes are near the Anglo-Saxons precisely because they are themselves superior to the other races of North America! Well, what has happened to these chosen peoples? The American Government took their ancient territories from both the tribes, and, by means of a special treaty, made them emigrate to a

---

[34] Prichard, "Natural History of Man," sec. 41.

[35] *Ibid.*

definite region, where separate places of settlement were marked out for them. Here, under the general superintendence of the Ministry of War and the direct guidance of Protestant missionaries, they were forced to take up their present mode of life, whether they liked it or not. The writer from whom I borrow these details—and who has himself taken them from the great work of Gallatin[36]—says the number of the Cherokees is continually increasing. His argument is that at the time when Adair visited them, their warriors were estimated at 2300, while today the sum-total of their population is calculated to be 15,000; this figure includes, it is true, the 1200 negro slaves who have become their property. He also adds, however, that their schools are, like their churches, in the hands of the missionaries, and that these missionaries, being Protestants, are for the most part married men with white children or servants, and probably also a sort of general staff of Europeans, acting as clerks, and the like. It thus becomes very difficult to establish the fact of any real increase in the number of the natives, while on the other hand it is very easy to appreciate the strong pressure that must be exerted by the European race over its pupils.[37]

---

[36] "Synopsis of the Indian Tribes of North America."

[37] I have discussed Prichard's facts without questioning their value. I might, however, have simply denied them, and should have had on my side the weighty authority of A. de Tocqueville, who in his great work on "Democracy in America" refers to the Cherokees in these words: "The presence of half-breeds has favored the very rapid development of European habits among the Indians. The half-breed shares the enlightenment of his father without entirely giving up the savage customs of his mother's race. He is thus a natural link between civilization and barbarism. Wherever half-breeds exist and multiply we see the savages gradually changing their customs and social conditions" ("Democracy in America," vol. iii). De Tocqueville ends by prophesying that although the Cherokees and the Creeks are half-breeds and not natives, as Prichard says, they will nevertheless disappear in a short time through the encroachment of the white race.

The possibility of making war is clearly taken away from them; they are exiled, surrounded on all sides by the American power, which is too vast for them to comprehend, and are, I believe, sincerely converted to the religion of their masters. They are kindly treated by their spiritual guides and convinced of the necessity for working, in the sense in which work is understood by their masters, if they are not to die of hunger. Under these conditions I can quite imagine that they will become successful agriculturists, and will learn to carry out the ideas that have been dinned into them, day in, day out, without ceasing.

By the exercise of a little patience and by the judicious use of hunger as a spur to greed, we can teach animals what they would never learn by instinct. But to cry out at our success would be to rate much lower than it is the intelligence even of the humblest member of the human family. When the village fairs are full of learned animals going through the most complicated tricks, can we be surprised that men, who have been submitted to a rigorous training and cut off from all means of escape or relaxation, should manage to perform those functions of civilized life which, even in a savage state, they might be able to understand, without having the desire to practice them? The result is a matter of course; and anyone who is surprised at it is putting man far below the card-playing dog or the horse who orders his dinner! By arbitrarily gathering one's premises from the "intelligent actions" of a few human groups, one ends in being too easily satisfied, and in coming to feel enthusiasms which are not very flattering even to those who are their objects.

I know that some learned men have given color to these rather obvious comparisons by asserting that between some human races and the larger apes there is only a slight difference of degree, and none of kind. As I absolutely reject such an insult to humanity, I may be also allowed to take no notice of the exaggerations by which it is usually answered. I believe, of course, that human races are unequal; but I do not think that any of them are like the brute, or to be classed with it. The lowest tribe, the most backward and miserable variety of the human species, is at least capable of imitation; and I have no doubt that if we take one of the most hideous bushmen, we could develop—I do not say in him, if he is already grown up, but in his son or at any rate his grandson—sufficient intelligence to make his acts correspond to a certain degree of civilization, even if this required some conscious effort of study on his part. Are we to infer that the people to which he belongs could be civilized on our model? This would be a hasty and superficial conclusion. From the practice of the arts and professions invented under an advanced civilization, it is a far cry to that civilization itself. Further, though the Protestant missionaries are an indispensable link between the savage tribe and the central civilizing power, is it certain that these missionaries are equal to the task imposed on them? Are they the masters of a complete system of social science? I doubt it. If communications were suddenly cut off between the American Government and its spiritual legates among the Cherokees, the traveller would find in the native farms, at the end of a few years, some new practices that he had not expected. These would result from the mixture of white and Indian blood; and our traveller would look in vain for anything more than a very pale copy of what is taught at New York.

We often hear of negroes who have learnt music, who are clerks in banking-houses, and who know how to read, write, count, dance, and speak, like white men. People are astonished at this, and conclude that the negro is capable of everything! And then, in the same breath, they will express surprise at the contrast between the Slav civilization and our own. The Russians, Poles, and Serbians (they will say), even though they are far nearer to us than the negroes, are only civilized on the surface; the higher classes alone participate in our ideas, owing to the continual admixture of English, French, and German blood. The masses, on the other hand, are invincibly ignorant of the Western world and its movements, although they have been Christian for so many centuries—in many cases before we were converted ourselves! The solution is simple. There is a great difference between imitation and conviction. Imitation does not necessarily imply a serious breach with hereditary instincts; but no one has a real part in any civilization until he is able to make progress by himself, without direction from others.[38] What is the use of telling me how clever some particular savages are in guiding the plough, in spelling, or reading, when they are only repeating the lessons they have learnt? Show me rather, among the many regions in which negroes have lived for ages in contact with Europeans, one single place where, in addition to the religious doctrines, the ideas, customs, and institutions of even one European people have been so completely assimilated that progress in them is made as naturally and spontaneously as among ourselves. Show me a place where the introduction of printing has had results, similar to those in Europe, where our sciences are brought to perfection, where new applications are made of our discoveries,

---

[38] In discussing the list of remarkable negroes which is given in the first instance by Blumenbach and could easily be supplemented, Carus well says that among the black races there has never been any politics or literature or any developed ideas of art, and that when any individual negroes have distinguished themselves it has always been the result of white influence. There is not a single man among them to be compared, I will not say to one of our men of genius, but to the heroes of the yellow races—for example, Confucius. (Carus, op. cit.)

where our philosophies are the parents of other philosophies, of political systems, of literature and art, of books, statues, and pictures!

But I am not really so exacting and narrow-minded as I seem. I am not seriously asking that a people should adopt our whole individuality at the same time as our faith. I am willing to admit that it should reject our way of thinking and strike out quite a different one. Well then! let me see our negro, at the moment when he opens his eyes to the light of the Gospel, suddenly realizing that his earthly path is as dark and perplexed as his spiritual life was before. Let me see him creating for himself a new social order in his own image, putting ideas into practice that have hitherto rusted unused, taking foreign notions and moulding them to his purpose. I will wait long for the work to be finished; I merely ask that it may be begun. But it has never been begun; it has never even been attempted. You may search through all the pages of history, and you will not find a single people that has attained to European civilization by adopting Christianity, or has been brought by the great fact of its conversion to civilize itself when it was not civilized already.

On the other hand, I shall find, In the vast tracts of Southern Asia and in certain parts of Europe, States fused together out of men of very different religions. The unalterable hostility of races, however, will be found side by side with that of cults; we can distinguish the Pathan who has become a Christian from the converted Hindu, just as easily as we separate today the Russian of Orenburg from the nomad Christian tribes among which he lives.

Once more, Christianity is not a civilizing power, and has excellent reasons for not being so.

CHAPTER VIII

DEFINITION OF THE WORD "CIVILIZATION"; SOCIAL DEVELOPMENT HAS A TWOFOLD ORIGIN

Here I must enter on a digression vital to my argument. At every turn I am using a word involving a circle of ideas which it is very necessary to define. I am continually speaking of "civilization," and cannot help doing so; for it is only by the existence in some measure, or the complete absence, of this attribute that I can gauge the relative merits of the different races. I refer both to European civilization and to others which may be distinguished from it. I must not leave the slightest vagueness on this point, especially as I differ from the celebrated writer who alone in France has made it his special business to fix the meaning and province of this particular word.

Guizot, if I may be allowed to dispute his great authority, begins his book on "Civilization in Europe" by a confusion of terms which leads him into serious error. He calls civilization an *event*.

The word *event* must be used by Guizot in a less positive and accurate way than it usually is—in a wide, uncertain, elastic sense that it never bears; otherwise, it does not properly define the meaning of the word *civilization* at all. Civilization is not an event, it is a *series,* a *chain* of events linked more or less logically together and brought about by the interaction of ideas which are often themselves very complex. There is a continual bringing to birth of further ideas and events. The result is sometimes incessant movement, sometimes stagnation. In either case, civilization is not an event, but an assemblage of events and ideas, a *state* in which a human society subsists, an *environment* with which it has managed to surround itself, which is created by it, emanates from it, and in turn reacts on it.

This state is universal in a sense in which an event never is. It admits of many variations which it could not survive if it were merely an event. Further, it is quite independent of all forms of government; it makes as much progress under a despotism as under the freest democracy, and it does not cease to exist when the conditions of political life are modified or even absolutely changed by civil war.

This does not mean that we may more or less neglect the forms of government. They are intimately bound up with the health of the social organism; its prosperity is impaired or destroyed if the choice of government is bad, favored and developed if the choice is good. But we are not concerned here with mere questions of prosperity. Our subject is more serious. It deals with the very existence of peoples and of civilization; and civilization has to do with certain elemental conditions which are independent of politics, and have to look far deeper for the motive-forces that bring them into being, direct, and expand them, make them fruitful or barren and, in a word, mould their whole life. In face of such root-questions as these, considerations of government, prosperity, and misery naturally take a second place. The first place is always and everywhere held by the question "to be or not to be," which is as supreme for a people as for an individual. As Guizot does not seem to have realized this, civilization is to him not a state or an environment, but an *event;* and he finds its generating principle in another event, of a purely political character.

If we open his eloquent and famous book, we shall come upon a mass of hypotheses calculated to set his leading idea into relief. After mentioning a certain number of situations to which human societies might come, the author asks "whether common instinct would recognize in these the conditions under which a people *civilizes* itself, in the natural sense of the word."

The first hypothesis is as follows: "Consider a people whose external life is easy and luxurious. It pays few taxes, and is in no distress. Justice is fairly administered between man and man. In fact, its material and moral life is carefully kept in a state of inertia, of torpor, I will not say of oppression, because there is no feeling of this, but at any rate of repression. The case is not unexampled. There have been a large number of little aristocratic republics, where the subjects have been treated in this way, like sheep, well looked after and, in a material sense, happy, but without any intellectual or moral activity. Is this civilization? And is such a people civilizing itself?"

I do not know whether it is actually civilizing itself; but certainly the people of whom he speaks might be very "civilized." Otherwise, we should have to rank among savage tribes or barbarians all the aristocratic republics, of ancient and modern times, which Guizot confessedly includes as instances of his hypothesis. The general instinct would certainly be offended by a method that forbids not only the Phoenicians, the Carthaginians, and the Spartans to enter the temple of civilization, but also the Venetians, the Genoese, the Pisans, and all the free Imperial cities of Germany, in a word all the powerful municipalities of the last few centuries. This conclusion seems in itself too violently paradoxical to be admitted by the common sense to which it appeals; but besides this, it has, I think, to face a still greater difficulty. These little aristocratic States which, owing to their form of government, Guizot refuses to accept as capable of civilization, have never, in most cases, possessed a special and unique culture. However powerful many of them may have been, they were in this respect assimilated to peoples who were differently governed, but very near them in race; they merely shared in a common civilization. Thus, though the Carthaginians and the Phoenicians were at a great distance from each other, they were nevertheless united by a similar form of culture, which had its prototype in Assyria. The Italian republics took part in the movement of ideas and opinions which were dominant in the neighboring monarchies. The Imperial towns of Swabia and Thuringia were quite independent politically, but were otherwise wholly within the sweep of the general progress or decadence of the German race. Hence while Guizot is distributing his orders of merit among the nations according to their degree of political liberty and their forms of government, he is really making cleavages, within races, that he cannot justify, and assuming differences that do not exist. A more detailed discussion of the point would hardly be in place here, and I pass on. If I did open such an argument, I should begin (and rightly I think) by refusing to admit that Pisa, Genoa, Venice, and the rest were in any way inferior to towns such as Milan, Naples, and Rome.

Guizot himself anticipates such an objection. He does not allow that a people is civilized, "which is governed mildly, but kept in a state of repression"; yet he also refuses civilization to another people "whose material life is less easy and luxurious, though still tolerable, yet whose moral and intellectual needs have not been neglected. ... In the people I am supposing," he says, "pure and noble sentiments are fostered. Their religious and ethical beliefs are developed to a certain degree, but the idea of freedom is extinct. Every one has his share of truth doled out to him; no one is allowed to seek it for himself. This is the condition into which most of the Asiatic nations, the Hindus, for example, have fallen; their manly qualities are sapped by the domination of the priests."

Thus into the same limbo as the aristocratic peoples must now be thrust the Hindus, the Egyptians, the Etruscans, the Peruvians, the Tibetans, the Japanese, and even the districts subject to modern Rome.

I will not touch on Guizot's last two hypotheses, for the first two have so restricted the meaning of civilization that scarcely any nation of the earth can rightly lay claim to it any more. In order to do so a people would have to live under institutions in which power and freedom were equally mingled, and material development and moral progress coordinated in one particular way. Government and religion would have strict limits drawn round them, beyond which they would not be allowed to advance. Finally, the subjects would necessarily possess rights of a very definite kind. On such an assumption, the only civilized peoples would be those whose government is both constitutional and representative. Thus, I should not be able to save any of the European nations from the indignity of being thrust into barbarism; and, as I should be always measuring the degree of civilization with reference to one single and unique political standard, I should gradually come to reject even those constitutional states that made a bad use of their Parliaments, and keep the prize exclusively for those which used them well. In the end I should be driven to consider only one nation, of all that have ever lived, as truly civilized—namely, the English.

I am, of course, full of respect and admiration for the great people whose power and prodigious deeds are witnessed in every corner of the world by their victories, their industry, and their commerce. I do not, however, feel that I am bound to respect and admire no other. It seems to me a confession altogether too cruel and humiliating to mankind, to say that, since the beginning of the ages, it has only succeeded in producing the full flower of civilization on a little island in the western ocean, and that even there the true principle was not discovered before the reign of William and Mary. Such a conception seems, you must allow, a little narrow. And then consider its danger. If civilization depends on a particular form of government, then reason, observation, and science will soon have no voice in the question at all; party-feeling alone will decide. Some bold spirits will be found to follow their own preferences, and refuse to the British institutions the honor of being the ideal of human perfection; all their enthusiasm will be given to the system established at Petrograd or Vienna. Many people, perhaps the majority of those living between the Rhine and the Pyrenees, will hold that, in spite of some defects, France is still the most civilized country in the world. The moment that a decision as to culture becomes a matter of personal feeling, agreement is impossible. The most highly developed man will be he who holds the same views as oneself as to the respective duties of ruler and subjects; while the unfortunate people who happen to think differently will be barbarians and savages. No one, I suppose, will question the logic of this, or dispute that a system that can lead to such a conclusion is, to say the least of it, very incomplete.

For my own part, Guizot's definition seems to me inferior even to that given by William von Humboldt: "Civilization is the humanizing of peoples both in their outward customs and institutions, and in the inward feelings that correspond to these."[39]

The defect here is the exact opposite of that which I have ventured to find in Guizot's formula. The cord is too loose, the field of application too wide. If civilization is acquired merely by softness of temper, more than one

---

[39] W. von Humboldt, *Über die Kawi-sprache auf der Insel Java,* Introduction, vol. i, p. 37.

very primitive tribe will have the right to claim it in preference to some European nation that may be rather rough in its character. There are some tribes, in the islands of the South Pacific Ocean and elsewhere, which are very mild and inoffensive, very easy of approach; and yet no one, even while praising them, has ever dreamed of setting them above the surly Norwegians, or even at the side of the ferocious Malays, who are clad in flaming robes made by themselves, who sail the seas in ships they have cleverly built with their own hands, and are the terror, and at the same time the most intelligent agents, of the carrying trade to the Eastern ports of the Indian Ocean. So eminent a thinker as von Humboldt could not fail to see this; by the side, therefore, of civilization, and just one grade above it, he places *culture.* "By culture," he says, "a people which is already humanized in its social relations attains to art and science."

According to this hierarchy, we find the second age of the world[40] filled with affectionate and sympathetic beings, poets, artists, and scholars. These, however, in their own nature, stand outside the grosser forms of work; they are as aloof from the hardships of war as they are from tilling the soil or practising the ordinary trades.

The leisure-time allowed for the exercise of the pure intellect is very small, even in times of the greatest happiness and stability; and there is an incessant struggle going on with Nature and the laws of the universe to gain even the bare means of subsistence. This being so, we can easily see that our Berlin philosopher is less concerned with describing realities than with taking certain abstractions which seem to him great and beautiful (as indeed they are), endowing them with life, and making them act and move in a sphere as ideal as

---

[40] *i.e.* the world in its second stage of improvement.

they are themselves. Any doubts that might remain on this point are soon dispelled when we come to the culminating-point of the system, which consists of a third grade, higher than the others. Here stands the "completely formed man," in whose nature is "something at once higher and more personal, a way of looking at the universe by which all the impressions gathered from the intellectual and moral forces at work around him are welded harmoniously together and taken up into his character and sensibility."

In this rather elaborate series the first stage is thus the "civilized man," that is, the softened or humanized man; the next is the "cultured man," the poet, artist, and scholar, and the last is the highest point of development of which our species is capable, the "completely formed man,"—of whom (if I understand the doctrine aright) we can gain an exact idea from what we are told of Goethe and his "Olympian calm." The principle at the base of this theory is merely the vast difference which von Humboldt sees between the general level of a people's civilization and the stage of perfection reached by a few great individuals. This difference is so great that civilizations quite foreign to our own—that of the Brahmans, for instance—have been able, so far as we know, to produce men far superior in some ways to those that are most admired among ourselves.

I quite agree with von Humboldt on this point. It is quite true that our European society gives us neither the most sublime thinkers, nor the greatest poets, nor even the cleverest artists. I venture to think, however, in spite of the great scholar's opinion, that in order to define and criticize civilization generally, we must, if only for a moment, be careful to shake off our prejudices with regard to the details of some particular type. We must not cast our net so widely as to include the man in von Humboldt's first stage, whom I refuse to call civilized merely because he happens to be mild in character. On the other hand we must not be so narrow as to reject every one but the philosopher of the third stage. This would limit too strictly the scope of all human endeavour after progress, and present its results as merely isolated and individual.

Von Humboldt's system does honor to the width and subtlety of a noble mind, and may be compared, in its essentially abstract nature, with the frail worlds, imagined by the Hindu philosophers, which are born from the brain of a sleeping god, rise into the aether like the rainbow-colored bubbles blown by a child, and then break and give place to others according to the dreams that lightly hover round the Divine slumber.

The nature of my investigations keeps me on a lower and more prosaic level; I wish to arrive at results that are a little more within the range of practical experience. The restricted angle of my vision forbids me to consider, as Guizot does, the measure of prosperity enjoyed by human societies, or to contemplate, with von Humboldt, the high peaks on which a few great minds sit in solitary splendor; my inquiries concern merely the amount of power, material as well as moral, that has been developed among the mass of a people. It has made me uneasy, I confess, to see two of the most famous men of the century losing themselves in by-ways; and if I am to trust myself to follow a different road from theirs, I must survey my ground, and go back as far as possible for my premises, in order to reach my goal without stumbling. I must ask the reader to follow me with patience and attention through the winding paths in which I have to walk, and I will try to illuminate, as far as I can, the inherent obscurity of my subject.

There is no tribe so degraded that we cannot discover in it the instinct to satisfy both its material and its moral needs. The first and most obvious difference between races lies in the various ways in which the two sides of this instinct are balanced. Among the most primitive peoples they are never of equal intensity. In some, the sense of the physical need is uppermost, in others, the tendency to contemplation. Thus the brutish hordes of the yellow race seem to be dominated by the needs of the body, though they are not quite without gleams of a spiritual world. On the other hand to most of the negro tribes that have reached the same stage of development, action is less than thought, and the imagination gives a higher value to the things unseen than those that can be handled. From the point of view of civilization, I do not regard this as a reason for placing the negroes on a higher level; for the experience of centuries shows that they are no more capable of being civilized than the others. Ages have passed without their doing anything to improve their condition; they are all equally powerless to mingle act and idea in sufficient strength to burst their prison walls and emerge from their degradation. But even in the lowest stages of human progress I always find this twofold stream of instinct, in which now one, now the other current predominates; and I will try to trace its path as I go up the scale of civilization.

Above the Samoyedes, as above some of the Polynesian negroes, come the tribes that are not quite content with a hut made of branches or with force as the only social relation, but desire something better. These tribes are raised one step above absolute barbarism. If they belong to those races to whom action is more than thought, we shall see them improving their tools, their arms, and their ornaments, setting up a government in which the warriors are more important than the priests, developing ideas of exchange, and already showing a fair aptitude for commerce. Their wars will still be cruel, but will tend more and more to become mere pillaging expeditions; in fact, material comfort and physical enjoyment will be the main aim of the people. I find this picture realized in many of the Mongolian tribes; also, in a higher form, among the Quichuas and Aymaras of Peru. The opposite condition, involving a greater detachment from mere bodily needs, will be found among the Dahomeys of West Africa, and the Kaffirs.

I now continue the journey upwards, and leave the groups in which the social system is not strong enough to impose itself over a large population, even after a fusion of blood. I pass to those in which the racial elements are so strong that they grip fast everything that comes within their reach, and draw it into themselves; they found over immense tracts of territory a supreme dominion resting on a basis of ideas and actions that are more or less perfectly coordinated. For the first time we have reached what can be called a *civilization*. The same internal differences that I brought out in the first two stages appear in the third; they are in fact far more marked than before, as it is only in this third stage that their effects are of any real importance. From the moment when an assemblage of men, which began as a mere tribe, has so widened the horizon of its social relations as to merit the name of a *people,* we see one of the two currents of instinct, the material and the intellectual, flowing with greater force than before, according as the separate groups, now fused together, were originally borne along by one or the other. Thus, different results will follow, and different qualities of a nation will come to the surface, according as the power of thought or that of action is dominant. We may use here the Hindu symbolism, and represent what I call the "intellectual current" by Prakriti, the female principle, and the "material current" by Purusha, the male principle. There is, of course, no blame or praise attaching to either of these phrases; they merely imply that the one principle is fertilized by the other.[41]

Further, we can see, at some periods of a people's existence, a strong oscillation between the two principles, one of which alternately prevails over the other. These changes depend on the mingling of blood that inevitably takes place at various times. Their consequences are very important, and sensibly alter the character of the civilization by impairing its stability.

I can thus divide peoples into two classes, as they come predominantly under the action of one or other of these currents; though the division is, of course, in no way absolute. At the head of the "male" category I put the Chinese; the Hindus being the prototype of the opposite class.

After the Chinese come most of the peoples of ancient Italy, the Romans of the Early Republic, and the Germanic tribes. In the opposite camp are ranged the nations of Egypt and Assyria. They take their place behind the men of Hindustan.

When we follow the nations down the ages, we find that the civilization of nearly all of them has been modified by their oscillation between the two principles. The peoples of Northern China were at first almost entirely materialistic. By a gradual fusion with tribes of different blood, especially those in the Yunnan, their outlook became less purely utilitarian. The reason why this development has been arrested, or at least has been very slow, for centuries past, is because the "male" constituents of the population are far greater in quantity than the slight "female" element in its blood.

---

[41] Klemm (*Allgemeine Kulturgeschichte der Menschheit*) divides the races of men into "active " and "passive." I do not know his book, and so cannot tell if his idea agrees with my own. But it is natural that if we follow the same path we should light upon the same truth.

In Northern Europe the materialistic strain, contributed by the best of the Germanic tribes, has been continually strengthened by the influx of Celts and Slavs. But as the white peoples drifted more and more towards the south, the male influences gradually lost their force and were absorbed by an excess of female elements, which finally triumphed. We must allow some exceptions to this, for example in Piedmont and Northern Spain.

Passing now to the other division, we see that the Hindus have in a high degree the feeling of the supernatural, that they are more given to meditation than to action. As their earliest conquests brought them mainly into contact with races organized along the same lines as themselves, the male principle could not be sufficiently developed among them. In such an environment their civilization was not able to advance on the material side as it had on the intellectual. We may contrast the ancient Romans, who were naturally materialistic, and only ceased to be so after a complete fusion with Greeks, Africans, and Orientals had changed their original nature and given them a totally new temperament. The internal development of the Greeks resembled that of the Hindus.

I conclude from such facts as these that every human activity, moral or intellectual, has its original source in one or other of these two currents, "male" or "female"; and only the races which have one of these elements in abundance (without, of course, being quite destitute of the other) can reach, in their social life, a satisfactory stage of culture, and so attain to civilization.

CHAPTER IX

DEFINITION OF THE WORD
"CIVILIZATION" (*continued*); DIFFERENT
CHARACTERISTICS OF CIVILIZED SOCIETIES;
OUR CIVILIZATION IS NOT SUPERIOR TO
THOSE WHICH HAVE GONE BEFORE

When a nation, belonging to either the male or female series, has the civilizing instinct so strongly that it can impose its laws on vast multitudes of men; when it is so fortunate as to be able to satisfy their inner needs, and appeal to their hearts as well as their heads; from this moment a culture is brought into being. This general appeal is the essential note of the civilizing instinct, and its greatest glory. This alone makes it a living and active force. The interests of individuals only flourish in isolation; and social life always tends, to some extent, to mutilate them. For a system of ideas to be really fruitful and convincing, it must suit the particular ways of thought and feeling current among the people to whom it is offered.

When some special point of view is accepted by the mass of a people as the basis of their legislation, it is really because it fulfills, in the main, their most cherished desires. The male nations look principally for material well-being, the female nations are more taken up with the needs of the imagination; but, I repeat, as soon as the multitudes enroll themselves under a banner, or—to speak more exactly—as soon as a particular form of administration is accepted, a civilization is born.

Another invariable mark of civilization is the need that is felt for stability. This follows immediately from what I have said above; for the moment that men have admitted, as a community, that some special principle is to govern and unite them, and have consented to make individual sacrifices to bring this about, their first impulse is to respect the governing principle—as much for what it brings as for what it demands—and to declare it unshakable. The purer a race keeps its blood, the less will its social foundations be liable to attack; for the general way of thought will remain the same. Yet the desire for stability cannot be entirely satisfied for long. The admixture of blood will be followed by some modifications in the fundamental ideas of the people, and these again by an itch for change in the building itself. Such change will sometimes mean real progress, especially in the dawn of a civilization, when the governing principle is usually rigid and absolute, owing to the exclusive predominance of some single race. Later, the tinkering will become incessant, as the mass is more heterogeneous and loses its singleness of aim; and the community will not always be able to congratulate itself on the result. So long, however, as it remains under the guidance of the original impulse, it will not cease, while holding fast to the idea of bettering its condition, to follow a chimera of stability. Fickle, unstable, changing every hour, it yet thinks itself eternal, and marches on, as towards some goal in Paradise. It clings to the doctrine (even while continually denying it in practice) that one of the chief marks of civilization is to borrow a part of God's immutability for the profit of man. When the likeness obviously does not exist, it takes courage, and consoles itself by the conviction that soon, at any rate, it will attain to the Divine attribute.

By the side of stability, and the co-operation of individual interests, which touch each other without being destroyed, we must put a third and a fourth characteristic of civilization, sociability, and the hatred of violence—in other words the demand that the head, and not the fists, shall be used for self-defense.

These last two features are the source of all mental improvement, and so of all material progress; it is to these especially that we look for the evidence as to whether a society is advanced or not.[42]

I think I may now sum up my view of civilization by defining it as *a state of relative stability, where the mass of men try to satisfy their wants by peaceful means, and are refitted in their conduct and intelligence.*

In this formula are comprised all the peoples whom I have mentioned up to now as being civilized, whether they belong to one or the other class. Assuming that the conditions are fulfilled, we must now inquire whether all civilizations are equal. I think not. The social needs of the chief peoples are not felt with the same intensity or directed towards the same objects; thus their conduct and intelligence will show great differences in kind, as well as in degree. What are the material needs of the Hindu? Rice and butter for his food, and a linen cloth for his raiment. We may certainly be tempted to ascribe this simplicity to conditions of climate. But the Tibetans live in a very severe climate, and are yet most remarkable for their abstinence. The main interest of both these peoples is in their religious and philosophical development, in providing for the very insistent demands of the mind and the spirit. Thus there is no balance kept between the male and female principles. The scale is too heavily weighted on the intellectual side, the consequence being that almost all the work done under this civilization is exclusively devoted to the one end, to the detriment of the other. Huge monuments,

---

[42] It is also in connection with these that we find the main cause of the false judgments passed on foreign peoples. Because the externals of their civilization are unlike the corresponding parts of our own, we are often apt to infer hastily that they are either barbarians or of less worth than ourselves. Nothing could be more superficial, and so more doubtful, than a conclusion drawn from such premises.

mountains of stone, are chiselled and set up, at a cost of toil and effort that staggers the imagination. Colossal buildings cover the ground—and with what object? to honor the gods. Nothing is made for man—except perhaps the tombs. By the side of the marvels produced by the sculptor, literature, with no less vigor, creates her masterpieces. The theology, the metaphysics, are as varied as they are subtle and ingenious, and man's thought goes down, without flinching, into the immeasurable abyss. In lyric poetry feminine civilization is the pride of humanity.

But when I pass from the kingdom of ideals and visions to that of the useful inventions, and the theoretical sciences on which they rest, I fall at once from the heights into the depths, and the brilliant day gives place to night. Useful discoveries are rare; the few that appear are petty and sterile; the power of observation practically does not exist. While the Chinese were continually inventing, the Hindus conceived a few ideas, which they did not take the trouble to work out. Again the Greeks had, as we know from their literature, many scientific notions that were unworthy of them; while the Romans, after passing the culminating-point in their history, could not advance very far, although they did more than the Greeks; for the mixture of Asiatic blood, that absorbed them with startling rapidity, denied them the qualities which are indispensable for a patient investigation of nature. Yet their administrative genius, their legislation, and the useful buildings that were set up throughout the Empire are a sufficient witness to the positive nature of their social ideas at a certain period; they prove that if Southern Europe had not been so quickly covered by the continual stream of colonists from Asia and Africa, positive science would have won the day, and the

THE INEQUALITY OF HUMAN RACES

Germanic pioneers would, in consequence, have lost a few of their laurels.

The conquerors of the fifth century brought into Europe a spirit of the same order as that of the Chinese, but with very different powers. It was equipped, to a far greater extent, with the feminine qualities, and united the two motive-forces far more harmoniously. Wherever this branch of the human family was dominant, the utilitarian tendencies, though in a nobler form, are unmistakable. In England, North America, Holland, and Hanover, they override the other instincts of the people. It is the same in Belgium, and also in the north of France, where there is always a wonderfully quick comprehension of anything with a practical bearing. As we go further south these tendencies become weaker. This is not due to the fiercer action of the sun, for the Catalans and the Piedmontese certainly live in a hotter climate than the men of Provence or Bas-Languedoc; the sole cause is the influence of blood.

The female or feminized races occupy the greater part of the globe, and, in particular, the greater part of Europe. With the exception of the Teutonic group and some of the Slavs, all the races in our part of the world have the material instincts only in a slight degree; they have already played their parts in former ages and cannot begin again. The masses, in their infinite gradations from Gaul to Celtiberian, from Celtiberian to the nameless mixture of Italians and other Latin races, form a descending scale, so far as the chief powers (though not all the powers) of the male principle are concerned.

Our civilization has been created by the mingling of the Germanic tribes with the races of the ancient world, the union, that is to say, of pre-eminently male groups with races and fragments of races clinging to the decayed remnants of the ancient ideas. The richness, variety, and fertility of invention for which we honor our modern societies, are the natural, and more or less successful, result of the maimed and disparate elements which our Germanic ancestors instinctively knew how to use, temper, and disguise.

Our own kind of culture has two general marks, wherever it is found; it has been touched, however superficially, by the Germanic element, and it is Christian. This second characteristic (to repeat what I have said already) is more marked than the other, and leaps first to the eye, because it is an outward feature of our modern State, a sort of varnish on its surface; but it is not absolutely essential, as many nations are Christian —and still more might become Christian—without forming a part of our circle of civilization. The first characteristic is, on the contrary, positive and decisive. Where the Germanic element has never penetrated, our special kind of civilization does not exist.

This naturally brings me to the question whether we can call our European societies entirely civilized; whether the ideas and actions that appear on the surface have the roots of their being deep down in the mass of the people, and therefore whether their effects correspond with the instincts of the greatest number. This leads to a further question: do the lower strata of our populations think and act in accordance with what we call European civilization?

Many have admired, and with good reason, the extraordinary unity of ideas and views that guided the whole body of citizens in the Greek states of the best period. The conclusions on every essential point were often hostile to each other; but they all derived from the same source. In politics, some wanted more or less democracy, some more or less oligarchy. In religion, some chose to worship the Eleusinian Demeter, others Athene Parthenos. As a matter of literary taste,

Æschylus might be preferred to Sophocles, Alcaeus to Pindar. But, at bottom, the ideas discussed were all such as we might call national; the disputes turned merely on points of proportion. The same was the case at Rome, before the Punic Wars; the civilization of the country was uniform and unquestioned. It reached the slave through the master; all shared in it to a different extent, but none shared in any other.

From the time of the Punic Wars among the Romans, and from that of Pericles, and especially of Philip, among the Greeks, this uniformity tended more and more to break down. The mixture of nations brought with it a mixture of civilizations. The result was a very complex and learned society, with a culture far more refined than before. But it had one striking disadvantage; both in Italy and in Hellas, it existed merely for the upper classes, the lower strata being left quite ignorant of its nature, its merits, and its aims. Roman civilization after the great Asiatic wars was, no doubt, a powerful manifestation of human genius; but it really embraced none but the Greek rhetoricians who supplied its philosophical basis, the Syrian lawyers who built up for it an atheistic legal system, the rich men who were engaged in public administration or money-making, and finally the leisured voluptuaries who did nothing at all. By the masses it was, at all times, merely tolerated. The peoples of Europe understood nothing of its Asiatic and African elements, those of Egypt had no better idea of what it brought them from Gaul and Spain, those of Numidia had no appreciation of what came to them from the rest of the world. Thus, below what we might call the social classes, lived innumerable multitudes who had a different civilization from that of the official world, or were not civilized at all. Only the minority of the Roman people held the secret, and attached any importance to it. We have here the example of a civilization that is accepted and dominant, no longer through the convictions of the peoples who live under it, but by their exhaustion, their weakness, and their indifference.

In China we find the exact contrary. The territory is of course immense, but from one end to the other there is the same spirit among the native Chinese—I leave the rest out of account—and the same grasp of their civilization. Whatever its principles may be, whether we approve of its aims or not, we must admit that the part played by the masses in their civilization shows how well they understand it. The reason is not that the country is free in our sense, that a democratic feeling of rivalry impels all to do their best in order to secure a position guaranteed them by law. Not at all; I am not trying to paint an ideal picture. Peasants and middle classes alike have little hope, in the Middle Kingdom at any rate, of rising by sheer force of merit. In this part of the Empire, in spite of the official promises with regard to the system of examinations by which the public services are filled, no one doubts that the places are all reserved for members of the official families, and that the decision of the professors is often affected more by money than by scholarship;[43] but though shipwrecked ambitions may bewail the evils of the system, they do not imagine that there could be a better one, and the existing state of things is the object of unshakable admiration to the whole people.

---

[43] "It is still only in China that a poor student can offer himself for the Imperial examination and come out a great man. This is a splendid feature of the social organization of the Chinese, and their theory is certainly better than any other. Unfortunately, its application is far from perfect. I am not here referring to the errors of judgment and corruption on the part of the examiners, or even to the sale of literary degrees, an expedient to which the Government is sometimes driven in times of financial stress ..." (F.J. Mohl, Annual Report of the Societe Asiatique," 1846).

Education in China is remarkably general and widespread; it extends to classes considerably below those which, in France, might conceivably feel the want of it. The cheapness of books,[44] the number and the low fees of the schools, bring a certain measure of education within the reach of everybody. The aims and spirit of the laws are generally well understood, and the government is proud of having made legal knowledge accessible to all. There is a strong instinct of repulsion against radical changes in the Government. A very trustworthy critic on this point, Mr. John F. Davis, the British Commissioner in China, who has not only lived in Canton but has studied its affairs with the closest application, says that the Chinese are a people whose history does not show a single attempt at a social revolution, or any alteration in the outward forms of power. In his opinion, they are best described as "a nation of steady conservatives."

The contrast is very striking, when we turn to the civilization of the Roman world, where changes of government followed each other with startling rapidity right up to the coming of the northern peoples. Everywhere in this great society, and at every time, we can find populations so detached from the existing order as to be ready for the wildest experiments. Nothing was left untried in this long period, no principle respected. Property, religion, the family were all called in question, and many, both in the North and South, were inclined to put the novel theories into practice. Absolutely nothing in the Graeco-Roman world rested on a solid

---

[44] John F. Davis, "The Chinese" (London, 1840): "Three or four volumes of any ordinary work of the octavo size and shape may be had for a sum equivalent to two shillings. A Canton bookseller's manuscript catalogue marked the price of the four books of Confucius, including the commentary, at a price rather under half-a-crown. The cheapness of their common literature is occasioned partly by the mode of printing, but partly also by the low price of paper."

foundation, not even the unity of the Empire, so necessary one would think for the general safety. Further, it was not only the armies, with their hosts of improvised Caesars, who were continually battering at this Palladium of society; the emperors themselves, beginning with Diocletian, had so little belief in the monarchy, that they established of their own accord a division of power. At last there were four rulers at once. Not a single institution, not a single principle, was fixed, in this unhappy society, which had no better reason for continuing to exist than the physical impossibility of deciding on which rock it should founder; until the moment came when it was crushed in the vigorous arms of the North, and forced at last to become something definite.

Thus we find a complete opposition between these two great societies, the Celestial and the Roman Empires. To the civilization of Eastern Asia I will add that of the Brahmans, which is also of extraordinary strength and universality. If in China every one, or nearly every one, has reached a certain level of knowledge, the same is the case among the Hindus. Each man, according to his caste, shares in a spirit that has lasted for ages, and knows exactly what he ought to learn, think, and believe. Among the Buddhists of Tibet and other parts of Upper Asia, nothing is rarer than a peasant who cannot read. Every one has similar convictions on the important matters of life.

Do we find the same uniformity among Europeans? The question is not worth asking. The Græco-Roman civilization has no definitely marked color, either throughout the nations as a whole, or even within the same people. I need not speak of Russia or most of the Austrian States; the proof would be too easy. But consider Germany or Italy (especially South Italy); Spain shows a similar picture, though in fainter lines; France is in the same position as Spain.

Take the case of France. I will not confine myself to the fact, which always strikes the most superficial observer, that between Paris and the rest of France there is an impassable gulf, and that at the very gates of the capital a new nation begins, which is quite different from that living within the walls. On this point there is no room for doubt, and those who base their conclusions, as to the unity of ideas and the fusion of blood, on the formal unity of our Government, are under a great illusion.

Not a single social law or root-principle of civilization is understood in the same way in all our departments. I do not refer merely to the peoples of Normandy, Brittany, Anjou, Limousin, Gascony, and Provence; every one knows how little one is like the other, and how they vary in their opinions. The important point is that, while in China, Tibet, and India the ideas essential to the maintenance of civilization are familiar to all classes, this is not at all the case among ourselves. The most elementary and accessible facts are sealed mysteries to most of our rural populations, who are absolutely indifferent to them; for usually they can neither read nor write, and have no wish to learn. They cannot see the use of such knowledge, nor the possibility of applying it. In such a matter, I put no trust in the promises of the law, or the fine show made by institutions, but rather in what I have seen for myself, and in the reports of careful observers. Different governments have made the most praiseworthy attempts to raise the peasants from their ignorance; not only are the children given every opportunity for being educated in their villages, but even adults, who are made conscripts at twenty, find in the regimental schools an excellent system of instruction in the most necessary subjects. Yet, in spite of these provisions, and the fatherly anxiety of the Government, in spite of the *compelle intrare*[45] which it is continually dinning into the ears of its agents, the agricultural classes learn nothing whatever. Like all those who have lived in the provinces, I have seen how parents never send their children to school without obvious reluctance, how they regard the hours spent there as a mere waste of time, how they withdraw them at once on the slightest pretext and never allow the compulsory number of years to be extended. Once he leaves school, the young man's first duty is to forget what he has learnt. This is, to a certain extent, a point of honor with him; and his example is followed by the discharged soldiers, who, in many parts of France, are not only ashamed of having learnt to read and write, but even affect to forget their own language, and often succeed in doing so. Hence I could more easily approve all the generous efforts that have been so fruitlessly made to educate our rural populations, if I were not convinced that the knowledge put before them is quite unsuitable, and that at the root of their apparent indifference there is a feeling of invincible hostility to our civilization. One proof lies in their attitude of passive resistance; but the spectre of another and more convincing argument appears before me, as soon as I see any instance of this obstinacy being overcome, under apparently favorable circumstances. In some respects the attempts at education are succeeding better than before. In our eastern departments and the great manufacturing towns there are many workmen who learn of their own accord to read and write. They live in a circle where such knowledge is obviously useful. But as soon as they have a sufficient grasp of the rudiments, how do they use them? Generally as a means of

---

[45] "Force them to enter."

acquiring ideas and feelings which are now no longer instinctively, but actively, opposed to the social order. The only exception is to be found in the agricultural and even the industrial population of the North-west, where knowledge up to an elementary point is far more widespread than in any other part, and where it is not only retained after the school time is over, but is usually made to serve a good end. As these populations have much more affinity than the others to the Germanic race, I am not surprised at the result. We see the same phenomenon in Belgium and the Netherlands.

If we go on to consider the fundamental beliefs and opinions of the people, the difference becomes still more marked. With regard to the beliefs we have to congratulate the Christian religion on not being exclusive or making its dogmas too narrow. If it had, it would have struck some very dangerous shoals. The bishops and the clergy have to struggle, as they have done for these five, ten, fifteen centuries, against the stream of hereditary tendencies and prejudices, which are the more formidable as they are hardly even admitted, and so can neither be fought nor conquered. There is no enlightened priest who does not know, after his mission-work in the villages, the deep cunning with which even the religious peasant will continue to cherish, in his inmost heart, some traditional idea that comes to the surface only at rare moments, in spite of himself. His complete confidence in his parish priest just stops short of what we might call his secret religion. Does he mention it to him? He denies it, will admit no discussion, and will not budge an inch from his convictions. This is the reason of the taciturnity that, in every province, is the main attitude of the peasant in face of the middle classes; it raises too an insuperable barrier between him and even the most popular landowners in his canton. With this view of civilization on the part of the majority of the people who are supposed to be most deeply attached to it, I can well believe that an approximate estimate of ten millions within our circle of culture, and twenty-six millions outside it, would be, if anything, an under-statement.

If our rural populations were merely brutal and ignorant, we might not take much notice of this cleavage, but console ourselves with the delusive hope of gradually winning them over, and absorbing them in the multitudes that are already civilized. But these peasants are like certain savage tribes: at first sight they seem brutish and unthinking, for they are outwardly self-effacing and humble. But if one digs even a little beneath the surface, into their real life, one finds that their isolation is voluntary, and comes from no feeling of weakness. Their likes and dislikes are not a matter of chance; everything obeys a logical sequence of definite ideas. When I spoke just now of religion, I might also have pointed out how very far removed our moral doctrines are from those of the peasants,[46] what a different sense they give to the word *delicacy*, how obstinately they cling to their custom of regarding every one who is not of peasant stock in the same way as the men of remote antiquity viewed the foreigner. It is true they do not murder him, thanks to the strange and mysterious terror inspired by laws they have not themselves made; but they do not conceal their hatred and distrust of him, and they take great pleasure in annoying him, if they can do it without risk. Does this mean that they are ill-natured? No, not among themselves—we may continually see them doing each

---

[46] A nurse of Touraine put a bird into the hands of the three-year-old boy of whom she was in charge, and encouraged him to pull out its wings and feathers. When the parents blamed her for teaching such wickedness, she replied, "It is to make him proud." This answer, given in 1847, goes back directly to the educational maxims in vogue at the time of Vercingetorix.

other little kindnesses. They simply look on themselves as a race apart, a race (if we may believe them) which is weak and oppressed, and obliged to deal crookedly, but which also keeps its stiff-necked and contemptuous pride. In some of our provinces the workman thinks himself of far better blood and older stock than his former master. Family pride, in some of the peasants, is at least equal to that of the nobility of the Middle Ages.[47]

We cannot doubt it; the lower strata of the French people have very little in common with the surface. They form an abyss over which civilization is suspended, and the deep stagnant waters, sleeping at the bottom of the gulf, will one day show their power of dissolving all that comes in their way. The most tragic crises of her history have deluged the country with blood, without the agricultural population playing any part except that which was forced on it. Where its immediate interests were not engaged, it let the storms pass by without troubling itself in the least. Those who are astonished and scandalized by such callousness say that the peasant is essentially immoral—which is both unjust and untrue. The peasants look on us almost in the light of enemies. They understand nothing of our civilization, they share

---

[47] A very few years ago there was a question of electing a churchwarden in a little obscure parish of French Brittany, that part of the old province which the true Bretons call the "Welsh," or "foreign," country. The church council, composed of peasants, deliberated for two days without being able to make up their minds; for the candidate before them, though rich and well esteemed as a good man and a good Christian, was a "foreigner." The council would not move from its opinion, although the "foreigner's" father, as well as himself, had been born in the district; it was still remembered that his grandfather, who had been dead for many years and had never known any member of the council, was an immigrant from another part of the country. The daughter of a peasant-proprietor makes a mésalliance if she marries a tailor or a miller or even a farmer, if he works for wages. It does not matter whether the husband is richer than she is; her crime is often punished, just the same, by a father's curse. Is not this case exactly like that of the churchwarden?

in it unwillingly, and think themselves justified in profiting, as far as they can, by its misfortunes. If we put aside this antagonism, which is sometimes active but generally inert, we need not hesitate to allow them some high moral qualities, however strangely these may, at times, be manifested.

I may apply to the whole of Europe what I have just said of France, and conclude that modern civilization includes far more than it absorbs; in this it resembles the Roman Empire. Hence one cannot be confident that our state of society will last; and I see a clear proof of this in the smallness of its hold even over the classes raised a little above the country population. Our civilization may be compared to the temporary islands thrown up in the sea by submarine volcanoes. Exposed as they are to the destructive action of the currents, and robbed of the forces that first kept them in position, they will one day break up, and their fragments will be hurled into the gulf of the all-conquering waves. It is a sad end, and one which many noble races before ourselves have had to meet. The blow cannot be turned aside; it is inevitable. The wise man may see it coming, but can do nothing more. The most consummate statesmanship is not able for one moment to counteract the immutable laws of the world.

But though thus unknown, despised, or hated by the majority of those who live under its shadow, our civilization is yet one of the most glorious monuments ever erected by the genius of man. It is certainly not distinguished by its power of invention; but putting this aside, we may say that it has greatly developed the capacity for understanding, and so for conquest. To mistake nothing is to take everything. If it has not founded the "exact sciences," it has at least made them exact, and freed them from errors to which, curiously enough, they were more liable than any other branch of knowledge. Thanks to its discoveries, it knows the material world better than all the societies which have gone before. It has guessed some of its chief laws, it can describe and explain them, and borrow from them a marvellous strength that passes a hundredfold the strength of a man. Little by little, by a skillful use of induction, it has reconstructed large periods of history of which the ancients never suspected the existence. The further we are from primitive times, the more clearly can we see them, and penetrate their mysteries. This is a great point of superiority, and one which we must, in fairness, allow to our civilization.

But when we have admitted this, should we be right in concluding, as is usually done, without reflexion, that it is superior to all the civilizations that have ever existed, and to all those that exist at the present day? Yes and no. Yes, because the extreme diversity of its elements allows it to rest on a powerful basis of comparison and analysis, and so to assimilate at once almost anything; yes, because this power of choice is favorable to its development in many different directions; yes again, because, thanks to the impulse of the Germanic element (which is too materialistic to be a destructive force) it has made itself a morality, the wise prescriptions of which were generally unknown before. If, however, we carry this idea of its greatness so far as to regard it as having an absolute and unqualified superiority, then I say no, the simple fact being that it excels in practically nothing whatever.

In politics, we see it in bondage to the continual change brought about by the different requirements of the races which it includes. In England, Holland, Naples, and Russia, its principles are still fairly stable, because the populations are more homogeneous, or at any rate form groups of the same kind, with similar instincts. But everywhere else, especially in France, Central Italy, and

Germany—where variations of race are infinite—
theories of government can never rise to the rank of
accepted truths, and political science is a matter of
continual experiment. As our civilization is unable to
have any sure confidence in itself, it is without the
stability that is one of the most important qualities
mentioned in my definition. This weakness is to be
found neither in the Buddhist and Brahman societies,
nor in the Celestial Empire; and these civilizations have
in this respect an advantage over ours. The whole people
is at one in its political beliefs. When there is a wise
government, and the ancient institutions are bearing
good fruit, every one is glad. When they are in clumsy
hands, and injure the commonwealth, they are pitied by
the citizens as a man pities himself; but they never cease
to be respected. There is sometimes a desire to purify
them, but never to sweep them away or replace them by
others. It does not need very keen eyes to see here a
guarantee of long life which our civilization is very far
from possessing.

In art, our inferiority to India, as well as to Egypt,
Greece, and America, is very marked. Neither in
sublimity nor beauty have we anything to compare with
the masterpieces of antiquity. When our day has drawn
to its close, and the ruins of our towns and monuments
cover the face of the land, the traveller will discover
nothing, in the forests and marshes that will skirt the
Thames, the Seine, and the Rhine, to rival the gorgeous
ruins of Philae, Nineveh, Athens, Salsette, and the valley
of Tenochtitlan. If future ages have something to learn
from us in the way of positive science, this is not the
case with poetry, as is clearly proved by the despairing
admiration that we so justly feel for the intellectual
wonders of foreign civilizations.

So far as the refinement of manners is concerned, we
have obviously changed for the worse. This is shown by

our own past history; there were periods when luxury, elegance, and sumptuousness were understood far better and practiced on a far more lavish scale than today. Pleasure was certainly confined to a smaller number. Comparatively few were in what we should call a state of *well-being*. On the other hand, if we admit (as we must) that refinement of manners elevates the minds of the multitudes who look on, as well as ennobling the life of a few favored individuals, that it spreads a varnish of beauty and grandeur over the whole country, and that these become the common inheritance of all—then our civilization, which is essentially petty on its external side, cannot be compared to its rivals.

I may add, finally, that the active element distinguishing any civilization is identical with the most striking quality, whatever it may be, of the dominant race. The civilization is modified and transformed according to the changes undergone by this race, and when the race itself has disappeared, carries on for some time the impulse originally received from it. Thus the kind of order kept in any society is the best index to the special capacities of the people and to the stage of progress to which they have attained: it is the clearest mirror in which their individuality can be reflected.

I see that the long digression, into which I have strayed, has carried me further than I expected. I do not regret it, for it has enabled me to vent certain ideas that the reader might well keep in mind. But it is now time to return to the main course of my argument, the chain of which is still far from being complete.

I established first that the life or death of societies was the result of internal causes. I have said what these causes are, and described their essential nature, in order that they may be more easily recognized. I have shown that they are generally referred to a wrong source; and in looking for some sign that could always distinguish them, and indicate their presence, I found it in the capacity to create a civilization. As it seemed impossible to discover a clear conception of this term, it was necessary to define it, as I have done. My next step must be to study the natural and unvarying phenomenon which I have identified as the latent cause of the life and death of societies. This, as I have said, consists in the relative worth of the different races. Logic requires me to make clear at once what I understand by the word *race*. This will be the subject of the following chapter.

CHAPTER X

SOME ANTHROPOLOGISTS REGARD MAN AS HAVING A MULTIPLE ORIGIN[48]

We must first discuss the word *race* in its physiological sense.

A good many observers, who judge by first impressions and so take extreme views, assert that there are such radical and essential differences between human families that one must refuse them any identity of origin.[49] The writers who adhere to such a notion assume many other genealogies by the side of that from Adam. To them there is no original unity in the species, or rather there is no single species; there are three or four, or even more, which produce perfectly distinct types, and these again have united to form hybrids.

The supporters of this theory easily win belief by citing the clear and striking differences between certain human groups. When we see before us a man with a yellowish skin, scanty hair and beard, a large face, a pyramidal skull, small stature, thick-set limbs, and slanting eyes with the skin of the eyelids turned so much outwards that the eye will hardly open[50]—we recognize a very well-marked type, the main features of which it is easy to bear in mind.

From him we turn to another—a negro from the West Coast of Africa, tall, strong-looking, with thick-set limbs and a tendency to fat. His color is no longer

---

[48] This chapter was, of course, written before the appearance of the "Origin of Species" or the "Descent of Man"; see author's preface.— Tr.

[49] These views are quoted by Flourens (*Eloge de Blumenbach, Mémoire de l'Academie des Sciences*), who himself dissents from them.

[50] This and the other illustrations in this chapter are taken from Prichard, "Natural History of Man."

yellowish, but entirely black; his hair no longer thin and wiry, but thick, coarse, woolly, and luxuriant; his lower jaw juts out, the shape of the skull is what is known as *prognathous.* "The long bones stand out, the front of the tibia and the fibula are more convex than in a European, the calves are very high and reach above the knee; the feet are quite flat, and the heel-bone, instead of being arched, is almost in a straight line with the other bones of the foot, which is very large. The hand is similarly formed."

When we look for a moment at an individual of this type, we are involuntarily reminded of the structure of the monkey, and are inclined to admit that the negro races of West Africa come from a stock that has nothing in common, except the human form, with the Mongolian.

We come next to tribes whose appearance is still less flattering to the self-love of mankind than that of the Congo negro. Oceania has the special privilege of providing the most ugly, degraded, and repulsive specimens of the race, which seem to have been created with the express purpose of forming a link between man and the brute pure and simple. By the side of many Australian tribes, the African negro himself assumes a value and dignity, and seems to derive from a nobler source. In many of the wretched inhabitants of this New World, the size of the head, the extreme thinness of the limbs, the famished look of the body, are absolutely hideous. The hair is flat or wavy, and generally woolly, the flesh is black on a foundation of grey.

When, after examining these types, taken from all the quarters of the globe, we finally come back to the inhabitants of Europe, and of South and West Asia, we find them so superior in beauty, in just proportion of limb and regularity of feature, that we are at once tempted to accept the conclusions of those who assert the multiplicity of races. Not only are these peoples more beautiful than the rest of mankind, which is, I confess, a pestilent congregation of ugliness;[51] not only have they had the glory of giving the world such admirable types as a Venus, an Apollo, a Farnese Hercules; but also there is a visible hierarchy of beauty established from ancient times even among themselves, and in this natural aristocracy the Europeans are the most eminent, by their grace of outline and strength of muscular development. The most reasonable view appears to be that the families into which man is divided are as distinct as are animals of different species. Such was the conclusion drawn from simple observation, and so long as only general facts were in question, it seemed irrefutable.

Camper was one of the first to reduce these observations to some kind of system. He was no longer satisfied with merely superficial evidence, but wished to give his proofs a mathematical foundation; he tried to define anatomically the differences between races. He succeeded in establishing a strict method that left no room for doubt, and his views gained the numerical accuracy without which there can be no science. His method was to take the front part of the skull and measure the inclination of the profile by means of two lines which he called the *facial lines*. Their intersection formed an angle, the size of which gave the degree of elevation attained by the race to which the skull belonged. One of these lines connected the base of the nose with the orifice of the ear; the other was tangential

---

[51] Meiners was so struck with the repulsive appearance of the greater part of humanity that he imagined a very simple system of classification, containing only two categories—the beautiful, namely the white race, and the ugly, which includes all the others (Grundriss der Geschichte der Menschheit). The reader will see that I have not thought it necessary to go through all the ethnological theories. I only mention the most important.

to the most prominent part of the forehead and the jut of the upper jaw. On the basis of the angle thus formed, he constructed a scale including not only man but all kinds of animals. At the top stood the European; and the more acute the angle, the further was the distance from the type which, according to Camper, was the most perfect. Thus birds and fishes showed smaller angles than the various mammals. A certain kind of ape reached 42°, and even 50°. Then came the heads of the African negro and the Kalmuck, which touched 70°. The European stood at 80°, and, to quote the inventor's own words, which are very flattering to our own type, "On this difference of 10° the superior beauty of the European, what one might call his 'comparative beauty,' depends; the 'absolute beauty' that is so striking in some of the works of ancient sculpture, as in the head of Apollo and the Medusa of Sosicles, is the result of a still greater angle, amounting in this instance to 100°."[52]

This method was attractive by its simplicity. Unhappily, the facts are against it, as against so many systems. By a series of accurate observations, Owen showed that, in the case of monkeys, Camper had studied the skulls only of the young animals; but since, in the adults, the growth of the teeth and jaws, and the development of the zygomatic arch, were not accompanied by a corresponding enlargement of the brain, the numerical difference between these and human skulls was much greater than Camper had supposed, since the facial angle of the black orangoutang or the highest type of chimpanzee was at most 30° or 35°. From this to the 70° of the negro and the Kalmuck the gap was too great for Camper's scale to have any significance.

---

[52] Prichard, op. cit. (2nd edition, 1845), p. 112.

Camper's theory made considerable use of phrenology. He attempted to discover a corresponding development of instinct as he mounted his scale from the animals to man. But here too the facts were against him. The elephant, for example, whose intelligence is certainly greater than the orangoutang's, has a far more acute facial angle; and even the most docile and intelligent monkeys do not belong to the species which are the "highest" in Camper's series.

Beside these two great defects, the method is very open to attack in that it does not apply to all the varieties of the human race. It leaves out of account the tribes with pyramidally shaped heads, who form, however, a striking division by themselves.

Blumenbach, who held the field against his predecessor, elaborated a system in his turn; this was to study a man's head from the top. He called his discovery *norma verticalis,* the "vertical method." He was confident that the comparison of heads according to their width brought out the chief differences in the general configuration of the skull. According to him, the study of this part of the body is so pregnant with results, especially in its bearing on national character, that it is impossible to measure all the differences merely by lines and angles; to reach a satisfying basis of classification, we must consider the heads from the point of view in which we can take in at one glance the greatest number of varieties. His idea was, in outline, as follows: "Arrange the skulls that you wish to compare in such a way that the jaw-bones are on the same horizontal line; in other words, let each rest on its lower jaw. Then stand behind the skulls and fix the eye on the vertex of each. In this way you will best see the varieties of shape that have most to do with national character; these consist either (1) in the direction of the jaw-bone and maxillary, or (2) in the breadth or narrowness of the oval outline presented by the top half of the skull, or (3) in the flattened or vaulted form of the frontal bone."[53]

Blumenbach's system resulted in the division of mankind into five main categories, which were in their turn subdivided into a certain number of types and classes.

This classification was of very doubtful value. Like that of Camper, it overlooked many important characteristics. It was partly to escape such objections that Owen proposed to examine skulls, not from the top, but from the bottom. One of the chief results of this new method was to show such a strong and definite line of difference between a man and an orangoutang that it became forever impossible to find the link that Camper imagined to exist between the two species. In fact, one glance at the two skulls, from Owen's point of view, is enough to bring out their radical difference. The diameter from front to back is longer in the orangoutang than in man; the zygomatic arch, instead of being wholly in the front part of the base, is in the middle, and occupies just a third of its diameter. Finally the position of the occipital orifice, which has such a marked influence on general structure and habits, is quite different. In the skull of a man, it is almost at the center of the base; in that of an orangoutang, it is a sixth of the way from the hinder end.[54]

Owen's observations have, no doubt, considerable value; I would prefer, however, the most recent of the craniological systems, which is at the same time, in many ways, the most ingenious, I mean that of the American

------

[53] Prichard, p. 116.

[54] *Ibid.*, pp. 117-18.

scholar Morton, adopted by Carus.[55] In outline this is as follows:

To show the difference of races, Morton and Carus started from the idea, that the greater the size of the skull, the higher the type to which the individual belonged, and they set out to investigate whether the development of the skull is equal in all the human races.

To solve this question, Morton took a certain number of heads belonging to whites, Mongols, negroes, and Redskins of North America. He stopped all the openings with cotton, except the *foramen magnum,* and completely filled the inside with carefully dried grains of pepper. He then compared the number of grains in each. This gave him the following table:

		Number of skulls measured.	Average number of grains.	Maximum number of grains.	Minimum number of grains.
White races		52	87	109	75
Yellow races { Mongols		10	83	93	69
{ Malays		18	81	89	64
Redskins		147	82	100	60
Negroes		29	78	94	65

The results set down in the first two columns are certainly very curious. On the other hand, I attach little importance to those in the last two; for if the extraordinary variations from the average in the second column are to have any real significance, Morton should have taken a far greater number of skulls, and further, have given details as to the social position of those to whom the skulls belonged. He was probably able to procure, in the case of the whites and the Redskins, heads which had belonged to men at any rate above the

[55] Carus, *op. cit.*, from which the following details are taken.

lowest level of society, while it is not likely that he had access to the skulls of negro chiefs, or of Chinese mandarins. This explains how he has been able to assign the number 100 to an American Indian, while the most intelligent Mongol whom he has examined does not rise above 93, and is thus inferior even to the negro, who reaches 94. Such results are a mere matter of chance. They are quite incomplete and unscientific; in such questions, however, one cannot be too careful to avoid judgments founded merely on individual cases. I am inclined therefore to reject altogether the second half of Morton's calculations.

I must also question one detail in the other half. In the second column, there is a clear gradation from the number 87, indicating the capacity of the white man's skull, to the numbers 83 and 78 for the yellow and black man respectively. But the figures 83, 81, 82, for the Mongols, Malays, and Redskins, give average results which evidently shade into one another; all the more so, because Carus does not hesitate to count the Mongols and Malays as the same race, and consequently to put the numbers 83 and 81 together. But, in that case, why allow the number 82 to mark a distinct race, and thus create arbitrarily a fourth great division of mankind?

This anomaly, however, actually buttresses the weak point in Carus' system. He likes to think that, just as we see our planet pass through the four stages of day and night, evening and morning twilight, so there *must* be in the human species four subdivisions corresponding to these. He sees here a symbol, which is always a temptation for a subtle mind. Carus yields to it, as many of his learned fellow-countrymen would have done in his place. The white races are the nations of the day; the black those of the night; the yellow those of the Eastern, and the red those of the Western twilight. We may easily guess the ingenious comparisons suggested by such a picture. Thus, the European nations, owing to the brilliance of their scientific knowledge and the clear outlines of their civilization, are obviously in the full glare of day, while the negroes sleep in the darkness of ignorance, and the Chinese live in a half-light that gives them an incomplete, though powerful, social development. As for the Redskins, who are gradually disappearing from the earth, where can we find a more beautiful image of their fate than the setting sun?

Unhappily, comparison is not proof, and by yielding too easily to this poetic impulse, Carus has a little damaged his fine theory. The same charge also may be leveled at this as at the other ethnological doctrines; Carus does not manage to include in a systematic whole the various physiological differences between one race and another.[56]

The supporters of the theory of racial unity have not failed to seize on this weak point, and to claim that, where we cannot arrange the observations on the shape of the skull in such a way as to constitute a proof of the original separation of types, we must no longer consider the variations as pointing to any radical difference, but merely regard them as the result of secondary and isolated causes, with no specific relevance.

The cry of victory may be raised a little too soon. It may be hard to find the correct method, without being necessarily impossible. The "Unitarians," however, do not admit this reservation. They support their view by observing that certain tribes that belong to the same

---

[56] There are some apparently trivial differences which are, however, very characteristic. A certain fullness at the side of the lower lip, that we see among Germans and English, is an example. This mark of Germanic origin may also be found in some faces of the Flemish School, in the Rubens *Madonna* at Dresden, in the *Satyrs and Nymphs* in the same collection, in a *Lute-player* of Mieris, etc. No craniological method can take account of such details, though they have a certain importance, in view of the mixed character of our races.

race show a very different physical type. They cite, for instance, the various branches of the hybrid Malayo-Polynesian family, without taking account of the proportion in which the elements are mingled in each case. If groups (they say) with a common origin can show quite a different conformation of features and skull, the unity of the human race cannot be disproved along these lines at all. However foreign the negro or Mongol type may appear to European eyes, this is no evidence of their different origin; the reasons why the human families have diverged will be found nearer to hand, and we may regard these physiological deviations merely as the result of certain local causes acting for a definite period of time.[57]

In face of so many objections, good and bad, the champions of multiplicity tried to extend the sphere of their arguments. Relying no longer on the mere study of skulls, they passed to that of the individual man as a

---

[57] Job Ludolf, whose data on this subject were necessarily very incomplete and inferior to those we have now, is none the less opposed to the opinion accepted by Prichard. His remarks on the black race are striking and unanswerable, and I cannot resist the pleasure of quoting them: "It is not my purpose to speak here about the blackness of the Ethiop; most people may, if they will, attribute it to the heat of the sun and the torrid zone. Yet even within the sun's equatorial path there are peoples who, if not white, are at least not quite black. Many who live outside either tropic are further from the Equator than the Persians or Syrians— for instance, the inhabitants of the Cape of Good Hope, who, however, are absolutely black. If you say that blackness belongs solely to Africa and the sons of Ham, you must still allow that the Malabars and the Cingalese and other even more remote peoples of Asia are equally black. If you regard the climate and soil as the reason, then why do not white men become black when they settle down in these regions? If you take refuge in 'hidden qualities,' you would do better to confess your ignorance at once" (Jobus Ludolfus, Commentarium ad Historiam Æthiopicam). I will add a short and conclusive passage of Mr. Pickering. He speaks of the regions inhabited by the black race in these words: "Excluding the northern and southern extremes, with the tableland of Abyssinia, it holds all the more temperate and fertile parts of the Continent." Thus it is just where we find most of the pure negroes that it is least hot … (Pickering, "The Races of Man and their Geographical Distribution." The essay is to be found in the "Records of the United States' Exploring Expedition during the Years 1838-42," vol. ix).

whole. In order to prove (as is quite true) that the differences do not merely lie in the facial appearance and the bony conformation of the head, they brought forward other important differences with regard to the shape of the pelvis, the proportions of the limbs, the color of the skin, and the nature of the capillary system.

Camper and other anthropologists had already recognized that the pelvis of the negro showed certain peculiarities. Dr. Vrolik pushed these inquiries further, and observed that the difference between the male and female pelvis was far less marked in the European, while in the negro race he saw in the pelvis of both sexes a considerable approximation to the brute. Assuming that the configuration of the pelvis necessarily affected that of the embryo, he inferred a difference of origin.[58]

Weber attacked this theory, with little result. He had to recognize that some formations of the pelvis were found in one race more frequently than in another; and all he could do was to show that there were some exceptions to Vrolik's rule, and that certain American, African, and Mongolian specimens showed formations that were usually confined to Europeans. This does not prove very much, especially as, in speaking of these exceptions, Weber does not seem to have inquired whether the peculiar configuration in question might not result from a mixture of blood.

With regard to the size of the limbs, the opponents of a common origin assert that the European is better proportioned. The answer—which is a good one—is that we have no reason to be surprised at the thinness of the extremities in peoples who live mainly on vegetables or have not generally enough to eat. But as against the argument from the extraordinary development of the bust among the Quichuas, the critics who refuse to

---

[58] Prichard, p. 124.

recognize this as a specific difference are on less firm ground. Their contention that the development among the mountaineers of Peru is explained by the height of the Andes, is hardly serious. There are many mountain-peoples in the world who arc quite differently constituted from the Quichuas.[59]

The next point is the color of the skin. The Unitarians deny this any specific influence, first because the color depends on facts of climate, and is not permanent—a very bold assertion; secondly because the color is capable of infinite gradation, passing insensibly from white to yellow, from yellow to black, without showing a really definite line of cleavage. This proves nothing but the existence of a vast number of hybrids, a fact which the Unitarians are continually neglecting, to the great prejudice of their theory.

As to the specific character of the hair, Flourens is of opinion, that this is no argument against an original unity of race.

After this rapid review of the divergent theories I come to the great scientific stronghold of the Unitarians, an argument of great weight, which I have kept to the end—I mean the ease with which the different branches of the human family create hybrids, and the fertility of these hybrids.

The observations of naturalists seem to prove that, in the animal or vegetable world, hybrids can be produced only from allied species, and that, even so, they are condemned to barrenness. It has also been observed that between related species intercourse, although possibly fertile, is repugnant, and usually has to be effected by trickery or force. This would tend to show

---

[59] Neither the Swiss nor the Tyrolese, nor the Highlanders of Scotland, nor the Balkan Slavs, nor the Himalaya tribes have the same hideous appearance as the Quichuas.

that in the free state the number of hybrids is even more limited than when controlled by man. We may conclude that the power of producing fertile offspring is among the marks of a distinct species.

As nothing leads us to believe that the human race is outside this rule, there is no answer to this argument, which more than any other has served to hold in check the forces opposed to unity. We hear, it is true, that in certain parts of Oceania the native women who have become mothers by Europeans are no longer fitted for impregnation by their own kind. Assuming this to be true, we might make it the basis of a more profound inquiry; but, so far as the present discussion goes, we could not use it to weaken the general principle of the fertility of human hybrids and the infertility of all others; it has no bearing on any conclusions that may be drawn from this principle.

CHAPTER XI

RACIAL DIFFERENCES ARE PERMANENT

The Unitarians say that the separation of the races is merely apparent, and due to local influences, such as are still at work, or to accidental variations of shape in the ancestor of some particular branch. All mankind is, for them, capable of the same improvement; the original type, though more or less disguised, persists in unabated strength, and the negro, the American savage, the Tungusian of Northern Siberia, can attain a beauty of outline equal to that of the European, and would do so, if they were brought up under similar conditions. This theory cannot be accepted.

We have seen above that the strongest scientific rampart of the Unitarians lay in the fertility of human hybrids. Up to now, this has been very difficult to refute, but perhaps it will not always be so; at any rate, I should not think it worth while to pause over this argument if it were not supported by another, of a very different kind, which, I confess, gives me more concern. It is said that Genesis does not admit of a multiple origin for our species.

If the text is clear, positive, peremptory, and incontestable, we must bow our heads; the greatest doubts must yield, reason can only declare herself imperfect and inferior, the origin of mankind is single, and everything that seems to prove the contrary is merely a delusive appearance. It is better to let darkness gather round a point of scholarship, than to enter the lists against such an authority. But if the Bible is not explicit, if the Holy Scriptures, which were written to shed light on quite other questions than those of race, have been misunderstood, and if without doing them violence one can draw a different meaning from them, then I shall not hesitate to go forward.

We must, of course, acknowledge that Adam is the ancestor of the white race. The scriptures are evidently meant to be so understood, for the generations deriving from him are certainly white. This being admitted, there is nothing to show that, in the view of the first compilers of the Adamite genealogies, those outside the white race were counted as part of the species at all. Not a word is said about the yellow races, and it is only an arbitrary interpretation of the text that makes us regard the patriarch Ham as black. Of course the translators and commentators, in calling Adam the common ancestor of all men, have had to enroll among his descendants all the peoples who have lived since his time. According to them, the European nations are of the stock of Japhet, hither Asia was occupied by the Semites, and the regions of Africa by the Hamites, who are, as I say, unreasonably considered to be of negro origin. The whole scheme fits admirably together—for one part of the world. But what about the other part? It is simply left out.

For the moment, I do not insist on this line of argument. I do not wish to run counter to even literal interpretations of the text, if they are generally accepted. I will merely point out that we might, perhaps, doubt their value, without going beyond the limits imposed by the Church; and then I will ask whether we may admit the basic principle of the Unitarians, such as it is, and yet somehow explain the facts otherwise than they do. In other words, Twill simply ask whether independently of any question of an original unity or multiplicity, there may not exist the most radical and far-reaching differences, both physical and moral, between human races.

The racial identity of all the different kinds of dog is admitted by Frédéric Cuvier among others;[60] but no one would say that in all dogs, without distinction of species, we find the same shapes, instincts, habits, and qualities. The same is true of horses, bulls, bears, and the like. Everywhere we see identity of origin, diversity of everything else, a diversity so deep that it cannot be lost except by crossing, and even then the products do not return to a real identity of nature. On the other hand, so long as the race is kept pure, the special characteristics remain unchanged, and are reproduced for generations without any appreciable difference.

This fact, which is indisputable, has led some to ask whether in the various kinds of domestic animals we can recognize the shapes and instincts of the primitive stock. The question seems forever insoluble. It is impossible to determine the form and nature of a primitive type, and to be certain how far the specimens we see today deviate from it. The same problem is raised in the case of a large number of vegetables. Man especially, whose origin offers a more interesting study than that of all the rest, seems to resist all explanation, from this point of view.

The different races have never doubted that the original ancestor of the whole species had precisely their own characteristics. On this point, and this alone, tradition is unanimous. The white peoples have made for themselves an Adam and an Eve that Blumenbach would have called Caucasian; whereas in the "Arabian Nights"—a book which, though apparently trivial, is a mine of true sayings and well-observed facts—we read that some negroes regard Adam and his wife as black, and since these were created in the image of God, God must also be black and the angels too, while the prophet

---

[60] *Annales du Muséum,* vol. xi, p. 458.

of God was naturally too near divinity to show a white skin to his disciples.

Unhappily, modern science has been able to provide no clue to the labyrinth of the various opinions. No likely hypothesis has succeeded in lightening this darkness, and in all probability the human races are as different from their common ancestor, if they have one, as they are from each other. I will therefore assume without discussion the principle of unity; and my only task, in the narrow and limited field to which I am confining myself, is to explain the actual deviation from the primitive type.

The causes are very hard to disentangle. The theory of the Unitarians attributes the deviation, as I have already said, to habits, climate, and locality. It is impossible to agree with this.[61] Changes have certainly been brought about in the constitution of races, since the dawn of history, by such external influences; but they do not seem to have been important enough to be able to explain fully the many vital divergences that exist. This will become clear in a moment.

I will suppose that there are two tribes which still bear a resemblance to the primitive type, and happen to

---

[61] The Unitarians are continually bringing forward comparisons between man and the animals in support of their theory; I have just been using such a line of argument myself. It only applies, however, within limits, and I could not honestly avail myself of it in speaking of the modification of species by climate. In this respect the difference between man and the animals is radical and (one might almost say) specific. There is a geography of animals, as there is of plants; but there is no geography of man. It is only in certain latitudes that certain vegetables, mammals, reptiles, fishes, and mollusks can exist; man, in all his varieties, can live equally well everywhere. In the case of the animals this fully explains a vast number of differences in organization; and I can easily believe that the species that cannot cross a certain meridian or rise to a certain height above sea-level without dying are very dependent upon the influence of climate and quick to betray its effects in their forms and instincts. It is just, however, because man is absolutely free from such bondage that I refuse to be always comparing his position, in face of the forces of nature, with that of the animals.

be living, the one in a mountainous country in the interior of a continent, the other on an island in the midst of the ocean. The atmosphere and the food conditions of each will be quite different. I will assume that the one has many ways of obtaining food, the other very few. Further, I will place the former in a cold climate, the second under a tropical sun. By this means the external contrast between them will be complete. The course of time will add its own weight to the action of the natural forces, and there is no doubt that the two groups will gradually accumulate some special characteristics which will distinguish them from each other. But even after many centuries no vital or organic change will have taken place in their constitution. This is proved by the fact that we find peoples of a very similar type, living on opposite sides of the world and under quite different conditions, of climate and everything else. Ethnologists are agreed on this point and some have even believed that the Hottentots are a Chinese colony—a hypothesis impossible on other grounds—on account of their likeness to the inhabitants of the Celestial Empire.[62] In the same way, some have seen a great resemblance between the portraits we have of the ancient Etruscans and the Araucans of South America. In features and general shape the Cherokees seem almost identical with many of the Italian peoples, such as the Calabrians. The usual type of face among the inhabitants of Auvergne, especially the women, is far less like the ordinary European's than that of many Indian tribes of North America. Thus when we grant that nature can produce similar types in widely separated

---

[62] Barrow is the author of this theory, which he bases on certain points of resemblance in the shape of the head and the yellowish color of the skin in the natives of the Cape of Good Hope. A traveller, whose name I forget, has even brought additional evidence by observing that the Hottentots usually wear a head-dress like the conical hat of the Chinese.

countries, under different conditions of life and climate, it becomes quite clear that the human races do not take their qualities from any of the external forces that are active at the present day.

I would not, however, deny that local conditions may favor the deepening of some particular skin-color, the tendency to obesity, the development of the chest muscles, the lengthening of the arms or the lower limbs, the increase or decrease of physical strength. But, I repeat, these are not essential points; and to judge from the very slight difference made by the alteration of local conditions in the shape of the body, there is no reason to believe that they have ever had very much influence. This is an argument of considerable weight.

Although we do not know what cataclysmal changes may have been effected in the physical organization of the races before the dawn of history, we may at least observe that this period extends only to about half the age attributed to our species. If for three or four thousand years the darkness is impenetrable, we still have another period of three thousand years, of which we can go right back to the beginning in the case of certain nations. Everything tends to show that the races which were then known, and which have remained relatively pure since that time, have not greatly changed in their outward appearance, although some of them no longer live in the same places, and so are no longer affected by the same external causes. Take, for example, the Arabs of the stock of Ishmael. We still find them, just as they are represented in the Egyptian monuments, not only in the parched deserts of their own land, but in the fertile, and often damp, regions of Malabar and the Coromandel Coast, in the islands of the Indies, and on many points of the north coast of Africa, where they are, as a fact, more mixed than anywhere else. Traces of them are still found in some parts of Roussillon, Languedoc, and the Spanish coast, although almost two centuries have passed away since their invasion. If the mere influence of environment had the power, as is supposed, of setting up and taking away the limits between organic types, it would have not allowed these to persist so long. The change of place would have been followed by a corresponding change of form.

After the Arabs, I will mention the Jews, who are still more remarkable in this connection, as they have settled in lands with very different climates from that of Palestine, and have given up their ancient mode of life. The Jewish type has, however, remained much the same; the modifications it has undergone are of no importance and have never been enough, in any country or latitude, to change the general character of the race. The warlike Rechabites of the Arabian desert, the peaceful Portuguese, French, German, and Polish Jews—they all look alike. I have had the opportunity of examining closely one of the last kind. His features and profile clearly betrayed his origin. His eyes especially were unforgettable. This denizen of the north, whose immediate ancestors had lived, for many generations, in the snow, seemed to have been just tanned by the rays of the Syrian sun. The Semitic face looks exactly the same, in its main characteristics, as it appears on the Egyptian paintings of three or four thousand years ago, and more; and we find it also, in an equally striking and recognizable form, under the most varied and disparate conditions of climate. The identity of descendant and ancestor does not stop at the features; it continues also in the shape of the limbs and the temperament. The German Jews are usually smaller and more slender in build than the men of European race among whom they have lived for centuries. Further, the marriageable age is much earlier among them than among their fellow-countrymen of another race.[63]

This, by the way, is an assertion diametrically opposed to the opinion of Prichard, who in his zeal for proving the unity of the species, tries to show that the age of puberty, for the two sexes, is the same everywhere and in all races.[64] The reasons which he advances are drawn from the Old Testament in the case of the Jews, and, in the case of the Arabs, from the religious law of the Koran, by which the age of marriage is fixed, for girls, at fifteen, and even (in the opinion of Abu-Hanifah) at eighteen.

These two arguments seem very questionable. In the first place, the Biblical evidence is not admissible on this point, as it often includes facts that contradict the ordinary course of nature. Sarah, for example, was brought to bed of a child in extreme old age, when Abraham himself had reached a hundred years;[65] to such an event ordinary reasoning cannot apply. Secondly, as to the views and ordinances of the Mohammedan law, I may say that the Koran did not intend merely to make sure of the physical fitness of the woman before authorizing the marriage. It wished her also to be far enough advanced in education and intelligence to be able to understand the serious duties of her new position. This is shown by the pains taken by the prophet to prescribe that the girl's religious instruction shall be continued to the time of her marriage. It is easy to see why, from this point of view, the day should have been put off as long as possible and why the law-giver thought it so important to develop the reasoning

---

[63] Müller, *Handbuch der Physiologie des Menschen,* vol. ii, p. 639.

[64] Prichard, "Natural History of Man," 2nd edition, pp. 484 *et sqq.*

[65] Genesis xxi, 5.

powers, instead of being as hasty in his ordinances as nature is in hers. This is not all. Against the serious evidence brought forward by Prichard, there are some conclusive arguments, though of a lighter nature, that decide the question in favor of my view.

The poets, in their stories of love, are concerned merely with showing their heroines in the flower of their beauty, without thinking of their moral development; and the Oriental poets have always made their girl-lovers younger than the age prescribed by the Koran. Zuleika and Leila are certainly not yet fourteen. In India, the difference is still more marked. Sakuntala would be a mere child in Europe. The best age of love for an Indian girl is from nine to twelve years. It is a very general opinion, long accepted and established among the Indian, Persian, and Arab races, that the spring of life, for a woman, flowers at an age that we should call a little precocious. Our own writers have for long followed the lead, in this matter, of their Roman models. These, like their Greek teachers, regarded fifteen as the best age. Since our literature has been influenced by Northern ideas,[66] we have seen in our novels nothing but girls of eighteen, or even older.

Returning now to more serious arguments, we find them equally abundant. In addition to what I have said about the German Jews, it may be mentioned that in many parts of Switzerland the sexual development of the people is so slow that, in the case of the men, it is not

---

[66] We must make an exception in the case of Shakespeare, who is painting a picture of Italy. Thus in *Romeo and Juliet* Capulet says:

> "My child is yet a stranger in the world,
> She hath not seen the change of fourteen years;
> Let two more summers wither in their pride
> Ere we may think her ripe to be a bride."

To which Paris answers:

> "Younger than she are happy mothers made."

always complete at twenty. The Bohemians, or Zingaris, yield another set of results, which are easily verified. They show the same early development as the Hindus, who are akin to them; and under the most inclement skies, in Russia and in Moldavia, they still keep the expression and shape of the face and the physical proportions, as well as the ideas and customs, of the pariahs.[67]

I do not, however, mean to oppose Prichard on every point. One of his conclusions I gratefully adopt, namely that "difference of climate occasions very little, if any, important diversity as to the periods of life and the physical changes to which the human constitution is subject."[68] This remark is very true, and I would not dream of contesting it. I merely add that it seems to contradict to some slight extent the principles otherwise upheld by the learned American physiologist and antiquary.

The reader will not fail to see that the question on which the argument here turns is that of the permanence of types. If we have shown that the human races are each, as it were, shut up in their own individuality, and can only issue from it by a mixture of blood, the Unitarian theory will find itself very hard-pressed. It will have to recognize that, if the types are

---

[67] According to Krapff, a Protestant missionary in East Africa, the Wanikas marry at twelve, boys and girls alike (*Zeitschrift der Deutschen Morgenländischen Gesellschaft,* vol. iii, p. 317). In Paraguay the Jesuits introduced the custom, which still holds among their disciples, of marrying the boys at thirteen and the girls at ten. Widows of eleven and twelve are to be seen in this country (A. d'Orbigny, *L'Homme américain,* vol. i, p. 40). In South Brazil the women marry at ten or eleven. Menstruation both appears and ceases at an early age (Martius and Spix, *Reise in Brasilien* vol. i, p. 382). Such quotations might be infinitely extended; I will only cite one more. In the novel of Yo-kiao-Li the Chinese heroine is sixteen years old, and her father is in despair that at such an age she is not yet married !

[68] Prichard, p. 486.

thus absolutely fixed, hereditary, and *permanent,* in spite of climate and lapse of time, mankind is no less completely and definitely split into separate parts, than it would be if specific differences were due to a real divergence of origin.

It now becomes an easy matter for us to maintain this important conclusion, which we have seen to be amply supported, in the case of the Arabs, by the evidence of Egyptian sculpture, and also by the observation of Jews and gypsies. At the same time there is no reason for rejecting the valuable help given by the paintings in the temples and underground chambers in the valley of the Nile, which equally show the permanence of the Negro type, with its woolly hair, prognathous head, and thick lips. The recent discovery of the bas-reliefs at Khorsabad confirm what was already known from the sculptured tombs of Persepolis, and themselves prove, with absolute certainty, that the Assyrians are physiologically identical with the peoples who occupy their territory at the present day.

If we had a similar body of evidence with regard to other races still living, the result would be the same. The fact of the permanence of types would merely be more fully demonstrated. It is enough however to have established it in all the cases where observation was possible. It is now for those who disagree to propose objections.

They have no means of doing so, and their line of defense shows them either contradicting themselves from the start, or making some assertion quite contrary to the obvious facts. For example, they say that the Jewish type has changed with the climate, whereas the facts show the opposite. They base their argument on the existence in Germany of many fair-haired Jews with blue eyes.[69] For this to have any value from the Unitarian point of view, climate would have to be regarded as the sole, or at any rate the chief, cause of the phenomenon; whereas the Unitarians themselves admit that the color of the skin, eyes, and hair in no way depends either on geographical situation or on the influence of cold or heat.[70] They rightly mention the presence of blue eyes and fair hair among the Cingalese;[71] they even notice a considerable variation from light brown to black. Again, they admit that the Samoyedes and Tungusians, although living on the borders of the Arctic Ocean, are very swarthy.[72] Thus the climate counts for nothing so far as the coloring of the skin, hair, and eyes is concerned. We must regard them either as having no significance at all, or as vitally bound up with race. We know, for example, that red hair is not, and never has been, rare in the East; and so no one need be surprised to find it today in some German Jews. Such a fact has no influence, one way or the other, on the theory of the permanence of types.

The Unitarians are no more fortunate when they call in history to help them. They give only two instances to

---

[69] It has been since discovered that this fairness, in certain Jews, is due to a mixture of Tartar blood; in the 9th century a tribe of Khazars went over to Judaism and intermarried with the German-Polish Jews (Kutschera, *Die Chasayen*).—Tr.

[70] *Edinburgh Review,* "Ethnology or the Science of Races," October 1848, pp. 444-8: "There is probably no evidence of original diversity of race which is so generally relied upon as that derived from the *color of the skin and the character of the hair* ... but it will not, we think, stand the test of a serious examination. ...

[71] *Ibid.*, p. 453: "The Cingalese are described by Dr. Davy as varying in color from light brown to black. The prevalent hue of their hair and eyes is black, but hazel eyes and brown hair are not very uncommon; grey eyes and red hair are occasionally seen, though rarely, and sometimes the light blue or red eye and flaxen hair of the Albino."

[72] *Edinburgh Review,* "The Samoyedes, Tungusians, and others living on the borders of the Icy Sea have a dirty brown or swarthy complexion."

prove their theory—the Turks and the Magyars. The Asiatic origin of the former is taken as self-evident, as well as their close relation to the Finnish stocks of the Ostiaks and the Laplanders. Hence they had in primitive times the yellow face, prominent cheekbones, and short stature of the Mongols. Having settled this point, our Unitarian turns to their descendants of today; and finding them of a European type, with long thick beards, eyes almond-shaped, but no longer slanting, he concludes triumphantly, from this utter transformation of the Turks, that there is no permanence in race.[73] "Some people," he says in effect, "have certainly supposed in them a mixture of Greek, Georgian, and Circassian blood. But this mixture has been only partial. Not all Turks have been rich enough to buy wives from the Caucasus; not all have had harems filled with white slaves. On the other hand, the hatred felt by the Greeks towards their conquerors, and religious antipathy in general, have been unfavorable to such alliances; though the two peoples live together, they are just as much separated in spirit at the present time as on the first day of the conquest."[74]

These reasons are more specious than solid. We can only admit provisionally the Finnish origin of the Turkish race. Up to now, it has been supported only by a single argument, the affinity of language. I will show later how the argument from language, when taken alone, is peculiarly open to doubt and criticism. Assuming however that the ancestors of the Turkish people belonged to the yellow race, we can easily show that they had excellent reasons for keeping themselves apart from it.

---

[73] *Ibid.*, p. 439.

[74] *Ibid.*, p. 439 (summarized).

From the time when the first Turanian hordes descended from the north-east to that when they made themselves masters of the city of Constantine, a period comprising many centuries, great changes passed over the world; and the Western Turks suffered many vicissitudes of fortune. They were in turn victors and vanquished, slaves and masters; and very diverse were the peoples among whom they settled. According to the annalists,[75] the Oghuzes, their ancestors, came down from the Altai Mountains, and, in the time of Abraham lived in the immense steppes of Upper Asia that extend from the Katai to Lake Aral, from Siberia to Tibet. This is the ancient and mysterious domain that was still inhabited by many Germanic peoples.[76] It is a curious fact that as soon as Eastern writers begin to speak of the peoples of Turkestan, they praise their beauty of face and stature.[77] Hyperbolic expressions are the rule, in this connection; and as these writers had the beautiful types of the ancient world before their eyes, as a standard, it is not very likely that their enthusiasm should have been aroused by the sight of creatures so incontrovertibly ugly and repulsive as the ordinary specimens of the Mongolian race. Thus in spite of the linguistic argument,

---

[75] Hammer, *Geschichte des Osmanischen Reichs,* vol. i, p. 2.

[76] Ritter, *Erdkunde, Asien,* vol. i, pp. 433, 1115, etc.; Tassen, *Zeitschrift für die Kunde des Morgenlandes,* vol. ii, p. 65; Benfey, Ersch and Gruber's *Encyclopädie, Indien,* p. 12. A. von Humboldt calls this fact one of the most important discoveries of our time (*Asie centrale,* vol. ii, p. 639). From the point of view of historical science this is absolutely true.

[77] Nushirwan, who reigned in the first half of the sixth century A.D., married Sharuz, daughter of the Turkish Khan. She was the most beautiful woman of her time (Haneberg, *Zeitschrift für die Kunde des Morgenlandes,* vol. i, p. 187). The Shahnameh gives many facts of the same kind.

which may itself be wrongly used,[78] we might still make out a good case for our view. But we will concede the point, and admit that the Oghuzes of the Altai were really a Finnish people; and we will pass on to the Mohammedan period, when the Turkish tribes were established, under different names and varied circumstances, in Persia and Asia Minor.

The Osmanlis did not as yet exist, and their ancestors, the Seljukians, were already closely connected in blood with the races of Islam. The chiefs of this people, such as Gayaseddin-Keikosrev, in 1237, freely intermarried with Arab women. They did better still; for Aseddin, the mother of another line of Seljukian princes, was a Christian. In all countries the chiefs watch more jealously than the common people over the purity of their race; and when a chief showed himself so free from prejudice, it is at least permissible to assume that his subjects were not more scrupulous. As the continual raids of the Seljukians offered them every opportunity to seize slaves throughout the vast territory which they overran, there is no doubt that, from the thirteenth century, the ancient Oghuz stock, with which the Seljukians of Rûm claimed a distant kinship, was permeated to a great extent with Semitic blood.

---

[78] Just as the Scythians, a Mongolian race, had adopted an Aryan tongue, so there would be nothing surprising in the view that the Oghouzes were an Aryan race, although they spoke a Finnish dialect. This theory is curiously supported by a naive phrase of the traveller Rubruquis, who was sent by St. Louis to the ruler of the Mongols. "I was struck," says the good monk, "by the likeness borne by this prince to the late M. Jean de Beaumont, who was equally ruddy and fresh-looking." Alexander von Humboldt, interested, as he well might be, by such a remark, adds with no less good sense, "This point of physiognomy is especially worth noting if we remember that the family of Tchingiz was probably Turkish, and not Mongolian." He confirms his conclusion by adding that "the absence of Mongolian characteristics strikes us also in the portraits which we have of the descendants of Baber, the rulers of India" (*Asie centrale,* vol. i, p. 248 *and note*).

From this branch sprang Osman, the son of Ortoghrul and father of the Osmanlis. The families that collected round his tent were not very numerous. His army was no more than a robber-band; and if the early successors of this nomad Romulus were able to increase it, they did so merely by following the practice of the founder of Rome, and opening their tents to anyone who wished to enter.

It may be assumed that the fall of the Seljukian Empire helped to send recruits of their own race to the Osmanlis. It is clear that this race had undergone considerable change; besides, even these new resources were not enough, for from this time the Turks began to make systematic slave-raids, with the express object of increasing their own population. At the beginning of the fourteenth century, Urkan, at the instance of Khalil Chendereli the Black, founded the Guard of Janissaries. At first these were only a thousand strong. But under Mohammed IV the new guard numbered 140,000; and as up to this time the Turks had been careful to fill up the ranks only with Christian children taken from Poland, Germany, and Italy, or from European Turkey itself, and then converted to Islam, there were in four centuries at least 5000 heads of families who infused European blood into the veins of the Turkish nation.

The racial admixture did not end here. The main object of the piracy practiced on such a large scale throughout the Mediterranean was to fill up the harems. Further (a still more conclusive fact) there was no battle, whether lost or won, that did not increase the number of the Faithful. A considerable number of the males changed their religion, and counted henceforth as Turks. Again, the country surrounding the field of battle was overrun by the troops and yielded them all the women they could seize. The plunder was often so abundant that they had difficulty in disposing of it; the most beautiful girl was bartered for a jack-boot.[79] When we consider this in connection with the population of Asiatic and European Turkey, which has, as we know, never exceeded twelve millions, we see clearly that the arguments for or against the permanence of racial type find no support whatever in the history of such a mixed people as the Turks. This is so self-evident, that when we notice, as we often do, some characteristic features of the yellow race in an Osmanli, we cannot attribute this directly to his Finnish origin; it is simply the effect of Slav or Tartar blood, exhibiting, at second hand, the foreign elements it had itself absorbed.

Having finished my observations on the ethnology of the Ottomans, I pass to the Magyars.

The Unitarian theory is backed by such arguments as the following: "The Magyars are of Finnish origin, and allied to the Laplanders, Samoyedes, and Eskimos. These are all people of low stature, with wide faces and prominent cheek-bones, yellowish or dirty brown in color. The Magyars, however, are tall and well set up; their limbs are long, supple and vigorous, their features are of marked beauty, and resemble those of the white nations. The Finns have always been weak, unintelligent, and oppressed. The Magyars take a high place among the conquerors of the world. They have enslaved others, but have never been slaves themselves. Thus, since the Magyars are Finns, and are so different, physically and

---

[79] Hammer, *op. cit.,* vol. i, p. 448: "The battle against the Hungarians was hotly contested and the booty considerable. So many boys and girls were seized that the most beautiful female slave was exchanged for a jackboot, and Ashik-Pacha-Zadeh, the historian, who himself took part in the battle and the plunder, could not sell five boy-slaves at Skopi for more than 500 piastres."

morally, from all the other branches of their primitive stock, they must have changed enormously."[80]

If such a change had really taken place, it would be so extraordinary as to defy all explanation, even by the Unitarians, however great the modifications that may be assumed in these particular types; for the transformation-scene would have taken place between the end of the ninth century and the present day, that is, in about 800 years. Further, we know that in this period St. Stephen's fellow countrymen have not intermarried to any great extent with the nations among whom they live. Happily for common sense, there is no need for surprise, as the argument, though otherwise perfect, makes one vital mistake—the Hungarians are certainly not Finns.

In a well-written article, A. de Gerando[81] has exploded the theories of Schlotzer and his followers. By weighty arguments drawn from Greek and Arab historians and Hungarian annalists, by facts and dates that defy criticism, he has proved the kinship of the Transylvanian tribe of the Siculi with the Huns, and the identity in primitive times of the former with the last invaders of Pannonia. Thus the Magyars are Huns.

Here we shall no doubt be met by a further objection, namely that though this argument may point to a different origin for the Magyars, it connects them just as intimately as the other with the yellow race. This is an error. The name "Huns" may denote a nation, but it is also, historically speaking, a collective word. The mass of tribes to which it refers is not homogeneous. Among

---

[80] "Ethnology," etc., p. 439: "The Hungarian nobility ... is proved by historical and philological evidence to have been a branch of the great Northern Asiatic stock, closely allied in blood to the stupid and feeble Ostiaks and the untamable Laplanders."

[81] *Essai historique sur l'origine des Hongrois* (Paris, 1844).

the crowd of peoples enrolled under the banner of Attila's ancestors, certain bands, known as the "White Huns," have always been distinguished. In these the Germanic element predominated.[82]

Contact with the yellow races had certainly affected the purity of their blood. There is no mystery about this; the fact is betrayed at once by the rather angular and bony features of the Magyar. The language is very closely related to some Turkish dialects. Thus the Magyars are White Huns, though they have been wrongly made out to be a yellow race, a confusion caused by their intermarriages in the past (whether voluntary or otherwise) with Mongolians. They are really, as we have shown, cross-breeds with a Germanic basis. The roots and general vocabulary of their language are quite different from those of the Germanic family; but exactly the same was the case with the Scythians, a yellow race speaking an Aryan dialect,[83] and with the Scandinavians of Neustria, who were, after some years of conquest, led to adopt the Celto-Latin dialect of their subjects.[84] Nothing warrants the belief that lapse of time, difference of climate, or change of customs should have

---

[82] The current opinions about the peoples of Central Asia will, it seems, have to be greatly modified. It can no longer be denied that the blood of the yellow races has been crossed more or less considerably by a white strain. This fact was not suspected before, but it throws a doubt on all the ancient notions on the subject, which must now be revised in the light of it. Alexander von Humboldt makes a very important observation with regard to the Kirghiz-Kasaks, who are mentioned by Menander of Byzantium and Constantine Porphyrogenetes. He rightly shows that when the former speaks of a Kirghiz (Χερχις) concubine given by the Turkish Shagan Dithubul to Zemarch, the envoy of the Emperor Justin II, in 569, he is referring to a girl of mixed blood. She corresponds exactly to the beautiful Turkish girls who are so praised by the Persians, and who were as little Mongolian in type as this Kirghiz *(Asie centrale,* vol. i, p. 237, etc.; vol. ii, pp. 130-31).

[83] Schaffarik, *Slavische Altertümer,* vol. i, p. 279 *et pass.*

[84] Aug. Thierry, *Histoire de la Conquête d'Angleterre,* vol. i, p. 155.

turned a Laplander or an Ostiak, a Tungusian or a Permian, into a St. Stephen. I conclude, from this refutation of the only arguments brought forward by the Unitarians, that the permanence of racial types is beyond dispute; it is so strong and indestructible that the most complete change of environment has no power to overthrow it, so long as no crossing takes place.

Whatever side, therefore, one may take in the controversy as to the unity or multiplicity of origin possessed by the human species, it is certain that the different families are today absolutely separate; for there is no external influence that could cause any resemblance between them or force them into a homogeneous mass.

The existing races constitute separate branches of one or many primitive stocks. These stocks have now vanished. They are not known in historical times at all, and we cannot form even the most general idea of their qualities. They differed from each other in the shape and proportion of the limbs, the structure of the skull, the internal conformation of the body, the nature of the capillary system, the color of the skin, and the like; and they never succeeded in losing their characteristic features except under the powerful influence of the crossing of blood.

This permanence of racial qualities is quite sufficient to generate the radical unlikeness and inequality that exists between the different branches, to raise them to the dignity of natural laws, and to justify the same distinctions being drawn with regard to the physiological life of nations, as I shall show, later, to be applicable to their moral life.

Owing to my respect for a scientific authority which I cannot overthrow, and, still more, for a religious interpretation that I could not venture to attack, I must resign myself to leaving on one side the grave doubts that are always oppressing me as to the question of original unity; and I will now try to discover as far as I can, with the resources that are still left to me, the probable causes of these ultimate physiological differences.

As no one will venture to deny, there broods over this grave question a mysterious darkness, big with causes that are at the same time physical and supernatural. In the inmost recesses of the obscurity that shrouds the problem, reign the causes which have their ultimate home in the mind of God; the human spirit feels their presence without divining their nature, and shrinks back in awful reverence. It is probable that the earthly agents to whom we look for the key of the secret are themselves but instruments and petty springs in the great machine. The origins of all things, of all events and movements, are not infinitely small, as we are often pleased to say, but on the contrary so vast, so immeasurable by the poor foot-rule of man's intelligence, that while we may perhaps have some vague suspicion of their existence, we can never hope to lay hands on them or attain to any sure discovery of their nature. Just as in an iron chain that is meant to lift up a great weight it frequently happens that the link nearest the object is the smallest, so the proximate cause may often seem insignificant; and if we merely consider it in isolation, we tend to forget the long series that has gone before. This alone gives it meaning, but this, in all its strength and might, derives from something that human eye has never seen. We must not therefore, like the fool in the old adage, wonder at the power of the roseleaf to make the water overflow; we should rather think that the reason of the accident lay in the depths of the water that filled the vessel to overflowing. Let us yield all respect to the primal and generating causes, that dwell far off in heaven, and without which nothing would exist; conscious of the Divine power that moves them, they rightly claim a part of the veneration we pay to their Infinite Creator. But let us abstain from speaking of them here. It is not fitting for us to leave the human sphere, where alone we may hope to meet with certainty. All we can do is to seize the chain, if not by the last small link, at any rate by that part of it which we can see and touch, without trying to catch at what is beyond our reach—a task too difficult for mortal man. There is no irreverence in saying this; on the contrary, it expresses the sincere conviction of a weakness that is insurmountable.

Man is a newcomer in this world. Geology— proceeding merely by induction, but attacking its problems in a marvelously systematic way—asserts that man is absent from all the oldest strata of the earth's surface. There is no trace of him among the fossils. When our ancestors appeared for the first time in an already aged world, God, according to Scripture, told them that they would be its masters and have dominion over everything on earth. This promise was given not so much to them as to their descendants; for these first feeble creatures seem to have been provided with very few means, not merely of conquering the whole of nature, but even of resisting its weakest attacks.[85] The ethereal heavens had seen, in former epochs, beings far more imposing than man rise from the muddy earth and the deep waters. Most of these gigantic races had, no doubt, disappeared in the terrible revolutions in which the inorganic world had shown a power so immeasurably beyond that possessed by animate nature. A great number, however, of these monstrous creatures were still living. Every region was haunted by herds of elephants

---

[85] Lyell, "Principles of Geology," vol. i, p. 178.

and rhinoceroses, and even the mastodon has left traces of its existence in American tradition.[86]

These last remnants of the monsters of an earlier day were more than enough to impress the first members of our species with an uneasy feeling of their own inferiority, and a very modest view of their problematic royalty. It was not merely the animals from whom they had to wrest their disputed empire. These could in the last resort be fought, by craft if not by force, and in default of conquest could be avoided by flight. The case was quite different with Nature, that immense Nature that surrounded the primitive families on all sides, held them in a close grip, and made them feel in every nerve her awful power.[87] The cosmic causes of the ancient cataclysms, although feebler, were always at work. Partial upheavals still disturbed the relative positions of earth and ocean. Sometimes the level of the sea rose and swallowed up vast stretches of coast; sometimes a terrible volcanic eruption would vomit from the depths of the waters some mountainous mass, to become part of a continent. The world was still in travail, and Jehovah had not calmed it by "seeing that it was good."

This general lack of equilibrium necessarily reacted on atmospheric conditions. The strife of earth, fire, and water brought with it complete and rapid changes of heat, cold, dryness, and humidity. The exhalations from the ground, still shaken with earthquake, had an irresistible influence on living creatures. The causes that enveloped the globe with the breath of battle and suffering could not but increase the pressure brought to bear by nature on man. Differences of climate and environment acted on our first parents far more

---

[86] Link, *Die Urwelt und das Altertum,* vol. i, p. 84.

[87] Link, *op. cit.*, vol. i, p. 91.

effectively than today. Cuvier, in his "Treatise on the revolutions of the globe," says that the inorganic forces of the present day would be quite incapable of causing convulsions and upheavals, or new arrangements of the earth's surface, such as those to which geology bears witness. The changes that were wrought in the past on her own body by the awful might of nature would be impossible today; she had a similar power over the human race, but has it no longer. Her omnipotence has been so lost, or at least so weakened and whittled away, that in a period of years covering roughly half the life of our species on the earth, she has brought about no change of any importance, much less one that can be compared to that by which the different races were forever marked off from each other.[88]

Two points are certain: first that the main differences between the branches of our race were fixed in the earliest epoch of our terrestrial life; secondly, that in order to imagine a period when these physiological cleavages could have been brought about, we must go back to the time when the influence of natural causes was far more active than it is now, under the normal and healthy conditions. Such a time could be none other than that immediately after the creation, when the earth was still shaken by its recent catastrophes and without any defense against the fearful effects of their last death-throes.

---

[88] Cuvier, *op. cit.* Compare also, on this point, the opinion of Alexander von Humboldt: "In the epochs preceding the existence of the human race the action of the forces in the interior of the globe must, as the earth's crust increased in thickness, have modified the temperature of the air and made the whole earth habitable by the products which we now regard as exclusively tropical. Afterwards the spatial relation of our planet to the central body (the sun) began, by means of radiation and cooling down, to be almost the sole agent in determining the climate at different latitudes. It was also in these primitive times that the elastic fluids, or volcanic forces, inside the earth, more powerful than they are today, made their way through the oxidized and imperfectly solidified crust of our planet" *(Asie centrale,* vol. i, p. 47).

Assuming the Unitarian theory, we cannot give any later date for the separation of types.

No argument can be based on the accidental deviations from the normal which are sometimes found in certain individual instances, and which, if transmitted, would certainly give rise to important varieties. Without including such deformities as a hump-back, some curious facts have been collected which seem, at first sight, to be of value in explaining the diversity of races. To cite only one instance, Prichard[89] quotes Baker's account of a man whose whole body, with the exception of his face, was covered with a sort of dark shell, resembling a large collection of warts, very hard and callous, and insensible to pain; when cut, it did not bleed. At different periods this curious covering, after reaching a thickness of three-quarters of an inch, would become detached, and fall off; it was then replaced by another, similar in all respects. Four sons were born to him, all resembling their father. One survived; but Baker, who saw him in infancy, does not say whether he reached manhood. He merely infers that since the father has produced such offspring, "a race of people may be propagated by this man, having such rugged coats and coverings as himself; and if this should ever happen, and the accidental original be forgotten, it is not improbable they might be deemed a different species of mankind."

Such a conclusion is possible. Individuals, however, who are so different as these from the species in general, do not transmit their characteristics. Their posterity either returns to the regular path or is soon extinguished. All things that deviate from the natural and normal order of the world can only borrow life for a time; they are not fitted to keep it. Otherwise, a succession of strange accidents would, long before this,

---

[89] Second edition, pp. 92-4. The man was born in 1727.

have set mankind on a road far removed from the physiological conditions which have obtained, without change, throughout the ages. We must conclude that impermanence is one of the essential and basic features of these anomalies. We could not include in such a category the woolly hair and black skin of the negro, or the yellow color, wide face, and slanting eyes of the Chinaman. These are all permanent characteristics; they are in no way abnormal, and so cannot come from an accidental deviation.

We will now give a summary of the present chapter.

In face of the difficulties offered by the most liberal interpretation of the Biblical text, and the objection founded on the law regulating the generation of hybrids, it is impossible to pronounce categorically in favor of a multiplicity of origin for the human species.

We must therefore be content to assign a lower cause to those clear-cut varieties of which the main quality is undoubtedly their permanence, a permanence that can only be lost by a crossing of blood. We can identify this cause with the amount of climatic energy possessed by the earth at a time when the human race had just appeared on its surface. There is no doubt that the forces that inorganic nature could bring into play were far greater then than anything we have known since, and under their pressure racial modifications were accomplished which would now be impossible. Probably, too, the creatures exposed to these tremendous forces were more liable to be affected by them than existing types would be. Man, in his earliest stages, assumed many unstable forms; he did not perhaps belong, in any definite manner, to the white, red, or yellow variety. The deviations that transformed the primitive characteristics of the species into the types established today were probably much smaller than those that would now be required for the black race, for example, to become assimilated to the white, or the yellow to the black. On this hypothesis, we should have to regard Adamite man as equally different from all the existing human groups; these would have radiated all around him, the distance between him and any group being double that between one group and another. How much of the primitive type would the peoples of the different races have subsequently retained? Merely the most general characteristics of our species, the vague resemblances of shape common to the most distant groups, and the possibility of expressing their wants by articulate sounds —but nothing more. The remaining features peculiar to primitive man would have been completely lost, by the black as well as the non-black races; and although we are all originally descended from him, we should have owed to outside influences everything that gave us our distinctive and special character. Henceforth the human races, the product of cosmic forces as well as of the primitive Adamic stock, would be very slightly, if at all, related to each other. The power of giving birth to fertile hybrids would certainly be a perpetual proof of original connection; but it would be the only one. As soon as the primal differences of environment had given each group its isolated character, as a possession forever—its shape, features, and color—from that moment the link of primal unity would have been suddenly snapped; the unity, so far as influence on racial development went, would be actually sterile. The strict and unassailable permanence of form and feature to which the earliest historical documents bear witness would be the charter and sign-manual of the eternal separation of races.

CHAPTER XII

HOW THE RACES WERE PHYSIOLOGICALLY SEPARATED, AND THE DIFFERENT VARIETIES FORMED BY THEIR INTERMIXTURE. THEY ARE UNEQUAL IN STRENGTH AND BEAUTY

The question of cosmic influences is one that ought to be fully cleared up, as I am confining myself to arguments based on it. The first problem with which I have to deal is the following: — "How could men, whose common origin implies a single starting-point, have been exposed to such a diversity of influences from without?" After the first separation of races, the groups were already numerous enough to be found under totally different conditions of climate; how then, considering the immense difficulties they had to contend against, the vast forests and marshy plains they had to cross, the sandy or snowy deserts, the rivers, lakes, and oceans— how, with all these obstacles, did they manage to cover distances which civilized man today, with all his developed power, can only surmount with great toil and trouble? To answer these objections, we must try to discover where the human species had its original home.

A very ancient idea, adopted also by some great modern minds, such as Cuvier, is that the different mountain-systems must have served as the point of departure for certain races. According to this theory, the white races, and even certain African varieties whose skull is shaped like our own, had their first settlement in the Caucasus. The yellow race came down from the ice-bound heights of the Altai. Again, the tribes of prognathous negroes built their first huts on the southern slopes of Mount Atlas, and made this the starting-point of their first migrations. Thus, the frightful places of the earth, difficult of access and full of gloomy horror—torrents, caverns, icy mountains, eternal snows, and impassable abysses—were actually more familiar to primitive ages than any others; while all the terrors of the unknown lurked, for our first ancestors, in the uncovered plains, on the banks of the great rivers, on the coasts of the lakes and seas.

The chief motive urging the ancient philosophers to put forward this theory, and the moderns to revive it, seems to have been the idea that, in order to pass successfully through the great physical crises of the world, mankind must have collected on the mountain heights, where the floods and inundations could not reach them. This large and general interpretation of the tradition of Ararat may suit perhaps the later epochs, when the children of men had covered the face of the earth; but it is quite inapplicable to the time of relative calm that marked their first appearance. It is also contrary to all theories as to the unity of the species. Again, mountains from the remotest times have been the object of profound terror and religious awe. On them has been set, by all mythologies, the abode of the gods. It was on the snowy peak of Olympus, it was on Mount Meru that the Greeks and the Brahmans imagined their divine synods. It was on the summit of the Caucasus that Prometheus suffered the mysterious punishment of his still more mysterious crime. If men had begun by making their home in the remote heights, it is not likely that their imagination would have caused them to raise these to the height of heaven itself. We have a scant respect for what we have seen and known and trodden underfoot. There would have been no divinities but those of the waters and the plains. Hence I incline to the opposite belief, that the flat and uncovered regions witnessed the first steps of man. This is, by the way, the Biblical notion.[90] After the first settlements were made in these parts, the difficulties of accounting for migrations are sensibly diminished; for flat regions are generally cut by rivers and reach down to the sea, and so there would have been no need to undertake the difficult task of crossing forests, deserts, and great marshes.

There are two kinds of migrations, the voluntary and the unexpected. The former are out of the question in very early times. The latter are more possible, and more probable too, among shiftless and unprepared savages than among civilized nations. A family huddled together on a drifting raft, a few unfortunate people surprised by an inrush of the sea, clinging to trunks of trees, and caught up by the currents—these are enough to account for a transplantation over long distances. The weaker man is, the more is he the sport of inorganic forces. The less experience he has, the more slavishly does he respond to accidents which he can neither foresee nor avoid. There are striking examples of the ease with which men can be carried, in spite of themselves, over considerable distances. Thus, we hear that in 1696 two large canoes from Ancorso, containing about thirty savages, men and women, were caught in a storm, and after drifting aimlessly some time, finally arrived at Samal, one of the Philippine Islands, three hundred leagues from their starting-point. Again, four natives of Ulea were carried out to sea in a canoe by a sudden squall. They drifted about for eight months, and reached at last one of the Radack Islands, at the eastern end of the Caroline Archipelago, after an involuntary voyage of 550 leagues. These unfortunate men lived solely on fish, and carefully collected every drop of rain they could. When rain failed them, they dived into the depths of

---

[90] *See* Genesis ii, 8, 10, 15.

the sea and drank the water there, which, they say, is less salt. Naturally, when they reached Radack, the travellers were in a deplorable state; but they soon rallied, and were eventually restored to health.[91]

These two examples are a sufficient witness for the rapid diffusion of human groups in very different regions, and under the most varied local conditions. If further proofs were required, we might mention the ease with which insects, plants, and testaceans are carried all over the world; it is, of course, unnecessary to show that what happens to such things may, a fortiori, happen more easily to man.[92] The land-testaceans are thrown into the sea by the destruction of the cliffs, and are then carried to distant shores by means of currents. Zoophytes attach themselves to the shells of mollusks or let their tentacles float on the surface of the sea, and so are driven along by the wind to form distant colonies. The very trees of unknown species, the very sculptured planks, the last of a long line, which were cast up on the Canaries in the fifteenth century, and by providing a text for the meditations of Christopher Columbus paved the way for the discovery of the New World—even these probably carried on their surface the eggs of insects; and these eggs were hatched, by the heat engendered by new sap, far from their place of origin and the land where lived the others of their kind.

Thus there is nothing against the notion that the first human families might soon have been separated,

[91] Lyell, "Principles of Geology," vol. ii, p. 119.

[92] Alexander von Humboldt does not think that this hypothesis can apply to the migration of plants. "What we know," he says, "of the deleterious action exerted by sea-water, during a voyage of 500 or 600 leagues, over the reproductive power of most grains, does not favor the theory of the migration of vegetables by means of ocean currents. Such a theory is too general and comprehensive " (*Examen critique de l'histoire de la géographie du nouveau continent,* vol. ii, p. 78).

and lived under very different conditions of climate, in regions far apart from each other. But it is not necessary, even under present circumstances, for the places to be far apart, in order to ensure a variation in the temperature, and in the local conditions resulting from it. In mountainous countries like Switzerland, the distance of a few miles makes such a difference in the soil and atmosphere, that we find the flora of Lapland and Southern Italy practically side by side; similarly in Isola Madre, on Lago Maggiore, oranges, great cacti, and dwarf palms grow in the open, in full view of the Simplon. We need not confine ourselves to mountains; the temperature of Normandy is lower than that of Jersey, while in the narrow triangle formed by the Western coasts of France, the vegetation is of the most varied character.[93]

The contrasts must have been tremendous, even over the smallest areas, in the days that followed the first appearance of our species on the globe. The selfsame

---

[93] Alexander von Humboldt gives the law determining these facts in the following passage (*Asie centrale,* vol. iii, p. 23): "The foundation of the science of climatology is the accurate knowledge of the inequalities of a continent's surface (hypsometry). Without this knowledge we are apt to attribute to elevation what is really the effect of other causes, acting, in low-lying regions, on a surface of which the curve is continuous with that of the sea, along the isothermic lines (i.e. lines along which the temperature is the same)." By calling attention to the multiplicity of influences acting on the temperature of any given geographical point, Von Humboldt shows how very different conditions of climate may exist in places that are quite near each other, independently of their height above sea-level. Thus in the north-east of Ireland, on the Glenarn coast, there is a region, on the same parallel of latitude as Konigsberg in Prussia, which produces myrtles growing in the open air quite as vigorously as in Portugal; this region is in striking contrast with those round it. "There are hardly any frosts in winter, and the heat in summer is not enough to ripen the grapes. ... The pools and small lakes of the Faroe Islands are not frozen over during the winter, in spite of the latitude (62°). ... In England, on the Devonshire coast, the myrtle, the camelia iaponica, the fuchsia coccinea, and the Boddleya globosa flourish in the open, unsheltered, throughout the winter. ... At Salcombe the winters are so mild that orange-trees have been seen, with fruit on them, sheltered by a wall and protected merely by screens" (pp. 147-48).

place might easily become the theater of vast atmospheric revolutions, when the sea retreated or advanced by the inundation or drying up of the neighboring regions; when mountains suddenly rose in enormous masses, or sank to the common level of the earth, so that the plains covered what once was their crests; and when tremors, that shook the axis of the earth, and by affecting its equilibrium and the inclination of the poles to the ecliptic, came to disturb the general economy of the planet.

We may now consider that we have met all the objections, that might be urged as to the difficulty of changing one's place and climate in the early ages of the world. There is no reason why some groups of the human family should not have gone far afield, while others were huddled together in a limited area and yet were exposed to very varied influences. It is thus that the secondary types, from which are descended the existing races, could have come into being. As to the type of man first created, the Adamite, we will leave him out of the argument altogether; for it is impossible to know anything of his specific character, or how far each of the later families has kept or lost its likeness to him. Our investigation will not take us further back than the races of the second stage.

I find these races naturally divided into three, and three only—the white, the black, and the yellow.[94] If I use a basis of division suggested by the color of the skin, it is not that I consider it either correct or happy, for the three categories of which I speak are not distinguished exactly by color, which is a very complex and variable

---

[94] I will explain in due course the reasons why I do not include the American Indian as a pure and primitive type. I have already given indications of my view. Here I merely subscribe to the opinion of Flourens, who also recognizes only three great subdivisions of the species—those of Europe, Asia, and Africa. The names call for criticism but the divisions axe in the main correct.

thing; I have already said that certain facts in the conformation of the skeleton are far more important. But in default of inventing new names—which I do not consider myself justified in doing—I must make my choice from the vocabulary already in use. The terms may not be very good, but they are at any rate less open to objection than any others, especially if they are carefully defined. I certainly prefer them to all the designations taken from geography or history, for these have thrown an already confused subject into further confusion. So I may say, once for all, that I understand by *white* men the members of those races which are also called Caucasian, Semitic, or Japhetic. By *black* men I mean the Hamites; by *yellow* the Altaic, Mongol, Finnish, and Tatar branches. These are the three primitive elements of mankind. There is no more reason to admit Blumenbach's twenty-eight varieties than Prichard's seven; for both these schemes include notorious hybrids. It is probable that none of the three original types was ever found in absolute simplicity. The great cosmic agents had not merely brought into being the three clear-cut varieties; they had also, in the course of their action, caused many sub-species to appear. These were distinguished by some peculiar features, quite apart from the general character which they had in common with the whole branch. Racial crossing was not necessary to create these specific modifications; they existed before any interbreeding took place at all. It would be fruitless to try to identify them today in the hybrid agglomeration that constitutes what we call the "white race." It would be equally impossible with regard to the yellow race. Perhaps the black type has to some extent kept itself pure; at any rate it has remained nearer its original form, and thus shows at first sight what, in the case of the other great human divisions, is not given by the testimony of our senses, but may be admitted on the strength of historical proof.

The negroes have always perpetuated the original forms of their race, such as the prognathous type with woolly hair, the Hindu type of the Kamaun and the Deccan, and the Pelagian of Polynesia. New varieties have certainly been created from their intermixture; this is the origin of what we may call the "tertiary types," which are seen in the white and yellow races, as well as the black.

Much has been made of a noteworthy fact, which is used today as a sure criterion for determining the racial purity of a nation. This fact is the resemblance of face, shape, and general constitution, including gesture and carriage. The further these resemblances go, the less mixture of blood is there supposed to be in the whole people. On the other hand, the more crossing there has been, the greater differences we shall find in the features, stature, walk, and general appearance of the individuals. The fact is incontestable, and valuable conclusions may be drawn from it; but the conclusions are a little different from those hitherto made.

The first series of observations by which the fact was discovered was carried out on the Polynesians. Now, these are far from being of pure race; they come from mixtures, in different proportions, of yellow and black. Hence the complete transmission of the type that we see today among the Polynesians shows, not the purity of the race, but simply that the more or less numerous elements of which it is composed have at last been fused in a full and homogeneous unity. Each man has the same blood in his veins as his neighbor, and so there is no reason why he should differ physically from him. Just as brothers and sisters are often much alike, as being produced from like elements, so, when two races have been so completely amalgamated that there is no group in the resulting people in which either race predominates, an artificial type is established, with a kind of factitious purity; and every new-born child bears its impress.

What I have defined as the "tertiary type" might in this way easily acquire the quality that is wrongly appropriated to a people of absolutely pure race—namely the likeness of the individual members to each other. This could be attained in a much shorter time at this stage, as the differences between two varieties of the same type are relatively slight. In a family, for example, where the father and mother belong to different nations, the children will be like one or the other, but there will be little chance of any real identity of physical characteristics between them. If, however, the parents are both from the same national stock, such an identity will be easily produced.

We must mention another law before going further. Crossing of blood does not merely imply the fusion of the two varieties, but also creates new characteristics, which henceforth furnish the most important standpoint from which to consider any particular sub-species. Examples will be given later; meanwhile I need hardly say that these new and original qualities cannot be completely developed unless there has previously been a perfect fusion of the parent-types; otherwise the tertiary race cannot be considered as really established. The larger the two nations are, the greater will naturally be the time required for their fusion. But until the process is complete, and a state of physiological identity brought about, no new sub-species will be possible, as there is no question of normal development from an original, though composite source, but merely of the confusion and disorder that are always engendered from the imperfect mixture of elements which are naturally foreign to each other.

Our actual knowledge of the life of these tertiary races is very slight. Only in the misty beginnings of human history can we catch a glimpse, in certain places, of the white race when it was still in this stage—a stage which seems to have been everywhere short-lived. The civilizing instincts of these chosen peoples were continually forcing them to mix their blood with that of others. As for the black and yellow types, they are mere savages in the tertiary stage, and have no history at all.[95]

To the tertiary races succeed others, which I will call "quaternary." The Polynesians, sprung from the mixture of black and yellow,[96] the mulattoes, a blend of white and black,—these are among the peoples belonging to the quaternary type. I need hardly say, once more, that the new type brings the characteristics peculiar to itself more or less into harmony with those which recall its two-fold descent.

When a quaternary race is again modified by the intervention of a new type, the resulting mixture has great difficulty in becoming stable; its elements are brought very slowly into harmony, and are combined in very irregular proportions. The original qualities of

---

[95] Carus gives his powerful support to the law I have laid down, namely that the civilizing races are especially prone to mix their blood. He points out the immense variety of elements composing the perfected human organism, as against the simplicity of the infinitesimal beings on the lowest step in the scale of creation. He deduces the following axiom: "Whenever there is an extreme likeness between the elements of an organic whole, its state cannot be regarded as the expression of a complete and final development, but is merely primitive and elementary " (*Über die ungleiche Befähigkeit dev verschiedenen Menschheitstämme für höhere geistige Entwickelung,* p. 4). In another place he says: "The greatest possible diversity (*i.e.* inequality) of the parts, together with the most complete unity of the whole, is clearly, in every sphere, the standard of the highest perfection of an organism." In the political world this is the state of a society where the governing classes are racially quite distinct from the masses, while being themselves carefully organized into a strict hierarchy.

[96] Flourens (*Eloge de Blumenbach,* p. xi) describes the Polynesian race as "a mixture of two others, the *Caucasian* and the Mongolian." *Caucasian* is probably a mere slip; he certainly meant *black*.

248

which it is composed are already weakened to a considerable extent, and become more and more neutralized. They tend to disappear in the confusion that has grown to be the main feature of the new product. The more this product reproduces itself and crosses its blood, the more the confusion increases. It reaches infinity, when the people is too numerous for any equilibrium to have a chance of being established— at any rate, not before long ages have passed. Such a people is merely an awful example of racial anarchy. In the individuals we find, here and there, a dominant feature reminding us in no uncertain way that blood from every source runs in their veins. One man will have the negro's hair, another the eyes of a Teuton, a third will have a Mongolian face, a fourth a Semitic figure; and yet all these will be akin! This is the state in which the great civilized nations are today; we may especially see proofs of it in their sea-ports, capitals, and colonies, where a fusion of blood is more easily brought about. In Paris, London, Cadiz, and Constantinople, we find traits recalling every branch of mankind, and that without going outside the circle of the walls, or considering any but the so-called "native population." The lower classes will give us examples of all kinds, from the prognathous head of the negro to the triangular face and slanting eyes of the Chinaman; for, especially since the Roman Empire, the most remote and divergent races have contributed to the blood of the inhabitants of our great cities. Commerce, peace, and war, the founding of colonies, the succession of invasions, have all helped in their turn to increase the disorder; and if one could trace, some way back, the genealogical tree of the first man he met, he would probably be surprised at the strange company of ancestors among whom he would find himself.[97]

We have shown that races differ physically from each other; we must now ask if they are also unequal in beauty and muscular strength. The answer cannot be long doubtful.

I have already observed that the human groups to which the European nations and their descendants belong are the most beautiful. One has only to compare the various types of men scattered over the earth's surface to be convinced of this. From the almost rudimentary face and structure of the Pelagian and the Pecheray to the tall and nobly proportioned figure of Charlemagne, the intelligent regularity of the features of Napoleon, and the imposing majesty that exhales from the royal countenance of Louis XIV, there is a series of gradations; the peoples who are not of white blood approach beauty, but do not attain it.

Those who are most akin to us come nearest to beauty; such are the degenerate Aryan stocks of India and Persia, and the Semitic peoples who are least infected by contact with the black race.[98] As these races recede from the white type, their features and limbs become incorrect in form; they acquire defects of proportion which, in the races that are completely foreign to us, end by producing an extreme ugliness.

---

[97] The physiological characteristics of the ancestors are reproduced in their descendants according to fixed rules. Thus we see in South America that though the children of a white man and a negress may have straight soft hair, yet the crisp woolly hair invariably appears in the second generation (A. d'Orbigny, *l'Homme américain,* vol. i, p. 143).

[98] It may be remarked that the happiest blend, from the point of view of beauty, is that made by the marriage of white and black. We need only put the striking charm of many mulatto, Creole, and quadroon women by the side of such mixtures of yellow and white as the Russians and Hungarians. The comparison is not to the advantage of the latter. It is no less certain that a beautiful Rajput is more ideally beautiful than the most perfect Slav.

This is the ancient heritage and indelible mark of the greater number of human groups. We can no longer subscribe to the doctrine (reproduced by Helvetius in his book on the "Human Intellect") which regards the idea of the beautiful as purely artificial and variable. All who still have scruples on that point should consult the admirable "Essay on the Beautiful" of the Piedmontese philosopher, Gioberti; and their doubts will be laid to rest. Nowhere is it better brought out that beauty is an absolute and necessary idea, admitting of no arbitrary application. I take my stand on the solid principles established by Gioberti, and have no hesitation in regarding the white race as superior to all others in beauty; these, again, differ among themselves in the degree in which they approach or recede from their model. Thus the human groups are unequal in beauty; and this inequality is rational, logical, permanent, and indestructible.

Is there also an inequality in physical strength? The American savages, like the Hindus, are certainly our inferiors in this respect, as are also the Australians. The negroes, too, have less muscular power;[99] and all these peoples are infinitely less able to bear fatigue. We must distinguish, however, between purely muscular strength, which merely needs to spend itself for a single instant of victory, and the power of keeping up a prolonged resistance. The latter is far more typical than the former, of which we may find examples even in notoriously feeble races. If we take the blow of the fist as the sole criterion of strength, we shall find, among very backward negro races, among the New Zealanders (who are usually

---

[99] *See* (among other authorities), for the American aborigine, Martius and Spix, *Reise in Brasilien,* vol. i, p. 259; for the negroes, Pruner, *Der Rieger, eine aphoristische Skizze aus der medizinischen Topographie von Cairo,* in the *Zeitschrift der Deutschen morgenlandischen Gesellschaft,* vol. i, p. 131; for the muscular superiority of the white race over all the others, Carus, *op. cit.,* p. 84.

of weak constitution), among Lascars and Malays, certain individuals who can deliver such a blow as well as any Englishman. But if we take the peoples as a whole, and judge them by the amount of labor that they can go through without flinching, we shall give the palm to those belonging to the white race.

The different groups within the white race itself are as unequal in strength as they are in beauty, though the difference is less marked. The Italians are more beautiful than the Germans or the Swiss, the French or the Spanish. Similarly, the English show a higher type of physical beauty than the Slav nations.

In strength of fist, the English are superior to all the other European races; while the French and Spanish have a greater power of resisting fatigue and privation, as well as the inclemency of extreme climates. The question is settled, so far as the French are concerned, by the terrible campaign in Russia. Nearly all the Germans and the northern troops, accustomed though they were to very low temperatures, sank down in the snow; while the French regiments, though they paid their awful tribute to the rigors of the retreat, were yet able to save most of their number. This superiority has been attributed to their better moral education and military spirit. But such an explanation is insufficient. The German officers, who perished by hundreds, had just as high a sense of honor and duty as our soldiers had; but this did not prevent them from going under. We may conclude that the French have certain physical qualities that are superior to those of the Germans, which allow them to brave with impunity the snows of Russia as well as the burning sands of Egypt.

CHAPTER XIII

THE HUMAN RACES ARE INTELLECTUALLY UNEQUAL; MANKIND IS NOT CAPABLE OF INFINITE PROGRESS

In order to appreciate the intellectual differences between races, we ought first to ascertain the degree of stupidity to which mankind can descend. We know already the highest point that it can reach, namely civilization.

Most scientific observers up to now have been very prone to make out the lowest types as worse than they really are.

Nearly all the early accounts of a savage tribe paint it in hideous colors, far more hideous than the reality. They give it so little power of reason and understanding, that it seems to be on a level with the monkey and below the elephant. It is true that we find the contrary opinion. If a captain is well received in an island, if he meets, as he believes, with a kind and hospitable welcome, and succeeds in making a few natives do a small amount of work with his sailors, then praises are showered on the happy people. They are declared to be fit for anything and capable of everything; and sometimes the enthusiasm bursts all bounds, and swears it has found among them some higher intelligences.

We must appeal from both judgments—harsh and favorable alike. The fact that certain Tahitians have helped to repair a whaler does not make their nation capable of civilization. Because a man of Tonga-Tabu shows goodwill to strangers, he is not necessarily open to ideas of progress. Similarly, we are not entitled to degrade a native of a hitherto unknown coast to the level of the brute, just because he receives his first visitors with a flight of arrows, or because he is found eating raw lizards and mud pies. Such a banquet does not certainly connote a very high intelligence or very cultivated manners. But even in the most hideous cannibal there is a spark of the divine fire, and to some extent the flame of understanding can always be kindled in him. There are no tribes so low that they do not pass some judgments, true or false, just or unjust, on the things around them; the mere existence of such judgments is enough to show that in every branch of mankind some ray of intelligence is kept alive. It is this that makes the most degraded savages accessible to the teachings of religion and distinguishes them in a special manner, of which they are themselves conscious, from even the most intelligent beasts.

Are however these moral possibilities, which lie at the back of every man's consciousness, capable of infinite extension? Do all men possess in an equal degree an unlimited power of intellectual development? In other words, has every human race the capacity for becoming equal to every other? The question is ultimately concerned with the infinite capacity for improvement possessed by the species as a whole, and with the equality of races. I deny both points.

The idea of an infinite progress is very seductive to many modern philosophers, and they support it by declaring that our civilization has many merits and advantages which our differently trained ancestors did not possess. They bring forward all the phenomena that distinguished our modern societies. I have spoken of these already; but I am glad to be able to go through them again.

We are told that our scientific opinions are truer than they were; that our manners are, as a rule, kindly, and our morals better than those of the Greeks and Romans. Especially with regard to political liberty, they say, have we ideas and feelings, beliefs and tolerances, that prove our superiority. There are even some hopeful theorists who maintain that our institutions should lead us straight to that garden of the Hesperides which was sought so long, and with such ill-success, since the time when the ancient navigators reported that it was not in the Canaries. ...

A little more serious consideration of history will show what truth there is in these high claims.

We are certainly more learned than the ancients. This is because we have profited by their discoveries. If we have amassed more knowledge than they, it is merely because we are their heirs and pupils, and have continued their work. Does it follow that the discovery of steam-power and the solution of a few mechanical problems have brought us on the way to omniscience? At most, our success may lead us to explore all the secrets of the material world. Before we achieve this conquest, there are many things to do which have not even been begun, nay of which the very existence is not yet suspected; but even when the victory is ours, shall we have advanced a single step beyond the bare affirmation of physical laws? We shall, I agree, have greatly increased our power of influencing nature and harnessing her to our service. We shall have found different ways of going round the world, or recognized definitely that certain routes are impossible. We shall have learnt how to move freely about in the air, and, by mounting a few miles nearer the limits of the earth's atmosphere, discovered or cleared up certain astronomical or other problems; but nothing more. All this does not lead us to infinity. Even if we had counted all the planetary systems that move through space, should we be any nearer? Have we learnt a single thing about the great mysteries that was unknown to the ancients? We have, merely, so far as I can see, changed the previous methods of circling the cave where the secret lies. We have not pierced its darkness one inch further.

Again, admitting that we are in certain directions more enlightened, yet we must have lost all trace of many things that were familiar to our remote ancestors. Can we doubt that at the time of Abraham far more was known about primeval history than we know today? How many of our discoveries, made by chance or with great labor, are merely re-discoveries of forgotten knowledge! Further, how inferior we are in many respects to those who have lived before us! As I said above, in a different connection, can one compare even our most splendid works to the marvels still to be seen in Egypt, India, Greece, and America? And these bear witness to the vanished magnificence of many other buildings, which have been destroyed far less by the heavy hand of time than by the senseless ravages of man. What are our arts, compared with those of Athens? What are our thinkers, compared with those of Alexandria and India? What are our poets, by the side of Valmiki, Kalidasa, Homer, and Pindar?

Our work is, in fact, different from theirs. We have turned our minds to other inquiries and other ends than those pursued by the earlier civilized groups of mankind. But while tilling our new field, we have not been able to keep fertile the lands already cultivated. We have advanced on one flank, but have given ground on the other. It is a poor compensation; and far from proving our progress, it merely means that we have changed our position. For a real advance to have been made, we should at least have preserved in their integrity the chief intellectual treasures of the earlier societies, and set up, in addition, certain great and firmly based conclusions at which the ancients had aimed as well as ourselves. Our arts and sciences, using theirs as the starting-point, should have discovered some new and profound truths about life and death, the genesis of living creatures, and the basic principles of the universe. On all these questions, modern science, as we imagine, has lost the visionary gleam that played round the dawn of antiquity, and its own efforts have merely brought it to the humiliating confession, "I seek and do not find." There has been no real progress in the intellectual conquests of man. Our power of criticism is certainly better than that of our forefathers. This is a considerable gain, but it stands alone; and, after all, criticism merely means *classification*, not *discovery*.

As for our so-called new ideas on politics, we may allow ourselves to be more disrespectful to them than to our sciences.

The same fertility in theorizing, on which we so pride ourselves, was to be found at Athens after the death of Pericles. Anyone may be convinced of this by reading again the comedies of Aristophanes, and allowing for satirical exaggeration; they were recommended by Plato himself as a guide to the public life of the city of Athene. We have always despised such comparisons, since we persuaded ourselves that a fundamental difference between our present social order and the ancient Greek State was created by slavery. It made for a more far-reaching demagogy, I admit; but that is all. People spoke of slaves in the same way as one speaks today of workmen and the lower classes; and, further, how very advanced the Athenians must have been, when they tried to please their servile population after the battle of Arginusæ!

Let us now turn to Rome. If you open the letters of Cicero, you will find the Roman orator a moderate Tory of today. His republic is exactly like our constitutional societies, in all that relates to the language of parties and Parliamentary squabbles. There too, in the lower depths, seethed a population of degraded slaves, with revolt ever in their hearts, and sometimes in their fists also. We will leave this mob on one side; and we can do it the more readily as the law did not recognize their civil existence. They did not count in politics, and their influence was limited to times of uproar. Even then, they merely carried out the commands of the revolutionaries of free birth.

Regarding, then, the slaves as of no account, does not the Forum offer us all the constituents of a modern social State? The populace, demanding bread and games, free doles and the right to enjoy them; the middle class, which succeeded in its aim of monopolizing the public services; the patriciate, always being transformed and giving ground, always losing its rights, until even its defenders agreed, as their one means of defense, to refuse all privileges and merely claim liberty for all;—have we not here an exact correspondence with our own time?

Does anyone believe that of the opinions we hear expressed today, however various they may be, there is a single one, or any shade of one, that was not known at Rome? I spoke above of the letters written from the Tusculan Villa: they contain the thoughts of a Conservative with progressive leanings. As against Sulla, Pompeius and Cicero were Liberals. They were not liberal enough for Caesar, and were too much so for Cato. Later, under the Principate, we find a moderate Royalist in Pliny the Younger, though one who loved tranquillity. He was against excessive liberty for the people, and excessive power for the Emperor. His views were positivist; he thought little of the vanished splendors of the age of the Fabii, and preferred the prosaic administration of a Trajan. Not everyone agreed with him. Many feared another insurrection like that of Spartacus, and thought that the Emperor could not make too despotic a use of his power. On the other hand, some of the provincials asked for, and obtained, what we should call constitutional guarantees; while Socialist opinions found so highly placed a representative as the Gallic Emperor Gaius Junius Postumus, who set down, among his subjects for declamation, *Dives et pauper inimici,* "The rich and the poor are natural enemies."

In fact, every man who had any claim to share in the enlightenment of the time strongly asserted the equality of the human race, the right of all men to have their part in the good things of this world, the obvious necessity of the Græco-Roman civilization, its perfection and refinement, its certainty of a future progress even beyond its present state, and, to crown all, its existence forever. These ideas were not merely the pride and consolation of the pagans; they inspired also the firm hopes of the first and most illustrious Fathers of the Church, of whose views Tertullian was the self-constituted interpreter.[100]

Finally—to complete the picture with a last striking trait—the most numerous party of all was formed by the indifferent, the people who were too weak or timid, too skeptical or contemptuous, to find truth in the midst of all the divergent theories that passed kaleidoscopically before their eyes; who loved order when it existed, and (so far as they could) endured disorder when it came; who were always wondering at the progress of material comforts unknown to their fathers, and who, without wishing to think too much of the other side, consoled themselves by repeating over and over again, "Wonderful are the works of today!"

There would be more reason to believe that we have made improvements in political science, if we had

---

[100] Amedee Thierry, *Histoire de la Gaule sous l'administration romaine,* vol. i, p. 241.

invented some machinery that was unknown, in its essentials, before our time. Such a glory is not ours. Limited monarchies, for example, have been familiar to every age, and curious instances can be seen among certain American tribes, which in other respects have remained savage. Democratic and aristocratic republics of all kinds, balanced in the most various ways, have existed in the New as well as the Old World. Tlaxcala is just as good an example as Athens, Sparta, and Mecca before Mohammed's time. Even if it were shown that we had ourselves made some secondary improvements in the art of government, would this be enough to justify such a sweeping assertion as that the human race is capable of unlimited progress? Let us be as modest as that wisest of kings, when he said, "There is nothing new under the sun."[101]

---

[101] One is sometimes led to consider the government of the United States of America as an original creation, peculiar to our time; its most remarkable feature is taken to be the small amount of opportunity left for Government initiative or even interference. Yet if we cast our eyes over the early years of all the States founded by the white race, we shall find exactly the same phenomenon. "Self-government" is no more triumphant in New York today, than it was in Paris, at the time of the Franks. It is true that the Indians are treated far less humanely by the Americans than the Gallo-Romans were by the nobles of Chlodwig. But we must remember that the racial difference between the enlightened Republicans of the New World and their victims is far greater than that between the Germanic conqueror and those he conquered.

In fact, all Aryan societies began by exaggerating their independence as against the law and the magistrates.

The power of political invention possessed by the world cannot, I think, travel outside the boundaries traced by two particular peoples, one of them living in the north-east of Europe, the other on the banks of the Nile, in the extreme south of Egypt. The Government of the first of these peoples (in Bolgari, near Kazan) was accustomed to "order men of intelligence to be hanged" as a preventive measure. We owe our knowledge of this interesting fact to the Arabian traveller Ibn Foszlan (A. von Humboldt, *Asie centrale,* vol. i, p. 494). In the other nation, living at Fazoql, whenever the king did not give satisfaction, his relations and ministers came and told him so. They informed him that since he no longer pleased "the men, women, children, oxen, asses," etc., the best thing he could do was to die; they then proceeded to help him to his death as speedily as possible (Lepsius, *Briefe aus Ägypten, Äthiopien, und der Halbinsel des Sinai;* Berlin, 1852).

We come now to the question of manners. Ours are said to be gentler than those of the other great human societies; but this is very doubtful.

There are some rhetoricians today who would like to abolish war between nations. They have taken this theory from Seneca. Certain wise men of the East had also, on this subject, views that are precisely similar to those of the Moravian brotherhood. But even if the friends of universal peace succeeded in making Europe disgusted with the idea of war, they would still have to bring about a permanent change in the passions of mankind. Neither Seneca nor the Brahmans obtained such a victory. It is doubtful whether we are to succeed where they failed; especially as we may still see in our fields and our streets the bloody traces left by our so-called "humanity."

I agree that our principles are pure and elevated. Does our practice correspond to them?

Before we congratulate ourselves on our achievements, let us wait till our modern countries can boast of two centuries of peace, as could Roman Italy,[102] the example of which has unfortunately not been followed by later ages; for since the beginning of modern civilization fifty years have never passed without massacres.

The capacity for infinite progress is, thus, not shown by the present state of our civilization. Man has been able to learn some things, but has forgotten many others. He has not added one sense to his senses, one limb to his limbs, one faculty to his soul. He has merely explored another region of the circle in which he is confined, and even the comparison of his destiny with that of many kinds of birds and insects does not always

---

[102] Amedée Thierry, *op. cit.,* vol. i, p. 241.

inspire very consoling thoughts as to his happiness in this life.

The bees, the ants, and the termites have found for themselves, from the day of their creation, the kind of life that suited them. The last two, in their communities, have invented a way of building their houses, laying in their provisions, and looking after their eggs, which in the opinion of naturalists could be neither altered nor improved.[103] Such as it is, it has always been sufficient for the small wants of the creatures who use it. Similarly the bees—with their monarchical government, which admits of the deposition of the sovereign but not of a social revolution—have never for a single day turned aside from the manner of life that is most suitable to their needs. Metaphysicians were allowed for a long time to call animals machines, and to assign the cause of their movements to God, who was the "soul of the brutes," *anima brutorum.* Now that the habits of these so-called automata are studied in a more careful way, we have not merely given up this contemptuous theory; we have even recognized that instinct has a capacity that raises it almost to the dignity of reason.

In the bee-kingdom, we see the queens a prey to the anger of their subjects; this implies either a spirit of mutiny in the latter, or the inability of the former to fulfil their lawful obligations. We see too the termites sparing their conquered enemies, and then making them prisoners, and employing them in the public service by giving them the care of the young. What are we to conclude from such facts as these?

Our modern States are certainly more complicated, and satisfy our needs in larger measure: but when I see the savage wandering on his way, fierce, sullen, idle, and dirty, lazily dragging his feet along his uncultivated

---

[103] Martius and Spix, *Reise in Brasilien,* vol. iii, p. 950, etc.

ground, carrying the pointed stick that is his only weapon, and followed by the wife whom he has bound to him by a marriage-ceremony consisting solely in an empty and ferocious violence;[104] when I see the wife carrying her child, whom she will kill with her own hands if he falls ill, or even if he worries her;[105] when I see this miserable group under the pressure of hunger, suddenly stop, in its search for food, before a hill peopled by intelligent ants, gape at it in wonder, put their feet through it, seize the eggs and devour them, and then withdraw sadly into the hollow of a rock,— when I see all this, I ask myself whether the insects that have just perished are not more highly gifted than the stupid family of the destroyer, and whether the instinct of the animals, restricted as it is to a small circle of wants, does not really make them happier than the faculty of reason which has left our poor humanity naked on the earth, and a thousand times more exposed than any other species to the sufferings caused by the united agency of air, sun, rain, and snow. Man, in his wretchedness, has never succeeded in inventing a way of providing the whole race with clothes or in putting them beyond the reach of hunger and thirst. It is true that the knowledge possessed by the lowest savage is more

---

[104] In many tribes of Oceania the institution of marriage is conceived as follows:—A man sees a maiden, who, he thinks, will suit him. He obtains her from her father, by means of a few presents, among which a bottle of brandy, if he has been able to get one, holds the most distinguished place. Then the young suitor proceeds to conceal himself in a thicket, or behind a rock. The maiden passes by, thinking no harm. He knocks her down with a blow of his stick, beats her until she becomes unconscious, and carries her lovingly to his house, bathed in her blood. The formalities have been complied with, and the legal union is accomplished.

[105] D'Orbigny tells how Indian mothers love their children to distraction, and take such care of them as to be really their slaves. If however the child annoys the mother at any time, then she drowns him or crushes him to death, or abandons him in the forest, without any regret. I know no other example of such an extraordinary change (D'Orbigny, *L'Homme américain*, vol. ii, p. 232).

extensive than that of any animal; but the animals know what is useful to them, and we do not. They hold fast to what knowledge they have, but we often cannot keep what we have ourselves discovered. They are always, in normal seasons, sure of satisfying their needs by their instincts. But there are numerous tribes of men that from the beginning of their history have never been able to rise above a stinted and precarious existence. So far as material well-being goes, we are no better than the animals; our horizon is wider than theirs, but, like theirs, it is still cramped and bounded.

I have hardly insisted enough on this unfortunate tendency of mankind to lose on one side what it gains on the other. Yet this is the great fact that condemns us to wander through our intellectual domains without ever succeeding, in spite of their narrow limits, in holding them all at the same time. If this fatal law did not exist, it might well happen that at some date in the dim future, when man had gathered together all the wisdom of all the ages, knowing what he had power to know and possessing all that was within his reach, he might at last have learnt how to apply his wealth, and live in the midst of nature, at peace with his kind and no longer at grips with misery; and having gained tranquillity after all his struggles, he might find his ultimate rest, if not in a state of absolute perfection, at any rate in the midst of joy and abundance.

Such happiness, with all its limitations, is not even possible for us, since man unlearns as fast as he learns; he cannot gain intellectually and morally without losing physically, and he does not hold any of his conquests strongly enough to be certain of keeping them always.

We moderns believe that our civilization will never perish, because we have discovered printing, steam, and gunpowder. Has printing, which is no less known to the inhabitants of Tonkin and Annam[106] than in Europe, managed to give them even a tolerable civilization? They have books, and many of them—books which are sold far cheaper than ours. How is it that these peoples are so weak and degraded, so near the point where civilized man, strengthless, cowardly, and corrupted, is inferior in intellectual power to any barbarian who may seize the opportunity to crush him?[107] The reason is, that printing is merely a means and not an end. If you use it to disseminate healthy and vigorous ideas, it will serve a most fruitful purpose and help to maintain civilization. If, on the other hand, the intellectual life of a people is so debased that no one any longer prints such works of philosophy, history, and literature, as can give strong nourishment to a nation's genius; if the degraded press merely serves to multiply the unhealthy and poisonous compilations of enervated minds, if its theology is the work of sectaries, it's politics of libelers, its poetry of libertines,—then how and why should the printing-press be the savior of civilization?

Because copies of the great masterpieces can be easily multiplied, it is supposed that printing helps to preserve them; and that in times of intellectual barrenness, when they have no other competitors, printing can at least make them accessible to the nobler minds of the age. This is of course true. Yet if a man is to trouble himself about an ancient book at all, or gain any

---

[106] "The native Indian trade in books is very active, and many of the works produced are never seen in the libraries of Europeans, even in India. Sprenger says, in a letter, that in Lucknow alone there are thirteen lithographic establishments occupied purely in printing school-books, and he gives a considerable list of works of which probably not one has reached Europe. The same is the case at Delhi, Agra, Cawnpore, Allahabad, and other towns" (Mohl, *Rapport annuel à la Société asiatique,* 1851, p. 92).

[107] "The Siamese are the most shameless people in the world. They are at the lowest point of Indo-Chinese civilization; and yet they can all read and write" (Ritter, *Erdkunde, Asien,* vol. iii, p. 1152).

improvement from it, he must already have the precious gift of an enlightened mind. In evil times, when public virtue has left the earth, ancient writings are of little account, and no one cares to disturb the silence of the libraries. A man must be already worth something before he thinks of entering these august portals; but in such times no one is worth anything. ...

Further, the length of life assured by Gutenberg's discovery to the achievements of the human mind is greatly exaggerated. With the exception of a few works which are from time to time reprinted, all books are dying today, as manuscripts died in the old days. Scientific works especially, which are published in editions of a few hundred copies, soon disappear from the common stock. They can still be found, though with difficulty, in large collections. The intellectual treasures of antiquity were in exactly the same case; and, I repeat, learning will not save a people which has fallen into its dotage.

What have become of the thousands of admirable books published since the first printing-press was set up? Most of them have been forgotten. Many of those that are still spoken of have no longer any readers, while the very names of the authors who were in demand fifty years ago are gradually fading from memory.

In the attempt to heighten the influence of printing, too little stress has been laid on the great diffusion of manuscripts that preceded it. At the time of the Roman Empire, opportunities for education were very general, and books must have been very common indeed, if we look at the extraordinary number of out-at-elbows grammarians, whose poverty, licentiousness, and passionate search for enjoyment live for us in the *Satyricon* of Petronius. They swarmed even in the smallest towns, and may be compared to the novelists, lawyers, and journalists of our own age. Even when the decadence was complete, anyone who wanted books could get them. Virgil was read everywhere. The peasants who heard his praises took him for a dangerous enchanter. The monks copied him. They copied also Pliny, Dioscorides, Plato, Aristotle, even Catullus and Martial. From the great number of medieval manuscripts that remain after so much war and pillage, after the burning of so many castles and abbeys, we may guess that far more copies than one thinks were made of contemporary works, literary, scientific, and philosophical. We exaggerate the real services done by printing to science, poetry, morality, and civilization; it would be better if we merely touched lightly on these merits and spoke more of the way in which the invention of printing is continually helping all kinds of religious and political interests. Printing, I say again, is a marvellous tool; but when head and hand fail, a tool cannot work by itself.

Gunpowder has no more power than printing to save a society that is in danger of death. The knowledge of how to make it will certainly never be forgotten. I doubt, however, whether the half-civilized peoples who use it today as much as we do ourselves, ever look upon it from any other point of view than that of destruction.

As for steam-power and the various industrial discoveries, they too, like printing, are most excellent means, but not ends in themselves. I may add that some processes which began as scientific discoveries ended as matters of routine, when the intellectual movement that gave them birth had stopped forever, and the theoretical secrets at the back of the processes had been lost. Finally, material well-being has never been anything but an excrescence on civilization; no one has ever heard of a society that persisted solely through its knowledge of how to travel quickly and make fine clothes.

All the civilizations before our own have thought, as we do, that they were set firmly on the rock of time by their unforgettable discoveries. They all believed in their immortality. The Incas and their families, who travelled swiftly in their palanquins on the excellent roads, fifteen hundred miles long, that still link Cuzco to Quito, were certainly convinced that their conquests would last forever. Time, with one blow of his wing, has hurled their empire, like so many others, into the uttermost abyss. These kings of Peru also had their sciences, their machinery, their powerful engines, at the work of which we still stand amazed without being able to guess their construction. They too knew the secret of carrying enormous masses from place to place. They built fortresses by piling, one upon the other, blocks of stone thirty-eight feet long and eighteen wide, such as may be seen in the ruins of Tihuanaco, to which these gigantic building-materials must have been brought from a distance of many miles. Do we know the means used by the engineers of this vanished people to solve such a problem? No more than we know how the vast Cyclopean walls were constructed, the ruins of which, in many parts of Southern Europe, still defy the ravages of time.

We must not confuse the causes of a civilization with its results. The causes disappear, and the results are forgotten, when the spirit that gave them birth has departed. If they persist, it is because of a new spirit that takes hold of them, and often succeeds in giving quite a new direction to their activities. The human mind is always in motion. It runs from one point to another, but cannot be in all places at once. It exalts what it embraces, and forgets what it has abandoned. Held prisoner forever within a circle whose bounds it may not overstep, it never manages to cultivate one part of its domain without leaving the others fallow. It is always at the same time superior and inferior to its forbears. Mankind never goes beyond itself, and so is not capable of infinite progress.

CHAPTER XIV

PROOF OF THE INTELLECTUAL INEQUALITY OF RACES *(continued)*. DIFFERENT CIVILIZATIONS ARE MUTUALLY REPULSIVE. HYBRID RACES HAVE EQUALLY HYBRID CIVILIZATIONS

If the human races were equal, the course of history would form an affecting, glorious, and magnificent picture. The races would all have been equally intelligent, with a keen eye for their true interests and the same aptitude for conquest and domination. Early in the world's history, they would have gladdened the face of the earth with a crowd of civilizations, all flourishing at the same time, and all exactly alike. At the moment when the most ancient Sanskrit peoples were founding their empire, and, by means of religion and the sword, were covering Northern India with harvests, towns, palaces, and temples; at the moment when the first Assyrian Empire was crowning the plains of the Tigris and Euphrates with its splendid buildings, and the chariots and horsemen of Nimroud were defying the four winds, we should have seen, on the African coast, among the tribes of the prognathous negroes, the rise of an enlightened and cultured social state, skillful in adapting means to ends, and in possession of great wealth and power.

The Celts, in the course of their migrations, would have carried with them to the extreme west of Europe the necessary elements of a great society, as well as some tincture of the ancient wisdom of the East; they would certainly have found, among the Iberian peoples spread over the face of Italy, in Gaul and Spain and the islands of the Mediterranean, rivals as well schooled as themselves in the early traditions, as expert as they in the arts and inventions required for civilization.

Mankind, at one with itself, would have nobly walked the earth, rich in understanding, and founding everywhere societies resembling each other. All nations would have judged their needs in the same way, asked nature for the same things, and viewed her from the same angle. A short time would have been sufficient for them to get into close contact with each other and to form the complex network of relations that is everywhere so necessary and profitable for progress.

The tribes that were unlucky enough to live on a barren soil, at the bottom of rocky gorges, on the shores of ice-bound seas, or on steppes forever swept by the north winds—these might have had to battle against the unkindness of nature for a longer time than the more favored peoples. But in the end, having no less wisdom and understanding than the others, they would not have been backward in discovering that the rigors of a climate has its remedies. They would have shown the intelligent activity we see today among the Danes, the Norwegians, and the Icelanders. They would have tamed the rebellious soil, and forced it, in spite of itself, to be productive. In mountainous regions, we should have found them leading a pastoral life, like the Swiss, or developing industries like those of Cashmere. If their climate had been so bad, and its situation so unfavorable, that there was obviously nothing to be done with it, then the thought would have struck them that the world was large, and contained many valleys and kindly plains; they would have left their ungrateful country, and soon have found a land where they could turn their energy and intelligence to good account.

Then the nations of the earth, equally enlightened and equally rich, some by the commerce of their seething maritime cities, some by the agriculture of their vast and flourishing prairies, others by the industries of a mountainous district, others again by the facilities for transport afforded them by their central position—all these, in spite of the temporary quarrels, civil wars, and seditions inseparable from our condition as men, might soon have devised some system of balancing their conflicting interests. Civilizations identical in origin would, by a long process of give and take, have ended by being almost exactly alike; one might then have seen established that federation of the world which has been the dream of so many centuries, and which would inevitably be realized if all races were actually gifted, in the same degree, with the same powers.

But we know that such a picture is purely fantastic. The first peoples worthy of the name came together under the inspiration of an idea of union which the barbarians who lived more or less near them not only failed to conceive so quickly, but never conceived at all. The early peoples emigrated from their first home and came across other peoples, which they conquered; but these again neither understood nor ever adopted with any intelligence the main ideas in the civilization which had been imposed on them. Far from showing that all the tribes of mankind are intellectually alike, the nations capable of civilization have always proved the contrary, first by the absolutely different foundations on which they based their states, and secondly by the marked antipathy which they showed to each other. The force of example has never awakened any instinct, in any people, which did not spring from their own nature. Spain and the Gauls saw the Phoenicians, the Greeks, and the Carthaginians, set up flourishing towns, one after the other, on their coasts. But both Spain and the Gauls refused to copy the manners and the government of these great trading powers. When the Romans came as conquerors, they only succeeded in introducing a different spirit by filling their new dominions with Roman colonies. Thus the case of the Celts and the Iberians shows that civilization cannot be acquired without the crossing of blood.

Consider the position of the American Indians at the present day. They live side by side with a people which always wishes to increase in numbers, to strengthen its power. They see thousands of ships passing up and down their waterways. They know that the strength of their masters is irresistible. They have no hope whatever of seeing their native land one day delivered from the conqueror; their whole continent is henceforth, as they all know, the inheritance of the European. A glance is enough to convince them of the tenacity of those foreign institutions under which human life ceases to depend, for its continuance, on the abundance of game or fish. From their purchases of brandy, guns, and blankets, they know that even their own coarse tastes would be more easily satisfied in the midst of such a society, which is always inviting them to come in, and which seeks, by bribes and flattery, to obtain their consent. It is always refused. They prefer to flee from one lonely spot to another; they bury themselves more and more in the heart of the country, abandoning all, even the bones of their fathers. They will die out, as they know well; but they are kept, by a mysterious feeling of horror, under the yoke of their unconquerable repulsion from the white race, and although they admire its strength and general superiority, their conscience and their whole nature, in a word, their blood, revolts from the mere thought of having anything in common with it.

In Spanish America less aversion is felt by the natives towards their masters. The reason is that they were formerly left by the central Government under the rule of their Caciques. The Government did not try to civilize them; it allowed them to keep their own laws and customs, and, provided they became Christians, merely required them to pay tribute. There was no question of colonization. Once the conquest was made, the Spaniards showed a lazy tolerance to the conquered, and only oppressed them spasmodically. This is why the Indians of South America are less unhappy than those of the north, and continue to live on, whereas the neighbors of the Anglo-Saxons will be pitilessly driven down into the abyss.

Civilization is incommunicable, not only to savages, but also to more enlightened nations. This is shown by the efforts of French goodwill and conciliation in the ancient kingdom of Algiers at the present day, as well as by the experience of the English in India, and the Dutch in Java. There are no more striking and conclusive proofs of the unlikeness and inequality of races.

We should be wrong to conclude that the barbarism of certain tribes is so innate that no kind of culture is possible for them. Traces may be seen, among many savage peoples, of a state of things better than that obtaining now. Some tribes, otherwise sunk in brutishness, hold to traditional rules, of a curious complexity, in the matter of marriage, inheritance, and government. Their rites are unmeaning today, but they evidently go back to a higher order of ideas. The Red Indians are brought forward as an example; the vast deserts over which they roam are supposed to have been once the settlements of the Alleghanians.[108] Others, such as the natives of the Marianne Islands, have methods of manufacture which they cannot have invented themselves. They hand them down, without thought, from father to son, and employ them quite mechanically.

---

[108] Prichard, "Natural History of Man," sec. 41.

When we see a people in a state of barbarism, we must look more closely before concluding that this has always been their condition. We must take many other facts into account, if we would avoid error.

Some peoples are caught in the sweep of a kindred race; they submit to it more or less, taking over certain customs, and following them out as far as possible. On the disappearance of the dominant race, either by expulsion, or by a complete absorption in the conquered people, the latter allows the culture, especially its root principles, to die out almost entirely, and retains only the small part it has been able to understand. Even this cannot happen except among nations related by blood. This was the attitude of the Assyrians towards the Chaldean culture, of the Syrian and Egyptian Greeks towards the Greeks of Europe, of the Iberians, Celts, and Illyrians in face of the Roman ideas. If the Cherokees, the Catawhas, the Muskhogees, the Seminoles, the Natchez, and the like, still show some traces of the Alleghanian intelligence, I cannot indeed infer that they are of pure blood, and directly descended from the originating stock—this would mean that a race that was once civilized can lose its civilization;—I merely say that if any of them derives from the ancient conquering type as its source, the stream is a muddy one, and has been mingled with many tributaries on the way. If it were otherwise, the Cherokees would never have fallen into barbarism. As for the other and less gifted tribes, they seem to represent merely the dregs of the indigenous population, which was forced by the foreign conquerors to combine together to form the basic elements of a new social state. It is not surprising that these remnants of civilization should have preserved, without understanding them, laws, rites, and customs invented by men cleverer than themselves; they never knew their meaning or theoretical principles, or regarded them as anything but objects of superstitious veneration. The same argument applies to the traces of mechanical skill found among them. The methods so admired by travelers may well have been ultimately derived from a finer race that has long disappeared. Sometimes we must look even further for their origin. Thus, the working of mines was known to the Iberians, Aquitanians, and the Bretons of the Stilly Isles; but the secret was first discovered in Upper Asia, and thence brought long ago by the ancestors of the Western peoples in the course of their migration.

The natives of the Caroline Islands are almost the most interesting in Polynesia. Their looms, their carved canoes, their taste for trade and navigation put a deep barrier between them and the other negroes. It is not hard to see how they come to have these powers. They owe them to the Malay blood in their veins; and as, at the same time, their blood is far from being pure, their racial gifts have survived only in a stunted and degraded form.

We must not therefore infer, from the traces of civilization existing among a barbarous people, that it has ever been really civilized. It has lived under the dominion of another tribe, of kindred blood but superior to it; or perhaps, by merely living close to the other tribe, it has, feebly and humbly, imitated its customs. The savage races of today have always been savage, and we are right in concluding, by analogy, that they will continue to be so, until the day when they disappear.

Their disappearance is inevitable as soon as two entirely unconnected races come into active contact; and the best proof is the fate of the Polynesians and the American Indians.

The preceding argument has established the following facts:

(i) The tribes which are savage at the present day have always been so, and always will be, however high the civilizations with which they are brought into contact.

(ii) For a savage people even to go on living in the midst of civilization, the nation which created the civilization must be a nobler branch of the same race.

(iii) This is also necessary if two distinct civilizations are to affect each other to any extent, by an exchange of qualities, and give birth to other civilizations compounded from their elements. That they should ever be fused together is of course out of the question.

(iv) The civilizations that proceed from two completely foreign races can only touch on the surface. They never coalesce, and the one will always exclude the other. I will say more about this last point, as it has not been sufficiently illustrated.

The fortune of war brought the Persian civilization face to face with the Greek, the Greek with the Roman, the Egyptian with both Roman and Greek; similarly the modern European civilization has confronted all those existing today in the world, especially the Arabian.

The relations of Greek with Persian culture were manifold and inevitable. A large part of the Hellenic population—the richest, if not the most independent—was concentrated in the towns of the Syrian littoral, and in the colonies of Asia Minor and the Euxine. These were, soon after their foundation, absorbed in the dominions of the Great King; the inhabitants lived under the eye of the satrap, though to a certain extent they retained their democratic institutions. Again, Greece proper, the Greece that was free, was always in close contact with the cities of the Asiatic coast.

Were the civilizations of the two countries ever fused into one? We know they were not. The Greeks regarded their powerful enemies as barbarians, and their contempt was probably returned with interest. The two nations were continually coming into contact, but their political ideas, their private habits, the inner meaning of their public rites, the scope of their art, and the forms of their government, remained quite distinct. At Ecbatana only one authority was recognized; it was hereditary, and limited in certain traditional ways, but was otherwise absolute. In Hellas the power was subdivided among a crowd of different sovereigns. The government was monarchical at Sparta, democratic at Athens, aristocratic at Sicyon, tyrannic in Macedonia—a strange medley! Among the Persians, the State-religion was far nearer to the primitive idea of *emanation;* it showed the same tendency to unity as the government itself did, and had a moral and metaphysical significance that was not without a certain philosophic depth. The Greek symbolism, on the other hand, was concerned merely with the various outward appearances of nature, and issued in a glorification of the human form. Religion left the business of controlling a man's conscience to the laws of the State; as soon as the due rites were performed, and his meed of honor paid to the local god or hero, the office of faith was complete. Further, the rites themselves, the gods, and the heroes, were different in places a few miles apart. If, in some sanctuaries like Olympia or Dodona, we seem to find the worship, not of some special force of nature, but of the cosmic principle itself, such a unity only makes the diversity of the rest more remarkable; for this kind of worship was confined to a few isolated places. Besides, the oracle of Dodona and the cult of the Olympian Zeus were foreign importations.

As for the private customs of the Greeks, it is hardly necessary to show how much they differed from those of the Persians. For a rich, pleasure-loving, and cosmopolitan youth to imitate the habits of rivals far more luxurious and outwardly refined than the Greeks, was to bring himself into public contempt. Until the time of Alexander—in other words, during the great, fruitful and glorious period of Hellenism—Persia, in spite of its continual pressure, could not convert Greece to its civilization.

With the coming of Alexander, this was curiously confirmed. Men believed for a moment, when they saw Hellas conquering the kingdom of Darius, that Asia was about to become Greek, or, still better, that the acts of violence wrought in the madness of a single night by the conqueror against the monuments of the country were, in their very excess, a proof of contempt as well as hatred. But the burner of Persepolis soon changed his mind. The change was so complete that his design at last became apparent; it was to substitute himself purely and simply for the dynasty of the Achaemenidae, and to rule like his predecessor or the great Xerxes, with Greece as an appanage of his empire. In this way, the Persian social system might have absorbed that of the Greeks.

In spite, however, of all Alexander's authority, nothing of the kind happened. His generals and soldiers never became used to seeing him in his long clinging robe, wearing a turban on his head, surrounded by eunuchs and denying his country. After his death, his system was continued by some of his successors; they were, however, forced to mitigate it. And why, as a fact, were they able to find the middle term which became the normal condition of the Asiatics of the coast and the Græco-Egyptians? Simply because their subjects consisted of a mixed population of Greeks, Syrians, and Arabs, who had no reason to refuse the compromise. Where, however, the races remained distinct, all terms of union were impossible, and each country held to its national culture.

Similarly, right up to the last days of the Roman Empire, the hybrid civilization that was dominant all over the East, including Greece proper, had become much more Asiatic than Greek, owing to the great preponderance of Asiatic blood in the mass of the people. The intellectual life, it is true, took pride in being Hellenic. But it is not hard to find, in the thought of the time, an Oriental strain vitalizing all the products of the Alexandrian school, such as the "centralized state" idea of the Græco-Syrian jurists. We see how the different racial elements were balanced, and to which side the scale inclined.

Other civilizations may be compared in the same way; and before ending this chapter, I will say a few words about the relation between Arab culture and our own.

No one can doubt their mutual repulsion. Our medieval ancestors had opportunities of seeing at close quarters the marvels of the Muslim State, when they willingly sent their sons to study in the schools of Cordova. Yet nothing Arabian remains in Europe outside the nations that have a tinge of Ishmaelitish blood. Brahmanic India showed no more eagerness than ourselves to come to terms with Islam, and has, like us, resisted all the efforts of its Mohammedan masters.

Today, it is our turn to deal with the remains of Arab civilization. We harry and destroy the Arabs, but we do not succeed in changing them, although their civilization is not itself original, and so should have less power of resistance. It is notorious that the Arabian people, itself weak in numbers, continually incorporated the remnants of the races it had conquered by the sword. The Muslims form a very mixed population, with an equally hybrid culture, of which it is easy to disentangle the elements. The conquering nucleus did not, before Mohammed, consist of a new or unknown people. Its traditions were held in common with the Semite and Hamite families from which it was originally derived. It was brought into conflict with the Phoenicians and the Jews, and had the blood of both in its veins. It played a middleman's part in their Red Sea trade, and on the eastern coasts of India and Africa. It did the same, later, for the Persians and the Romans. Many Arab tribes took part in the political life of Persia under the Arsacidae and Sassanidae, while some of their princes, like Odenathus,[109] were proclaimed Caesar, some of their princesses, like Zenobia, daughter of Amru and Queen of Palmyra, won a glory that was distinctively Roman, and some of their adventurers, like Philip, even raised themselves to the Imperial purple. Thus this hybrid nation had never ceased, from the most ancient times, to make itself felt among the powerful societies among which it lived. It had associated itself with their work, and like a body half sunk in water, half exposed to the sun, contained at one and the same time elements of barbarism and of an advanced civilization.

Mohammed invented the religion that was best fitted to the mental state of his people, where idolatry found many followers, but where Christianity, distorted by heretics and Judaizers, made just as many proselytes. In the religious system of the Prophet of Koresh the reconciliation between the law of Moses and the Christian faith was more complete than in the doctrines of the Church. This problem had greatly exercised the minds of the early Catholics, and was always present to the Oriental conscience. Hence Mohammed's gift had already an appetizing appearance, and besides, any theological novelty had a good chance of gaining

---

[109] King of Palmyra in Syria, and husband of Zenobia. He was recognized by the Emperor Gallienus as co-regent of the East in 267, and was murdered in the same year.—Tr.

converts among the Syrians and Egyptians. To crown all, the new religion came forward sword in hand; this was another guarantee of success among the masses, who had no common bond of union, other than the strong conviction of their helplessness.

It was thus that Islam came forth from the desert. Arrogant, uninventive, and with a civilization that was already, for the most part, Græco-Asiatic, it found the ground prepared for it. Its recruits, on the East and South coasts of the Mediterranean, had already been saturated with the complex product which it was bringing to them, and which in turn it reabsorbed. The new cult, that had borrowed its doctrines from the Church, the Synagogue, and the garbled traditions of the Hedjaz and the Yemen, extended from Bagdad to Montpellier; and with the cult came its Persian and Roman laws, its Græco-Syrian[110] and Egyptian science, and its system of administration, which was tolerant from the first, as is natural where there is no unity in the State organism. We need not be astonished at the rapid progress in refinement made by the Muslims. The greater part of the people had merely changed their habits for the time being. When they began to play the part of apostles in the world, their identity was not at once recognized; they had not been known under their old names for some time. Another important point must be remembered. In this varied collection of peoples, each no doubt contributed its share to the common welfare. But which of them had given the first push to the machine, and which directed its motion for the short time it lasted? Why, the little nucleus of Arab

---

[110] "The impulse towards this science given them by their kinship with the Græco-Syrians made them capable of really absorbing the Greek language and spirit; for the Arabs preferred to confine themselves to the purely scientific results of Greek speculation" (W. von Humboldt, *Über die Kawi-Sprache,* Introduction, p. cclxiii).

tribes that had come from the interior of the peninsula, and consisted, not of philosophers, but of fanatics, soldiers, conquerors, and rulers.

Arab civilization was merely the old Græco-Syrian civilization, modified by Persian admixture, and revived and rejuvenated by the new, sharp breath of a genius. Hence, although ready to make concessions, it could not come to terms with any form of society that had a different origin from its own, any more than the Greek culture could with the Roman, although these were so near to each other and lived side by side for so many centuries within the same Empire.

The preceding paragraphs are enough to show how impossible it is that the civilizations belonging to racially distinct groups should ever be fused together. The irreconcilable antagonism between different races and cultures is clearly established by history, and such innate repulsion must imply unlikeness and inequality. If it is admitted that the European cannot hope to civilize the negro, and manages to transmit to the mulatto only a very few of his own characteristics; if the children of a mulatto and a white woman cannot really understand anything better than a hybrid culture, a little nearer than their father's to the ideas of the white race,—in that case, I am right in saying that the different races are unequal in intelligence.

I will not adopt the ridiculous method that is unhappily only too dear to our ethnologists. I will not discuss, as they do, the moral and intellectual standing of individuals taken one by one.

I need, not indeed speak of morality at all, as I have already admitted the power of every human family to receive the light of Christianity in its own way. As to the question of intellectual merit, I absolutely refuse to make use of the argument, "every negro is a fool."[111] My main reason for avoiding it is that I should have to recognize, for the sake of balance, that every European is intelligent; and heaven keep me from such a paradox!

I will not wait for the friends of equality to show me such and such passages in books written by missionaries or sea-captains, who declare that some Yolof is a fine carpenter, some Hottentot a good servant, that some Kaffir dances and plays the violin, and some Bambara knows arithmetic.

I am ready to admit without proof all the marvels of this kind that anyone can tell me, even about the most degraded savages. I have already denied that even the lowest tribes are absolutely stupid. I actually go further than my opponents, as I have no doubt that a fair number of negro chiefs are superior, in the wealth of their ideas, the synthetic power of their minds, and the strength of their capacity for action, to the level usually reached by our peasants, or even by the average specimens of our half-educated middle class. But, I say again, I do not take my stand on the narrow ground of individual capacity. It seems to me unworthy of science to cling to such futile arguments. If Mungo Park or Lander have given a certificate of intelligence to some negro, what is to prevent another traveller, who meets the same phoenix, from coming to a diametrically opposite conclusion? Let us leave these puerilities, and compare together, not men, but groups. When, as may happen some day, we have carefully investigated what the different groups can and cannot do, what is the limit of their faculties and the utmost reach of their intelligence, by what nations they have been dominated

---

[111] The severest judgment on the negro that has perhaps been passed up to now comes from one of the pioneers of the doctrine of equality. Franklin defines the negro as "an animal who eats as much, and works as little, as possible."

since the dawn of history—then and then only shall we have the right to consider why the higher individuals of one race are inferior to the geniuses of another. We may then go on to compare the powers of the average men belonging to these types, and to find out where these powers are equal and where one surpasses the other. But this difficult and delicate task cannot be performed until the relative position of the different races has been accurately, and to some extent mathematically, gauged. I do not even know if we shall ever get clear and undisputed results, if we shall ever be free to go beyond a mere general conclusion and come to such close grips with the minor varieties as to be able to recognize, define, and classify the lower strata and the average minds of each nation. If we can do this, we shall easily be able to show that the activity, energy, and intelligence of the least gifted individuals in the dominant races, are greater than the same qualities in the corresponding specimens produced by the other groups.[112]

Mankind is thus divided into unlike and unequal parts, or rather into a series of categories, arranged, one above the other, according to differences of intellect.

In this vast hierarchy there are two great forces always acting on each member of the series. These forces are continually setting up movements that tend to fuse the races together; they are, as I have already indicated, (i) resemblance in general bodily structure and (ii) the common power of expressing ideas and sensations by the modulation of the voice.

I have said enough about the first of these, and have shown the true limits within which it operates.

---

112 I have no hesitation in regarding the exaggerated development of instinct among savage races as a specific mark of intellectual inferiority. The sharpening of certain senses can only be gained by the deterioration of the mental facilities. On this point, compare what Lesson says of the Papuans, in a paper printed in the *Annales des sciences naturelles,* vol. x.

I will now discuss the second point, and inquire what is the relation between the power of a race and the merit of its language; in other words, whether the strongest races have the best idioms, and if not, how the anomaly may be explained.

CHAPTER XV

THE DIFFERENT LANGUAGES ARE UNEQUAL,
AND CORRESPOND PERFECTLY IN RELATIVE
MERIT TO THE RACES THAT USE THEM

If a degraded people, at the lowest rung of the racial ladder, with as little significance for the "male" as for the "female" progress of mankind, could possibly have invented a language of philosophic depth, of aesthetic beauty and flexibility, rich in characteristic forms and precise idioms, fitted alike to express the sublimities of religion, the graces of poetry, the accuracy of physical and political science,—such a people would certainly possess an utterly useless talent, that of inventing and perfecting an instrument which their mental capacity would be too weak to turn to any account.

We should have, in such a case, to believe that our observation has been suddenly brought to a stop, not by something unknown or unintelligible (as often happens) but by a mere absurdity.

At first sight, this tantalizing answer seems the correct one. If we take the races as they are today, we must admit that the perfection of idiom is very far from corresponding, in all cases, to the degree of civilization reached. The tongues of modern Europe, to speak of no others, are unequal in merit, and the richest and most beautiful do not necessarily belong to the most advanced people. Further, they are one and all vastly inferior to many languages which have been at different times spoken in the world.

A still more curious fact is that the languages of whole groups of peoples which have stopped at a low level of culture may be of considerable merit. Thus the net of language, with its varied meshes, might seem to have been cast over mankind at random, the silk and the gold sometimes covering rude, ferocious, and miserable tribes, while wise and learned peoples are still caught in the hemp, the wool, and the horsehair. Happily, this is so only in appearance. If, with the aid of history, we apply our doctrine of the difference of races, we shall soon find that our proofs of their intellectual inequality are even strengthened.

The early philologists were doubly in error, when they thought, first that all languages are formed on the same principle, secondly that language was invented merely under the stress of material needs. In the former point they were influenced by the Unitarian doctrine that all human groups have a common origin.

With regard to language, doubt is not even possible. The modes of formation are completely different; and whether the classifications of philology require revision or not, we cannot believe for a moment that the Altaic, Aryan, and Semitic families were not from the first absolutely foreign to each other. Nothing is the same. The vocabulary has its own peculiar character in each of these groups. There is a different modulation of the voice in each. In one, the lips are used to produce the sounds; in another, the contraction of the throat; in another the nasal passage and the upper part of the head. The composition of the parts of speech, according as they confuse or distinguish the various shades of thought, points equally to a difference of origin. The most striking proof of the divergence in thought and feeling between one group and another are seen in the inflections of the substantive and the conjugations of the verb. When, therefore, the philosopher tries to give an account of the origin of language by a process of purely abstract conjecture, and begins by conceiving an "original man," without any specific racial or linguistic character, he starts from an absurdity, and continues on the same lines. There is no such being as "man" in the abstract; and I am especially sure that he will not be discovered by the investigation of language. I cannot argue on the basis that mankind started from some one point in its creation of idiom. There were many points of departure, because there were many forms of thought and feeling.[113]

The second view, I think, is just as false. According to this theory, there would have been no development save as dictated by necessity. The result would be that the "male" races would have a richer and more accurate language than the "female"; further, as material needs are concerned with objects apprehended by the senses, and especially with actions, the main factor of human speech would be vocabulary.

There would be no necessity for the syntax and grammatical structure to advance beyond the simplest and most elementary combinations. A series of sounds more or less linked together is always enough to express a need; and a gesture, as the Chinese know well, is an obvious form of commentary, when the phrase is obscure without it.[114] Not only would the synthetic power of language remain undeveloped; it would also be the poorer for dispensing with harmony, quantity, and rhythm. For what is the use of melody when the sole object is to obtain some positive result? A language, in fact, would be a mere chance collection of arbitrary sounds.

---

113 W. von Humboldt, in one of the most brilliant of his minor works, has admirably expressed this fact, in its essentials. "In language," he says, "the work of time is helped everywhere by national idiosyncrasies. The characteristic features in the idioms of the warrior hordes of America and Northern Asia were not necessarily those of the primitive races of India and Greece. It is not possible to trace a perfectly equal, and as it were natural, development of any language, whether it was spoken by one nation or many" (W. von Humboldt, *Über das Entstehen der grammatischen Formen, und ihren Einfluss auf die Ideenentwickelung*).

114 W. von Humboldt, *Über die Kawi-Sprache*, Introduction.

Certain questions are apparently cleared up by such a theory. Chinese, the tongue of a masculine race, seems to have been at first developed with a purely utilitarian aim. The word has never risen above a mere sound, and has remained monosyllabic. There is no evolution of vocabulary, no root giving birth to a family of derivatives. All the words are roots; they are not modified by suffixes, but by each other, according to a very crude method of juxtaposition. The grammar is extremely simple; which makes the phraseology very monotonous. The very idea of aesthetic value is excluded, at any rate for ears that are accustomed to the rich, varied, and abundant forms, the inexhaustible combinations of happier tongues. We must however add that this may not be the impression produced on the Chinese themselves; and their spoken language certainly aims at some kind of beauty, since there are definite rules governing the melodic sequence of sounds. If it does not succeed in being so euphonious as other languages, we must still recognize that it aims at euphony no less than they. Further, the primary elements of Chinese are something more than a mere heaping together of useful sounds.[115]

I admit that the masculine races may be markedly inferior in aesthetic power to the others,[116] and their inferiority may be reproduced in their idioms. This is shown, not merely by the relative poverty of Chinese, but also by the careful way in which certain Western races have robbed Latin of its finest rhythmic qualities, and Gothic of its sonority. The inferiority of our modern languages, even the best of them, to Sanskrit, Greek, and Latin, is self-evident, and corresponds exactly to the mediocrity of the Chinese civilization and our own, so

---

[115] I am inclined to believe that the monosyllabic quality of Chinese is not really a specific mark of the language at all; and though a striking characteristic, it does not seem to be an essential one. If it were, Chinese would be an "isolating" language, connected with others having the same structure. We know that this is not so. Chinese belongs to the Tatar or Finnish system, of which some branches are polysyllabic. On the other hand, we find monosyllabic languages among groups with quite a different origin. I do not lay any stress on the example of Othomi, a Mexican dialect which, according to du Ponceau, has the monosyllabic quality of Chinese, and yet in other respects belongs to the American family among which it is found, as Chinese does to the Tatar group (see Morton, "An Inquiry into the Distinctive Characteristics of the aboriginal race of America," Philadelphia, 1844). My reason for neglecting this apparently important example is that these American languages may one day be recognized as forming merely a vast branch of the Tatar family; and thus any conclusion I might draw from them would simply go to confirm what I have said as to the relation of Chinese to the surrounding dialects, a relation which is in no way disproved by the peculiar character of Chinese itself.

I find therefore a more conclusive instance in Coptic, which will not easily be shown to have any relation to Chinese. But here also every syllable is a root; and the simple affixes that modify the root are so independent that even the determining particle that marks the time of the verb does not always remain joined to the word. Thus *hon* means "to command"; *a-hon,* "he commanded"; but *a Moyses hon,* "Moses commanded" (see E. Meier, *Hebräisches Wurzelwörterbuch*).

Thus it seems possible for monosyllabism to appear in every linguistic family. It is a kind of infirmity produced by causes which are not yet understood; it is not however a specific feature, separating the language in which it occurs from the rest, and setting it in a class by itself.

[116] Goethe says in *Wilhelm Meister:* "Few Germans, and perhaps few men of modern nations, have the sense of an aesthetic whole. We only know how to praise and blame details, we can only show a fragmentary admiration."

far as art and literature are concerned. I admit that this difference, alone with others, may serve to mark off the languages of the masculine races. They still, however, have a feeling for rhythm (less than that of the ancient tongues, but still powerful), and make a real attempt to create and obey laws of correspondence between sounds and the forms by which thought is modified in speech. I conclude that even in the languages of masculine races there still flickers the intellectual spark, the feeling for beauty and logic; this feeling, as well as that of material need, must preside at the birth of every language.

I said above that if material need had reigned alone, a set of any chance sounds would have been enough for human necessities, in the first ages of man's existence. Such a theory cannot be maintained.

Sounds are not assigned to ideas by pure chance. The choice is governed by the instinctive recognition of a certain logical relation between noises heard outwardly by man's ear and ideas that his throat or tongue wishes to express. In the eighteenth century men were greatly struck by this truth. Unfortunately, it was caught in the net of etymological exaggeration so characteristic of the time; and its results were so absurd that they justly fell into disrepute. For a long time the best minds were warned off the land that had been so stupidly exploited by the early pioneers. They are now beginning to return to it again, and if they have learnt prudence and restraint in the bitter school of experience, they may arrive at valuable conclusions. Without pushing a theory, true in itself, into the realm of chimeras, we may allow that primitive speech knew how to use as far as possible the different impressions received by the ear, in order to form certain classes of words; in creating others it was guided by the feeling of a mysterious relation between certain abstract ideas and some particular noises. Thus, for example, the sound of *e* seems to suggest death and dissolution, that of *v* or *w*, vagueness in the moral or physical realm, vows, wind, and the like; *s* suggests starkness and standing fast, *m* maternity, and so on.[117] Such a theory is sufficiently well founded for us to take it seriously, if kept within due limits. But it must be used with great circumspection, if we are not to find ourselves in the dark paths where even common sense is soon led astray.

The last paragraph may show, however imperfectly, that material need is not the only element that produces a language, but that the best of man's powers have helped in the task. Sounds were not applied arbitrarily to ideas and objects, and in this respect men followed a pre-established order, one side of which was manifested in themselves. Thus the primitive tongues, however crude and poor they may have been, contained all the elements from which their branches might at a later time be developed in a logical and necessary sequence.

W. von Humboldt has observed, with his usual acuteness, that every language is independent of the will of those who speak it. It is closely bound up with their intellectual condition, and is beyond the reach of arbitrary caprice. It cannot be altered at will, as is curiously shown by the efforts that have been made to do so.

The Bushmen have invented a system of changing their language, in order to prevent its being understood by the uninitiated. We find the same custom among certain tribes of the Caucasus. But all their efforts come to no more than the mere insertion of a subsidiary syllable at the beginning, middle, or end of words. Take

---

117 *Cf.* W. von Humboldt, *Über die Kawi-Sprache,* Introduction, p. xcv: "We may call the sound that imitates the meaning of a word *symbolic,* although the symbolic element in speech goes far deeper than this. ... This kind of imitation undoubtedly had a great, and perhaps exclusive, influence over the early attempts at word-building."

away this parasitic element, and the language remains the same, changed neither in forms nor syntax.

De Sacy has discovered a more ambitious attempt, in the language called "Balaibalan." This curious idiom was invented by the Sufis, to be used in their mystical books, with the object of wrapping the speculations of their theologians in still greater mystery. They made up, on no special plan, the words that seemed to them to sound most strangely to their ears. If however this so-called language did not belong to any family and if the meaning given to its sounds was entirely arbitrary, yet the principles of euphony, the grammar and the syntax, everything in fact which gives a language its special character, bore the unmistakable stamp of Arabic and Persian. The Sufis produced a jargon at once Aryan and Semitic, and of no importance whatever. The pious colleagues of Jalāl ad-Dīn Rūmī were not able to invent a language; and clearly this power has not been given to any single man.[118]

Hence the language of a race is closely bound up with its intelligence, and has the power of reflecting its

---

[118] There is probably another jargon of the same kind as Balaibalan. This is called "Afnskoë," and is spoken by the peddlers and horse-dealers of Greater Russia, especially in the province of Vladimir. It is confined to men. The grammar is entirely Russian, though the roots are foreign. (*See* Pott, Ersch and Gruber's *Encyclopädie, Indogermanischer Sprachstamm*, p. 110.)

various mental stages, as they are reached. This power may be at first only implicit.[119]

Where the mental development of a race is faulty or imperfect, the language suffers to the same extent. This is shown by Sanskrit, Greek, and the Semitic group, as well as by Chinese, in which I have already pointed out a utilitarian tendency corresponding to the intellectual bent of the people. The superabundance of philosophical and ethnological terms in Sanskrit corresponds to the genius of those who spoke it, as well as its richness and rhythmic beauty. The same is the case with Greek; while the lack of precision in the Semitic tongues is exactly paralleled by the character of the Semitic peoples.

If we leave the cloudy heights of the remoter ages, and come down to the more familiar regions of modern history, we shall be, as it were, presiding at the birth of many new tongues; and this will make us see with even greater clearness how faithfully language mirrors the genius of a race.

As soon as two nations are fused together, a revolution takes place in their respective languages; this is sometimes slow, sometimes sudden, but always inevitable. The languages are changed and, after a

---

[119] C.O. Müller, in an admirable passage which I cannot resist the temptation of transcribing, shows the true nature of language: "Our age has learnt, by the study of the Hindu and especially the Germanic languages, that the laws of speech are as fixed as those of organic life. Between different dialects, developing independently after their separation, there are still mysterious links, which reciprocally determine the sounds and their sequences. Literature and science set limits to this growth, and arrest perhaps some of its richer developments; but they cannot impose any law on it higher than that ordained by nature, mother of all things. Even a long time before the coming of decadence and bad taste, languages may fall sick, from outward or inward causes, and suffer vast changes; but so long as life remains in them, their innate power is enough to heal their wounds, to set their torn limbs, and to restore unity and regularity, even when the beauty and perfection of the noble plants has almost entirely disappeared" {*Die Etrusker,* p. 65).

certain time, die out as separate entities. The new tongue is a compromise between them, the dominant element being furnished by the speech of the race that has contributed most members to the new people.[120] Thus, from the thirteenth century, the Germanic dialects of France have had to yield ground, not to Latin, but to the *lingua romana,* with the revival of the Gallo-Roman power.[121] Celtic, too, had to retreat before the Italian colonists. It did not yield to Italian civilization; in fact, one might say, that, thanks to the number of those who spoke it, Celtic finally gained a kind of victory. For after the complete fusion of the Gauls, the Romans, and the northern tribes, it was Celtic that laid the foundations of modern French syntax, abolished the strong accentuation of Germanic as well as the sonority of Latin, and introduced its own equable rhythm. The gradual development of French is merely the effect of this patient labor, that went on, without ceasing, under the surface. Again, the reason why modern German has lost the striking forms to be seen in the Gothic of Bishop Ulfilas lies in the presence of a strong Cymric element in the midst of the small Germanic population that was still left to the east of the Rhine,[122] after the great migrations of the sixth and following centuries of our era.

---

[120] Pott, *op. cit.*, p. 74.

[121] That the mixture of idioms is proportionate to that of the races constituting a nation had already been noticed before philology, in the modern sense, existed at all. Kämpfer for example says in his "History of Japan" (published in 1729): "We may take it as a fixed rule that the settlement of foreigners in a country will bring a corresponding proportion of foreign words into the language; these will be naturalized by degrees, and become as familiar as the native words themselves."

[122] Keferstein shows that German is merely a hybrid language made up of Celtic and Gothic *(Ansichten über die keltischen Altertümer,* Halle, 1846-51; Introduction, p. xxxviii). Grimm is of the same opinion.

The linguistic results of the fusion of two peoples are as individual as the new racial character itself. One may say generally that no language remains pure after it has come into close contact with a different language. Even when their structures are totally unlike each other, the vocabulary at any rate suffers some changes. If the parasitic language has any strength at all, it will certainly attack the other in its rhythmic quality, and even in the unstable parts of its syntax. Thus language is one of the most fragile and delicate forms of property; and we may often see a noble and refined speech being affected by barbarous idioms and passing itself into a kind of relative barbarism. By degrees it will lose its beauty; its vocabulary will be impoverished, and many of its forms obsolete, while it will show an irresistible tendency to become assimilated to its inferior neighbor. This has happened in the case of Wallachian and Rhsetian, Kawi and Birman. The two latter have been leavened with Sanskrit elements; but in spite of this noble alliance, they have been declared by competent judges to be inferior to Delaware.[123]

The group of tribes speaking this dialect are of the Lenni-Lenapes family, and they originally ranked higher than the two yellow peoples who were caught in the sweep of Hindu civilization. If, in spite of their primitive superiority, they are now inferior to the Asiatics, it is because these live under the influence of the social institutions of a noble race and have profited by them, though in themselves they are of slight account. Contact

---

[123] W. von Humboldt says: "Languages, that are apparently crude and unrefined, may show some striking qualities in their structure, and often do so. In this respect they may quite possibly surpass more highly developed tongues. The comparison of Birman with Delaware, not to speak of Mexican, can leave no doubt of the superiority of the latter; yet a strand of Indian culture has certainly been interwoven into Birman by Pali" *(Über die Kawi-Sprache,* Introduction, p. xxxiv).

with the Hindus has been enough to raise them some way in the scale, while the Lenapes, who have never been touched by any such influence, have not been able to rise above their present civilization. In a similar way (to take an obvious example) the young mulattoes who have been educated in London or Paris may show a certain veneer of culture superior to that of some Southern Italian peoples, who are in point of merit infinitely higher: for once a mulatto, always a mulatto. When therefore we come upon a savage tribe with a language better than that of a more civilized nation, we must examine carefully whether the civilization of the latter really belongs to it, or is merely the result of a slight admixture of foreign blood. If so, a low type of native language helped out by a hybrid mixture of foreign idioms may well exist side by side with a certain degree of social culture.[124]

I have already said that, as each civilization has a special character, we must not be surprised if the poetic and philosophic sense was more developed among the Hindus and the Greeks than among ourselves; whereas our modern societies are marked rather by their practical, scientific, and critical spirit. Taken as a whole, we have more energy and a greater genius for action than the conquerors of Southern Asia and Hellas. On the other hand, we must yield them the first place in the kingdom of beauty, and here our languages naturally mirror our humble position. The style of the Indian and Ionian writers takes a more powerful flight towards the

---

[124] This difference of level between the intellect of the conqueror and that of the conquered is the cause of the "sacred languages" that we find used in the early days of an empire; such as that of the Egyptians, or the Incas of Peru. These languages are the object of a superstitious veneration; they are the exclusive property of the upper classes, and often of a sacerdotal caste, and they furnish the strongest possible proof of the existence of a foreign race that has conquered the country where they are found.

sphere of the ideal. Language, in fact, while being an excellent index of the general elevation of races, is in a special degree the measure of their aesthetic capacities. This is the character it assumes when we use it as a means of comparing different civilizations.

To bring out this point further, I will venture to question a view put forward by Wilhelm von Humboldt, that in spite of the obvious superiority of the Mexican to the Peruvian language, the civilization of the Incas was yet far above that of the people of Anahuac.[125]

The Peruvian customs were certainly more gentle than the Mexican; and their religious ideas were as inoffensive as those of Montezuma's subjects were ferocious. In spite of this, their social condition was marked by far less energy and variety. Their crude despotism never developed into more than a dull kind of communism; whereas the Aztec civilization had made various political experiments of great complexity. Its military system was far more vigorous; and though the use of writing was equally unknown in both empires, it seems that poetry, history, and ethics, which were extensively studied at the time of Cortés, would have advanced further in Mexico than in Peru, the institutions of which were colored by an Epicurean indifferentism that was highly unfavorable to intellectual progress. Clearly we must regard the more active people as superior.

Von Humboldt's view is simply a consequence of the way in which he defines civilization. Without going over the same ground again, I was yet bound to clear up this point; for if two civilizations had really been able to develop in inverse ratio to the merits of their respective languages, I should have had to give up the idea of any necessary connection between the intelligence of a

---

[125] W. von Humboldt, *Über die Kawi-Sprache,* Introduction, p. xxxiv

people and the value of the language spoken by it. But I cannot do this, in view of what I have already said about Greek and Sanskrit, as compared with English, French, and German.

It would be, however, a very difficult task to assign a reason, along these lines, for the exact course taken by the language of a hybrid people. We have seldom sufficient knowledge either of the quantity or quality of the intermixture of blood to be able properly to trace its effects. Yet these racial influences persist, and if they are not unravelled, we may easily come to false conclusions. It is just because the connection between race and language is so close, that it lasts much longer than the political unity of the different peoples, and may be recognized even when the peoples are grouped under new names. The language changes with their blood, but does not die out until the last fragment of the national life has disappeared. This is the case with modern Greek. Sadly mutilated, robbed of its wealth of grammar, impoverished in the number of its sounds, with the pure stream of its vocabulary troubled and muddy, it has none the less retained the impress of its original form.[126] In the intellectual world it corresponds to the sullied and deflowered Parthenon, which first became a church for the Greek popes, and then a powder-magazine; which had its pediments and columns shattered in a thousand places by the Venetian bullets of Morosini; but which still stands, for the wonder and adoration of the ages, as a model of pure grace and unadorned majesty.

Not every race has the power of being faithful to the tongue of its ancestors. This makes our task still more

---

[126] Ancient Greece contained many dialects, but not so many as the Greece of the sixteenth century, when seventy were counted by Simeon Kavasila; further we may notice (in connection with the following paragraph) that in the thirteenth century French was spoken throughout Greece, and especially in Attica (Heilmayer, quoted by Pott, *op. cit.,* p. 73).

difficult, when we try to determine the origin or relative value of different human types by the help of philology. Not only do languages change without any obvious reason, at any rate from the racial point of view; but there are also certain nations which give up their own language altogether, when they are brought for some time into contact with a foreign race. This happened, after the conquests of Alexander, in the case of the more enlightened nations of Western Asia, such as the Carians, Cappadocians, and Armenians. The Gauls are another instance, as I have already said. Yet all these peoples brought a foreign element into the conquering tongue, which was transformed in its turn. Thus they could all be regarded as using their own intellectual tools, though to a very imperfect extent; while others, more tenacious of theirs, such as the Basques, the Berbers of Mount Atlas, and the Ekkhilis of Southern Arabia, speak even at the present day the same tongue as was spoken by their most primitive ancestors. But there are certain peoples, the Jews for example, who seem never to have held to their ancestral speech at all; and we can discover this indifference from the time of their earliest migrations. When Terah left the land of his fathers, Ur of the Chaldees, he certainly had not learnt the Canaanitish tongue that henceforth became the national speech of the children of Israel. It was probably influenced to some extent by their earlier recollections, and in their mouth became a special dialect of the very ancient language which was the mother of the earliest Arabic we know, and the lawful inheritance of tribes closely allied to the black Hamites.[127] Yet not even to this language were the Jews to remain faithful. The

---

[127] The Hebrews themselves did not call their language "Hebrew"; they called it, quite properly, the "language of Canaan" (Isaiah xix, 18). Compare Roediger's preface to the Hebrew grammar of Gesenius (16th edition, Leipzig, 1851, p. 7 *et passim*).

tribes who were brought back from captivity by Zerubbabel had forgotten it during their short stay of sixty-two years by the rivers of Babylon. Their patriotism was proof against exile, and still burned with its original fire; but the rest had been given up, with remarkable facility, by a people which is at the same time jealous of its own traditions and extremely cosmopolitan. Jerusalem was rebuilt, and its inhabitants reappeared, speaking an Aramaic or Chaldaean jargon, which may have had some slight resemblance to the speech of the fathers of Abraham.

At the time of Christ, this dialect offered only a feeble resistance to the invasion of Hellenistic Greek, which assailed the Jewish mind on all sides. Henceforth all the works produced by Jewish writers appeared in the new dress, which fitted them more or less elegantly, and copied to some extent the old Attic fashions. The last canonical books of the Old Testament, as well as the works of Philo and Josephus, are Hellenistic in spirit.

When the Holy City was destroyed, and the Jewish nation scattered, the favor of God departed from them, and the East came again into its own. Hebrew culture broke with Athens as it had broken with Alexandria, and the language and ideas of the Talmud, the teaching of the school of Tiberias, were again Semitic, sometimes in the form of Arabic, sometimes in that of the "language of Canaan," to use Isaiah's phrase. I am speaking of what was henceforth to be the sacred language of religion and the Rabbis, and was regarded as the true national speech. In their everyday life, however, the Jews used the tongue of the country where they settled; and, further, these exiles were known everywhere by their special accent. They never succeeded in fitting their vocal organs to their adopted language, even when they had learnt it from childhood. This goes to confirm what Wilhelm von Humboldt says as to the connection between race and language being so close that later generations never get quite accustomed to pronounce correctly words that were unknown to their ancestors.[128]

Whether this be true or not, we have in the Jews a remarkable proof of the fact that one must not always assume, at first sight, a close connection between a race and its language, for the language may not have belonged to it originally.[129]

We see how cautiously we must tread if we attempt to infer an identity of race from the affinity, or even the resemblance, of languages. Not only have most of the nations of Western Asia and nearly all those of Southern Europe merely adapted the speech of others to their own use, while leaving its main elements untouched; but there are also some who have taken over languages absolutely foreign to them, to which they have made no contribution whatever. The latter case is certainly rarer, and may even be regarded as an anomaly. But its mere existence is enough to make us very careful in admitting a form of proof in which such exceptions are possible. On the other hand, since they *are* exceptions, and are not met with so often as the opposite case, of a national tongue being preserved for centuries by even a weak nation; since we also see how a language is assimilated to the particular character of the people that has created it, and how its changes are in exact proportion to the successive modifications in the people's blood; since the part played by a language in forming its derivatives varies

---

[128] This is also the view of W. Edwards ("Physical Characteristics of the Human Races ").

[129] Besides the Jews, I might also mention the Gypsies. There is, further, the case where a people speaks two languages. In Grisons almost all the peasants of the Engadine speak Roumansch and German with equal facility, the former among themselves, the latter to foreigners. In Courland there is a district where the peoples speak Esthonian (a Finnish dialect) to each other and Lithuanian to every one else (Pott, *op. cit.,* p. 104).

with the numerical strength, in the new groups, of the race that speaks it, we may justly conclude that no nation can have a language of greater value than itself, except under special circumstances. As this point is of considerable importance, I will try to bring it out by a new line of proof.

We have already seen that the civilization of a composite people does not include all its social classes. The racial influences that were at work in the lower strata from the first still go on; and they prevent the directing forces of the national culture from reaching the depths at all,—if they do, their action is weak and transitory. In France, about five-eighths of the total population play merely an unwilling and passive part in the development of modern European culture, and that only by fits and starts. With the exception of Great Britain, of which the insular position produces a greater unity of type, the proportion is even higher in the rest of the Continent. I will speak of France at greater length, as an instance of the exact correspondence between language and racial type; for in France we have a particular instance that strikingly confirms our main thesis.

We know little, or rather we have no real evidence at all, of the phases which Celtic and rustic Latin[130] passed through before they met and coalesced. Nevertheless, St. Jerome and his contemporary Sulpicius Severus tell us (the former in his "Commentaries" on St. Paul's Epistle to the Galatians, the second in his "Dialogue on the virtues of the Eastern Monks") that in their time at least

---

[130] The way was not so long from rustic Latin, *lingua rustica Romanorum,* to the *lingua romana* and thence to corruption, as it was from the classical tongue, the precise and elaborate forms of which offered more resistance to decay. We may add that, as every foreign legionary brought his own provincial patois into the Gallic colonies, the advent of a common dialect was hastened, not merely by the Celts, but by the immigrants themselves.

two languages were generally spoken in Gaul. There was, first, Celtic, which was preserved on the banks of the Rhine in so pure a form, that it remained identical with the language spoken by the Galatians of Asia Minor, who had been separated from their mother country for more than six centuries.[131] Secondly, there was the language called "Gallic," which according to a commentator, can only have been a form, already broken down, of Popular Latin. This fourth century dialect, while different from the Gallic of Treves, was spoken neither in the West nor in Aquitaine. It was found only in the center and south of what is now France, and was itself probably split up into two great divisions. It is the common source of the currents, more or less Latinized, which were mingled with other elements in different proportions, and formed later the *langue d'oil* and the *lingua romana,* in the narrower sense. I will speak first of the latter.

In order to bring it into being, all that was necessary was a slight alteration in the vocabulary of Latin, and the introduction of a few syntactical notions borrowed from Celtic and other languages till then unknown in the West of Europe. The Imperial colonies had brought in a fair number of Italian, African, and Asiatic elements. The Burgundian, and especially the Gothic, invasions added another, which was marked by considerable harmony, liveliness, and sonority. Its vocabulary was further increased after the inroads of the Saracens. Thus the *lingua romana* became, in its rhythmic quality, quite distinct from Gallic, and soon assumed a character of its own. It is true that we do not find this in its perfection, in the "Oath of the Sons of Ludwig the Pious," as we do later in the poems of Raimbaut de Vaqueiras or Bertran

131 Sulp. Severus, *Dial. I de virtutibus monachorum orientalium.*

de Born.[132] Yet even in the "Oath" we can recognize the language for what it is; it has already acquired its main features, and its future path is clearly mapped out. It formed henceforth (in its different dialects of Limousin, Provençal, and Auvergnat) the speech of a people of as mixed an origin as any in the world. It was a refined and supple language, witty, brilliant, and satirical, but without depth or philosophy. It was of tinsel rather than gold, and had never been able to do more than pick up a few ingots on the surface of the rich mines that lay open to it. Without any serious principles, it was destined to remain an instrument of indifference, of universal skepticism and mockery. It did not fail to be used as such. The people cared for nothing but pleasure and parade. Brave to a fault, beyond measure gay, spending their passion on a dream, and their vitality on idle toys, they had an instrument that was exactly suited to their character, and which, though admired by Dante, was put to no better use in poetry than to tag satires, love-songs, and challenges, and in religion to support heresies such as that of the Albigenses, a pestilent Manichaeism, without value even for literature, from which an English author, in no way Catholic in his sympathies, congratulates the Papacy on having delivered the Middle Ages.[133] Such was the *lingua romana* of old, and such do we find it even today. It is pretty rather than beautiful, and shows on the surface how little it is fitted to serve a great civilization.

---

[132] Both troubadours who flourished in the latter half of the twelfth century.—Tr.

[133] Macaulay, "History of England," *ad init.* The Albigenses are the special favorites of revolutionary writers, especially in Germany (*see* Lenau's poem, *Die Albigenser*). Nevertheless the sectaries of Languedoc were recruited mainly from the knightly orders and the dignitaries of the Church. Their doctrines were indeed antisocial; and for this reason much may be pardoned to them.

Was the *langue d'oil* formed in a similar way? Obviously not. However the Celtic, Latin, and Germanic elements were fused (for we cannot be certain on this point, in the absence of records going back to the earliest period of the language[134]), it is at any rate clear that it rose from a strongly marked antagonism between the three tongues, and that it would thus have a character and energy quite incompatible with such compromises and adaptations as those which gave birth to the *lingua romana*. In one moment of its life, the *langue d'oil* was partly a Germanic tongue. In the written remains that have survived, we find one of the best qualities of the Aryan languages, the power of forming compounds. This power, it is true, is limited; and though still considerable, is less than in Sanskrit, Greek, and German. In the nouns, we find a system of inflection by suffix, and, in consequence, an ease in inverting the order which modern French has lost, and which the language of the sixteenth century retained only to a slight extent, its inversions being gained at the expense of clearness. Again, the vocabulary of the *langue d'oil* included many words brought in by the Franks.[135] Thus it began by being almost as much Germanic as Gallic; Celtic elements appeared in its second stage, and perhaps fixed the melodic principles of the language. The best possible tribute to its merits is to be found in the successful experiment of Littré,[136] who translated the first book of the *Iliad* literally, line for line, into French

---

134 See the curious remarks of Génin in his preface to the *Chanson de Roland* (edited 1851).

135 *See* Hickes, *Thesaurus litteraturæ septentrionalis;* also *L'Histoire littéraire de France,* vol. xvii, p. 633.

136 Published in the *Revue des Deux Mondes.*

of the thirteenth century. Such a *tour de force* would be impossible in modern French.

Such a language belonged to a people that was evidently very different from the inhabitants of Southern Gaul. It was more deeply attached to Catholicism; its politics were permeated by a lively idea of freedom, dignity, and independence, its institutions had no aim but utility. Thus the mission set before the popular literature was not to express the fancies of the mind or heart, the freakishness of a universal skepticism, but to put together the annals of the nation, and to set down what was at that time regarded as the truth. It is to this temper of the people and their language that we owe the great rhymed chronicles, especially "Garin le Loherain," which bear witness, though it has since been denied, to the predominance of the North. Unfortunately, since the compilers of these traditions, and even their original authors, mainly aimed at preserving historical facts or satisfying their desire for positive and solid results, poetry in the true sense, the love of form and the search for beauty, does not always bulk as large as it should in their long narratives. The literature of the *langue d'oil* was, above all, utilitarian; and so the race, the language, and the literature were in perfect harmony.

The Germanic element in the race, however, being far less than the Gallic basis or the Roman accretions, naturally began to lose ground. The same thing took place in the language; Celtic and Latin advanced, Germanic retreated. That noble speech, which we know only at its highest stage, and which might have risen even higher, began to decline and become corrupted towards the end of the thirteenth century. In the fifteenth, it was no more than a patois, from which the Germanic elements had completely disappeared. The treasury was exhausted; and what remained was an illogical and barbarous anomaly in the midst of the progress of Celtic and Latin. Thus in the sixteenth century the revival of classical studies found the language in ruins, and tried to remodel it on the lines of Greek and Latin. This was the professed aim of the writers of this great age. They did not succeed, and the seventeenth century, wisely seeing that the irresistible march of events could in no wise be curbed by the hand of man, set itself merely to improve the language from within; for every day it was assuming more and more the forms best suited to the dominant race, the forms, in other words, into which the grammatical life of Celtic had formerly been cast.

Although both the *langue d'oil* and French proper are marked by a greater unity than the *lingua romana* (since the mixture of races and languages that gave birth to them was less complex) yet they have produced separate dialects which survive to this day. It is not doing these too much honor to call them dialects, not patois. They arose, not from the corruption of the dominant type, with which they were at least contemporary, but from the different proportions in which the Celtic, Latin, and Germanic elements, that still make up the French nationality, were mingled.

To the north of the Seine, we find the dialect of Picardy; this is, in vocabulary and rhythmic quality, very near Flemish, of which the Germanic character is too obvious to be dwelt upon. Flemish, in this respect, shows the same power of choice as the *langue d'oil,* which could in a certain poem, without ceasing to be itself, admit forms and expressions taken bodily from the language spoken at Arras.[137]

As we go south of the Seine towards the Loire, the Celtic elements in the provincial dialects grow more

---

[137] P. Pâris, *Garin le Loherain,* preface.

numerous. In Burgundian, and the dialects of Vaud and Savoy, even the vocabulary has many traces of Celtic; these are not found in French, where the predominant factor is rustic Latin.[138]

I have shown above how from the sixteenth century the influence of the north had given ground before the growing preponderance of the peoples beyond the Loire. The reader has merely to compare the present sections on language with my former remarks on blood to see how close is the relation between the speech of a people and its physical constitution.[139]

I have dealt in detail with the special case of France, but the principle could easily be illustrated from the rest of Europe; and it would be seen, as a universal rule, that the successive changes and modifications of a language are not, as one usually hears, the ' work of centuries. If they were, Ekkhili, Berber, Euskara, and Bas-Breton would long have disappeared; and yet they still survive. The changes in language are caused by corresponding changes in the blood of successive generations, and the parallelism is exact.

I must here explain a phenomenon to which I have already referred, namely the renunciation by certain racial groups (under pressure of special necessity, or their own nature) of their native tongue in favor of one which is more or less foreign to them. I took the Jews and the Parsees as examples. There are others more remarkable still; for we find, in America, savage tribes speaking languages superior to themselves.

---

[138] It may however be observed that the accent of Vaud and Savoy has a southern ring, strongly reminiscent of the colony of Aventicum.

[139] Pott brings out very well the fact that the different dialects maintain the balance between the blood of a race and its language, when he says, "Dialects are the diversity in unity, the prismatic sections of the monochromatic light and the primordial One" (Ersch and Gruber's *Encyclopädie,* p. 66). The phraseology is obscure; but it shows his meaning clearly enough.

310

In America, by a curious stroke of fate, the most energetic nations have developed, so to speak, in secret. The art of writing was unknown to them, and their history proper begins very late and is nearly always very obscure. The New World contains a great number of peoples which, though they are neighbors and derive in different directions from a common origin, have very little resemblance to each other.

According to d'Orbigny, the so-called "Chiquitean group" in Central America is composed of tribes, of which the largest contain about 1500 souls, and the least numerous 50 and 300. All these, even the smallest, have distinct languages. Such a state of things can only be the result of a complete racial anarchy.

On this hypothesis, I am not at all surprised to see many of these tribes, like the Chiquitos, in possession of a complicated and apparently scientific language. The words used by the men are sometimes different from those of the women; and in every case when a man borrows one of the women's phrases, he changes the terminations. Where such luxury in vocabulary is possible, the language has surely reached a very refined stage. Unfortunately, side by side with this we find that the table of numerals does not go much further than ten. Such poverty, in the midst of so much careful elaboration, is probably due to the ravaging hand of time, aided by the barbarous condition of the natives today. When we see anomalies like these, we cannot help recalling the sumptuous palaces, once marvels of the Renaissance, which have come, by some revolution, into the hands of rude peasants. The eye may rove with admiration over delicate columns, elegant trellis-work, sculptured porches, noble staircases, and striking gables —luxuries which are useless to the wretchedness that lives under them; for the ruined roofs let in the rain, the floors crack, and the worm eats into the mouldering walls.

I can now say with certainty that, with regard to the special character of races, philology confirms all the facts of physiology and history. Its conclusions however must be handled with extreme care, and when they are all we have to go upon, it is very dangerous to rest content with them. Without the slightest doubt, a people's language corresponds to its mentality, but not always to its real value for civilization. In order to ascertain this, we must fix our eyes solely on the race by which, and for which, the language was at first designed. Now with the exception of the negroes, and a few yellow groups, we meet only quaternary races in recorded history. All the languages we know are thus derivative, and we cannot gain the least idea of the laws governing their formation except in the comparatively later stages. Our results, even when confirmed by history, cannot be regarded as infallibly proved. The further we go back, the dimmer becomes the light, and the more hypothetical the nature of any arguments drawn from philology. It is exasperating to be thrown back on these when we try to trace the progress of any human family or to discover the racial elements that make it up. We know that Sanskrit and Zend are akin. That is something; but their common roots are sealed to us. The other ancient tongues are in the same case. We know nothing of Euskara except itself. As no analogue to it has been discovered up to now, we are ignorant of its history, and whether it is to be regarded as itself primitive or derived. It yields us no positive knowledge as to whether the people who speak it are racially simple or composite.

Ethnology may well be grateful for the help given by philology. But the help must not be accepted unconditionally, or any theories based on it alone.[140]

This rule is dictated by a necessary prudence. All the facts, however, mentioned in this chapter go to prove that, originally, there is a perfect correspondence between the intellectual virtues of a race and those of its native speech; that languages are, in consequence, unequal in value and significance, unlike in their forms and basic elements, as races are also; that their modifications, like those of races, come merely from intermixture with other idioms; that their qualities and merits, like a people's blood, disappear or become absorbed, when they are swamped by too many heterogeneous elements; finally, that when a language of a higher order is used by some human group which is unworthy of it, it will certainly become mutilated and die out. Hence, though it is often difficult to infer at once, in a particular case, the merits of a people from those of its language, it is quite certain that in theory this can always be done.

I may thus lay it down, as a universal axiom, that the hierarchy of languages is in strict correspondence with the hierarchy of races.

---

[140] This caution applies only when the history of a single people is in question, not that of a group of peoples. Although one nation may sometimes change its language, this never happens, and could not happen, in the case of a complex of nationalities, racially identical though politically independent. The Jews have given up their national speech; but the Semitic nations as a whole can neither lose their native dialects nor acquire others.

CHAPTER XVI

RECAPITULATION; THE RESPECTIVE CHARACTERISTICS OF THE THREE GREAT RACES; THE SUPERIORITY OF THE WHITE TYPE, AND, WITHIN THIS TYPE, OF THE ARYAN FAMILY

I have shown the unique place in the organic world occupied by the human species, the profound physical, as well as moral, differences separating it from all other kinds of living creatures. Considering it by itself, I have been able to distinguish, on physiological grounds alone, three great and clearly marked types, the black, the yellow, and the white. However uncertain the aims of physiology may be, however meagre its resources, however defective its methods, it can proceed thus far with absolute certainty.

The negroid variety is the lowest, and stands at the foot of the ladder. The animal character, that appears in the shape of the pelvis, is stamped on the negro from birth, and foreshadows his destiny. His intellect will always move within a very narrow circle. He is not however a mere brute, for behind his low receding brow, in the middle of his skull, we can see signs of a powerful energy, however crude its objects. If his mental faculties are dull or even non-existent, he often has an intensity of desire, and so of will, which may be called terrible. Many of his senses, especially taste and smell, are developed to an extent unknown to the other two races.[141]

The very strength of his sensations is the most striking proof of his inferiority. All food is good in his

---

[141] "Taste and smell in the negro are as powerful as they are undiscriminating. He eats everything, and odors which are revolting to us are pleasant to him" (Pruner).

eyes, nothing disgusts or repels him. What he desires is to eat, to eat furiously, and to excess; no carrion is too revolting to be swallowed by him. It is the same with odors; his inordinate desires are satisfied with all, however coarse or even horrible. To these qualities may be added an instability and capriciousness of feeling, that cannot be tied down to any single object, and which, so far as he is concerned, do away with all distinctions of good and evil. We might even say that the violence with which he pursues the object that has aroused his senses and inflamed his desires is a guarantee of the desires being soon satisfied and the object forgotten. Finally, he is equally careless of his own life and that of others: he kills willingly, for the sake of killing; and this human machine, in whom it is so easy to arouse emotion, shows, in face of suffering, either a monstrous indifference or a cowardice that seeks a voluntary refuge in death.

The yellow race is the exact opposite of this type. The skull points forward, not backward. The forehead is wide and bony, often high and projecting. The shape of the face is triangular, the nose and chin showing none of the coarse protuberances that mark the negro. There is further a general proneness to obesity, which, though not confined to the yellow type, is found there more frequently than in the others. The yellow man has little physical energy, and is inclined to apathy; he commits none of the strange excesses so common among negroes. His desires are feeble, his will-power rather obstinate than violent; his longing for material pleasures, though constant, is kept within bounds. A rare glutton by nature, he shows far more discrimination in his choice of food. He tends to mediocrity in everything; he understands easily enough anything not too deep or sublime.[142] He has a love of utility and a respect for order, and knows the value of a certain amount of freedom. He is practical, in the narrowest sense of the word. He does not dream or theorize; he invents little, but can appreciate and take over what is useful to him. His whole desire is to live in the easiest and most comfortable way possible. The yellow races are thus clearly superior to the black. Every founder of a civilization would wish the backbone of his society, his middle class, to consist of such men. But no civilized society could be created by them; they could not supply its nerve-force, or set in motion the springs of beauty and action.

We come now to the white peoples. These are gifted with reflective energy, or rather with an energetic intelligence. They have a feeling for utility, but in a sense far wider and higher, more courageous and ideal, than the yellow races; a perseverance that takes account of obstacles and ultimately finds a means of overcoming them; a greater physical power, an extraordinary instinct for order, not merely as a guarantee of peace and tranquillity, but as an indispensable means of self-preservation. At the same time, they have a remarkable, and even extreme, love of liberty, and are openly hostile to the formalism under which the Chinese are glad to vegetate, as well as to the strict despotism which is the only way of governing the negro.

The white races are, further, distinguished by an extraordinary attachment to life. They know better how to use it, and so, as it would seem, set a greater price on it; both in their own persons and those of others, they are more sparing of life. When they are cruel, they are conscious of their cruelty; it is very doubtful whether such a consciousness exists in the negro. At the same

---

142 Carus, *op. cit.*, p. 60.

time, they have discovered reasons why they should surrender this busy life of theirs, that is so precious to them. The principal motive is honor, which under various names has played an enormous part in the ideas of the race from the beginning. I need hardly add that the word honor, together with all the civilizing influences connoted by it, is unknown to both the yellow and the black man.

On the other hand, the immense superiority of the white peoples in the whole field of the intellect is balanced by an inferiority in the intensity of their sensations. In the world of the senses, the white man is far less gifted than the others, and so is less tempted and less absorbed by considerations of the body, although in physical structure he is far the most vigorous.[143]

Such are the three constituent elements of the human race. I call them secondary types, as I think myself obliged to omit all discussion of the Adamite man. From the combination, by intermarriage, of the varieties of these types come the tertiary groups. The quaternary formations are produced by the union of one of these tertiary types, or of a pure-blooded tribe, with another group taken from one of the two foreign species.

Below these categories others have appeared—and still appear. Some of these are very strongly characterized, and form new and distinct points of departure, coming as they do from races that have been completely fused. Others are incomplete, and ill-ordered, and, one might even say, anti-social, since their elements, being too numerous, too disparate, or too barbarous, have had neither the time nor the opportunity for combining to any fruitful purpose. No

---

[143] Martius observes that the European is superior to the colored man in the pressure of the nervous fluid *(Reise in Brasilien,* vol. i, p. 259).

limits, except the horror excited by the possibility of infinite intermixture, can be assigned to the number of these hybrid and checkered races that make up the whole of mankind.

It would be unjust to assert that every mixture is bad and harmful. If the three great types had remained strictly separate, the supremacy would no doubt have always been in the hands of the finest of the white races, and the yellow and black varieties would have crawled forever at the feet of the lowest of the whites. Such a state is so far ideal, since it has never been beheld in history; and we can imagine it only by recognizing the undisputed superiority of those groups of the white races which have remained the purest.

It would not have been all gain. The superiority of the white race would have been clearly shown, but it would have been bought at the price of certain advantages which have followed the mixture of blood. Although these are far from counterbalancing the defects they have brought in their train, yet they are sometimes to be commended. Artistic genius, which is equally foreign to each of the three great types, arose only after the intermarriage of white and black. Again, in the Malayan variety, a human family was produced from the yellow and black races that had more intelligence than either of its ancestors. Finally, from the union of white and yellow, certain intermediary peoples have sprung, who are superior to the purely Finnish tribes as well as to the negroes.

I do not deny that these are good results. The world of art and great literature that comes from the mixture of blood, the improvement and ennoblement of inferior races—all these are wonders for which we must needs be thankful. The small have been raised. Unfortunately, the great have been lowered by the same process; and this is an evil that nothing can balance or repair. Since I am putting together the advantages of racial mixtures, I will also add that to them is due the refinement of manners and beliefs, and especially the tempering of passion and desire. But these are merely transitory benefits, and if I recognize that the mulatto, who may become a lawyer, a doctor, or a business man, is worth more than his negro grandfather, who was absolutely savage, and fit for nothing, I must also confess that the Brahmans of primitive India, the heroes of the *Iliad* and the Shahnameh, the warriors of Scandinavia—the glorious shades of noble races that have disappeared—give us a higher and more brilliant idea of humanity, and were more active, intelligent, and trusty instruments of civilization and grandeur than the peoples, hybrid a hundred times over, of the present day. And the blood even of these was no longer pure.

However it has come about, the human races, as we find them in history, are complex; and one of the chief consequences has been to throw into disorder most of the primitive characteristics of each type. The good as well as the bad qualities are seen to diminish in intensity with repeated intermixture of blood; but they also scatter and separate off from each other, and are often mutually opposed. The white race originally possessed the monopoly of beauty, intelligence, and strength. By its union with other varieties, hybrids were created, which were beautiful without strength, strong without intelligence, or, if intelligent, both weak and ugly. Further, when the quantity of white blood was increased to an indefinite amount by successive infusions, and not by a single admixture, it no longer carried with it its natural advantages, and often merely increased the confusion already existing in the racial elements. Its strength, in fact, seemed to be its only remaining quality, and even its strength served only to promote disorder. The apparent anomaly is easily explained. Each stage of a perfect mixture produces a new type from diverse elements, and develops special faculties. As soon as further elements are added, the vast difficulty of harmonizing the whole creates a state of anarchy. The more this increases, the more do even the best and richest of the new contributions diminish in value, and by their mere presence add fuel to an evil which they cannot abate. If mixtures of blood are, to a certain extent, beneficial to the mass of mankind, if they raise and ennoble it, this is merely at the expense of mankind itself, which is stunted, abased, enervated, and humiliated in the persons of its noblest sons. Even if we admit that it is better to turn a myriad of degraded beings into mediocre men than to preserve the race of princes whose blood is adulterated and impoverished by being made to suffer this dishonorable change, yet there is still the unfortunate fact that the change does not stop here; for when the mediocre men are once created at the expense of the greater, they combine with other mediocrities, and from such unions, which grow ever more and more degraded, is born a confusion which, like that of Babel, ends in utter impotence, and leads societies down to the abyss of nothingness whence no power on earth can rescue them.

Such is the lesson of history. It shows us that all civilizations derive from the white race, that none can exist without its help, and that a society is great and brilliant only so far as it preserves the blood of the noble group that created it, provided that this group itself belongs to the most illustrious branch of our species.

Of the multitude of peoples which live or have lived on the earth, ten alone have risen to the position of complete societies. The remainder have gravitated round these more or less independently, like planets round their suns. If there is any element of life in these ten civilizations that is not due to the impulse of the white races, any seed of death that does not come from the inferior stocks that mingled with them, then the whole theory on which this book rests is false. On the other hand, if the facts are as I say, then we have an irrefragable proof of the nobility of our own species. Only the actual details can set the final seal of truth on my system, and they alone can show with sufficient exactness the full implications of my main thesis, that peoples degenerate only in consequence of the various admixtures of blood which they undergo; that their degeneration corresponds exactly to the quantity and quality of the new blood, and that the rudest possible shock to the vitality of a civilization is given when the ruling elements in a society and those developed by racial change have become so numerous that they are clearly moving away from the homogeneity necessary to their life, and it therefore becomes impossible for them to be brought into harmony and so acquire the common instincts and interests, the common logic of existence, which is the sole justification for any social bond whatever. There is no greater curse than such disorder, for however bad it may have made the present state of things, it promises still worse for the future.

NOTE. — The "ten civilizations" mentioned in the last paragraph are as follows. They are fully discussed in the subsequent books of the "Inequality of Races," of which the present volume forms the first.

I. The Indian civilization, which reached its highest point round the Indian Ocean, and in the north and east of the Indian Continent, south-east of the Brahmaputra. It arose from a branch of a white people, the Aryans.

II. The Egyptians, round whom collected the Ethiopians, the Nubians, and a few smaller peoples to the west of the oasis of Ammon. This society was created by an Aryan colony from India, that settled in the upper valley of the Nile.

III. The Assyrians, with whom may be classed the Jews, the Phoenicians, the Lydians, the Carthaginians, and the Hymiarites. They owed their civilizing qualities to the great white invasions which may be grouped under the name of the descendants of Shem and Ham. The Zoroastrian Iranians who ruled part of Central Asia under the names of Medes, Persians, and Bactrians, were a branch of the Aryan family.

IV. The Greeks, who came from the same Aryan stock, as modified by Semitic elements.

V. The Chinese civilization, arising from a cause similar to that operating in Egypt. An Aryan colony from India brought the light of civilization to China also. Instead however of becoming mixed with black peoples, as on the Nile, the colony became absorbed in Malay and yellow races, and was reinforced, from the north-west, by a fair number of white elements, equally Aryan but no longer Hindu.

VI. The ancient civilization of the Italian peninsula, the cradle of Roman culture. This was produced by a mixture of Celts, Iberians, Aryans, and Semites.

VII. The Germanic races, which in the fifth century transformed the Western mind. These were Aryans.

VIII.-X. The three civilizations of America, the Alleghanian, the Mexican, and the Peruvian.

Of the first seven civilizations, which are those of the Old World, six belong, at least in part, to the Aryan race, and the seventh, that of Assyria, owes to this race the Iranian Renaissance, which is, historically, its best title to fame. Almost the whole of the Continent of

Europe is inhabited at the present time by groups of which the basis is white, but in which the non-Aryan elements are the most numerous. There is no true civilization, among the European peoples, where the Aryan branch is not predominant.

In the above list no negro race is seen as the initiator of a civilization. Only when it is mixed with some other can it even be initiated into one.

Similarly, no spontaneous civilization is to be found among the yellow races; and when the Aryan blood is exhausted stagnation supervenes.

APPENDIX:

The Structure of the
Essay on the Inequality of Human Races
Vol. I-IV.

Of the four volumes of the Essay, only Volume 1 has been translated into English.

VOLUME I (1853)

Dedication

Book One

Preliminary Considerations - Definitions, Investigation and Exposition of the Natural Laws governing Social Existence

1. The mortal condition of civilization results from a general and common cause.

2. Fanaticism, luxury, the corruption of manners, and irreligion do not necessarily bring about the fall of societies.

3. The relative merit of governments has no influence upon the longevity of peoples.

4. Concerning what is meant by the word 'degeneration'; and regarding the mixture of ethnic elements, and how societies form and dissolve.

5. Ethnic inequalities are not the result of institutions.

6. In progress or stagnation, peoples are independent of the places they inhabit.

7. Christianity neither creates nor transforms the aptitude for civilization.

8. Definition of the word 'civilization'; social development results from a double source.

9. Definition of 'civilization' continued; the different characteristics of human society; our civilization is not superior to those existing earlier.

10. Some anatomists ascribe to humanity multiple origins.

11. Ethnic differences are permanent.

12. How races were physiologically separated and what varieties they subsequently formed through their mixtures. They are unequal in strength and beauty.

13. The human races are intellectually unequal; humanity is not infinitely perfectible.

14 Demonstration of the intellectual inequality of races continued. Different civilizations are in mutual repulsion. Mongrel races have civilizations equally mongrelized.

15. Languages, being unequal among themselves, are completely linked to the relative merit of races.

16. Recapitulation; respective characteristics of the three basic races; social effects of race-mixture; superiority of the white stock and, within this type, of

the Aryan family.

Book Two

Ancient Civilization spreading from Central Asia to the South-West

1. The Hamites.
2. The Semites.
3. The Maritime Canaanites.
4. The Assyrians; the Hebrews; the Choreans.
5. The Egyptians; the Ethiopians.

VOLUME II (1853)

6. The Egyptians were not conquerors; why their civilization remained stationary.

7 Ethnic connection between the Assyrian and Egyptian nations. The arts and lyric poetry are produced by the mingling of white and black peoples.

Book Three

Civilization spreading from Central Asia to the South and South-East.

1. The Aryans; the Brahmins and their social system.
2. Developments in Brahminism.
3. Buddhism, its defeat; modern India.
4. The yellow race.
5. The Chinese.
6. The origins of the white race.

Book Four

Semitized Civilizations of the South-West

1. History exists only amongst the white nations. Why nearly all civilizations have been developed in the western hemisphere.
2. The Zoroastrians.
3. The autochthonous Greeks; the Semite settlers; the Aryan-Hellenes.
4. The Semitic Greeks

VOLUME III (1855)

Book Five

Semitized European Civilization

1.   The first peoples of Europe.
2.   The Thracians; the Illyrians; the Etruscans; the Iberians.
3.   The Gauls.
4.   The aboriginal Italiot peoples.
5.   The Tyrrhenian Etruscans; Etruscan Rome.
6.   Italiot Rome.
7.   Semitic Rome.

Book Six

Western Civilization

1. The Slavs; Domination by some pre-Germanic Aryan peoples.

VOLUME IV (1855)

2.   The Aryan-Germans.
3.   The capacity of native Germanic races.
4.   Germanic Rome; the Romano-Celtic and Romano-Germanic armies; the German emperors.
5.   The final Aryan-Scandinavian migrations.

6. The final developments of Germano-Roman society.
7. The indigenous Americans.
8. European colonization in America.

General Conclusion

Made in the USA
Middletown, DE
06 October 2023

40348971R00186